Imaginative Resistance, Queer Fiction and the Law

I0602941

Imaginative Resistance, Queer Fiction and the Law develops a novel account of how heteronormative sociolegal orders undermine the well-being of same-sex attracted people, even when these normative orders may fall short of coercively interfering with their choices.

Queer well-being is generally studied from psychological perspectives, through the concept of 'minority stress.' Taking four texts of mid-century Anglo-American queer fiction as illustrative case studies, this book argues – in a philosophical rather than a psychological register – that heteronormativity also affects queer well-being in more intangible ways. The central claim is that heteronormativity shackles the imagination: it curtails no less the imaginative reach of authors of queer fiction, than our ability – engaged as we are in projects of self-authorship – to make-believe personal futures in which same-sex intimacy is brought to bear on our well-being. The book's central claim re-works a concept central to the philosophy of fiction – 'imaginative resistance' – and puts it into service of questions raised in moral philosophy. Apart from its political and normative implications – strengthening the case for at least some global gay rights – and from challenging some of queer theory's orthodoxies, the book also makes contributions to queer literary history, criticism and biography. Drawing on archival material and personal interviews, fresh readings are offered of Charles Jackson's *The Fall of Valor* (1946), Gillian Freeman's *The Leather Boys* (1961), and Patricia Highsmith's *The Price of Salt* (1952) and *The Talented Mr Ripley* (1955), making a case for their inclusion in the queer literary canon.

Imaginative Resistance, Queer Fiction and the Law will appeal to students of literary criticism, queer sociolegal history, law & literature, the philosophy of fiction, and queer theory, politics and ethics.

Aleardo Zanghellini is Professor of Law & Social Theory at the University of Reading. His academic writing is in the fields of legal, political and moral philosophy; the politics and governance of sexuality and gender; and law & literature.

Imaginative Resistance, Queer Fiction and the Law

Same-Sex Desire and the Good Life in Heteronormative Orders

Aleardo Zanghellini

Routledge
Taylor & Francis Group
a GlassHouse Book

First published 2022
by Routledge
2 Park Square, Milton Park, Abingdon, Oxon OX14 4RN

and by Routledge
605 Third Avenue, New York, NY 10158

a GlassHouse book

Routledge is an imprint of the Taylor & Francis Group, an informa business

© 2022 Aleardo Zanghellini

The right of Aleardo Zanghellini to be identified as author of this work has been asserted by him in accordance with sections 77 and 78 of the Copyright, Designs and Patents Act 1988.

British Library Cataloguing-in-Publication Data
A catalogue record for this book is available from the British Library

Library of Congress Cataloging-in-Publication Data
A catalog record has been requested for this book

ISBN: 978-1-032-03747-9 (hbk)
ISBN: 978-1-032-03750-9 (pbk)
ISBN: 978-1-003-18879-7 (ebk)

DOI: 10.4324/9781003188797

Typeset in Bembo
by Taylor & Francis Books

In memory of Gillian Freeman, who found artistic inspiration in desire between men; of Colonel Vincent Kramer, who unwittingly inspired Charles Jackson's novel of same-sex desire; and of Barbara Kramer, without whose testimony to her son Ray Kramer the real-life story behind Jackson's novel would be lost to us.

Contents

Figure

Acknowledgements

First and foremost, I want to thank Ray Kramer and Edward Thorpe. Ray graciously consented to being interviewed about the autobiographical basis of Charles Jackson's *The Fall of Valor*, and Mr Thorpe about the context to Gillian Freeman's *The Leather Boys*. I am deeply grateful to both. I also gratefully acknowledge the financial assistance provided by Reading Law School, which topped up my research allowance so as to enable me to interview Ray in New York in 2018. Staff at both the Rauner Special Collections (Dartmouth College) and The University of Reading Special Collections were a pleasure to deal with, and I thank them for their assistance with my archival research. I recall with particular fondness my time at the Rauner Library, and am grateful for the chance to use, in this work, the many letters and other documents collected in the voluminous papers of Charles Jackson. Many thanks also to the staff at Routledge – but especially Colin Perrin – for their help during the book's acquisition and production process, as well as to the reviewers of the book proposal and manuscript for their support. If this book is any good, I owe it in part to colleagues and friends who have kindly discussed it with me, but also to loved ones: H. Kojima and Momotaro (a non-human animal) ground me in ways that make intellectual work feel far less effortful than it might otherwise be. Love, boundless, to them both.

Introduction

Queer fiction's tragic endings, 1946–1961

In recalling his experiences as a reader of queer novels, John D'Emilio (2014: 169) recounts:

> First was *Advise and Consent,* a wildly popular novel from the late 1950s that I read before starting high school. The main character, a senator who had a gay affair while in the army, commits suicide when he's threatened with exposure. From there I moved on to *Another Country,* by James Baldwin. One gay character kills himself. Another finds happiness, but only by moving to France. My life prospects had now improved to 50–50, but how would I get to France? ... Books were letting me imagine that there were other homosexuals in the world. They were even giving me the words to defend my feelings and attractions. But jolly and hopeful they weren't.

Patricia Highsmith (2010: 311), in the afterword to the re-issued edition of her 1952 lesbian novel *The Price of Salt* puts it with even blunter humour:

> Prior to this book, homosexuals male and female in American novels had had to pay for their deviation by cutting their wrists, drowning themselves in a swimming pool, or by switching to heterosexuality (so it was stated), or by collapsing – alone and miserable and shunned – into a depression equal to hell.

Similarly, Bergman (2004: 46) reports queer writer George Whitmore to have declared that 'the last-chapter suicide was an obligatory fixture of gay novels of the late forties and early fifties'.

Whitmore and Highsmith may have exaggerated, but not by much. It is virtually a cliché that twentieth century, pre-sexual revolution, gay- or lesbian-themed Anglo-American fiction tends to end badly. This is variously ascribed to authors' internalised homophobia, publishers' pressures, or a novel's political aspiration to contribute to social change, either by manipulating mainstream

DOI: 10.4324/9781003188797-1

readers into feeling pity and sympathy for unfortunate queers (Bergman, 2004: 50), or by attempting a fictional portrayal of respectable queerness deserving of decriminalisation (Dines, 2019: 123). Bergman (2004: 50) also argues that a happy ending is what marks out – or was taken to mark out – a pre-Stonewall US queer text as pulp or porn rather than as serious literature, so that 'work that aspired to literary respectability took on the tragic story of gay life' (52).

Yet none of these explanations is very satisfactory. Much queer-authored or queer-themed fiction from this era does show a degree of ambivalence towards same-sex desire, but hardly the kind of internalised homophobia or self-loathing that would call for inflicting death or misery on its queer characters. As we will see in this book, there was also never a generalised requirement – whether implicit or explicit – on the part of publishers of serious queer-themed works of fiction that these works should end tragically, either to appease censors or an assumedly homophobic reading public. And finally, there is little reason to suppose that writers should *invariably* bend their creative output quite so deliberately in the service of instrumental considerations – be they other-regarding (a reformist agenda) or self-regarding (one's career aspirations).

This book proposes a different explanation for pre-sexual revolution queer novels' endings. My explanation invokes the idea of authorial resistance to imagining happy endings. 'Imaginative resistance' is a concept drawn from the philosophy of fiction. It refers to readers finding certain features of a story hard to make-believe, resulting in the story failing to do its work for the reader. Philosophers of fiction point out that imaginative resistance tends to be less of an issue when it comes to factual improbabilities than normative ones: readers readily accept fantastical beasts or superheroes, but they will have trouble cathecting with morally deviant fictional worlds.

In this book, I extend the concept of imaginative resistance – thus far treated in the literature as something relevant to the experience of *reading* fiction – in two ways. First, I use the concept of imaginative resistance to account for *authors'* own resistance to producing certain outcomes in their own fiction. Specifically, I use it to explain why authors of mid-century queer-themed fiction infrequently concluded their stories with a happy, or at least non-tragic, ending. Second, I extend the concept of imaginative resistance so as to account for how heteronormativity may impair queer people's success in make-believing, and therefore pursuing, life projects in which same-sex desire can be integrated with central aspects of their lives, and thereby be brought to bear on their well-being.

The philosophical literature on imaginative resistance, which I review fairly systematically in Chapter 1, already recognises that imaginability puzzles are not confined to fiction, but also affect our experience in the real world. Surprisingly, however, there is less recognition that, in the domain of fiction, imaginative resistance structures not only readers' experience, but also authorial choices. This book draws attention to this phenomenon. Additionally, it highlights the symmetry existing between imaginative resistance to certain possible fictional outcomes as it plays out in the context of authorial choice in fiction, and imaginative resistance to certain real-world outcomes on the part of individuals conceived as authors of their own lives. In this latter respect, the concept of imaginative resistance captures something akin to the phenomenon that popular psychological literature describes in terms of one's failing to give oneself permission to do (or to be) something that it might enhance one's well-being to do (or to be).

In more concrete terms, the book will discuss four Anglo-American novels, to illustrate that authorial imaginative resistance better explains mid-century queer fiction's endings than either a cruder appeal to internalised homophobia, or the assumption of a non-existent publishers' conspiracy to veto happy endings, or, finally, the ascription of political, reform-oriented goals to the novels' authors. From here, the argument about the ways in which imaginative resistance may also affect one's life plans is developed by analogy, relying on the symmetry between the creation of fictional worlds and creative self-authorship in the real world. The symmetry has to do with how imaginative resistance effectively makes certain outcomes unavailable – whether it disqualifies them from the range of endings that could conclude a novel, or from the life choices that one could pursue. In either case, it is normative constraints that have the effect of disqualifying those outcomes, be they fictional or real-world ones. Since my focus is on queer books and queer people's lives, the normative constraint I foreground is the regulatory regime of heteronormativity – the complex array of legal and non-legal norms 'through which heterosexuality is normalized, naturalized and privileged as an institution, and … homosexual practices and relationships are excluded, stigmatized, marginalized and minoritized' (Roseneil, 2013: 66).

The novels I analyse date from a period of fifteen years, when the pressures of heteronormativity, in both their legal and non-legal dimensions, were particularly intense in both Britain and America. These are the years between 1946 to 1961, spanning, therefore, the immediate aftermath of WWII through to the years immediately preceding the sexual revolution of the 1960s and 1970s. As I explain in Chapter 2, the war years had partially disrupted heteronormativity, affording people unprecedented opportunities for satisfying and experimenting with same-sex desire, and offering novel paradigms for queer self-understanding. While this destabilisation triggered, already during the war years, the near-immediate re-organisation of heteronormative forces, it was in the post-war period that this backlash gained momentum and effectiveness. In both Britain and the US, institutional and non-institutional actors – including the government, law-enforcement agencies, psychiatry, and the popular press – contributed to this process of (re-)entrenchment of heteronormativity.

It is easy, of course, to characterise this period as one of untrammelled repression. Yet, repression went hand-in-hand with, and even generated, queer networks, the beginnings of the gay and lesbian movement, and the development of what Weeks (2012: 534) 'described, borrowing from Peter Wildeblood, a prominent victim of the notorious Montagu-Wildeblood trials of the early 1950s, as "a way of life"'. Despite these complexities, and despite the fact that the post-war mobilisation of heteronormative discourses and practices did not necessarily blight the lives of each and every queer person, they did affect many negatively, as we will see in detail in Chapter 2.

In setting out, respectively, the account of imaginative resistance relied upon in the book and in detailing the processes through which hetero-normativity was stabilised and mobilised in Britain and the United States during the post-war period, Chapter 1 and Chapter 2 set the stage for the analysis that follows in the next three chapters. Each of these is devoted to the work of an author of mid-century Anglo-American queer fiction.

The selection of the four texts I use as case studies in these chapters was partly fortuitous. Chapter 3 analyses *The Fall of Valor,* Charles Jackson's heavily autobiographical 1946 novel about a middle-aged, married university professor, who falls in love with a Marine on a honeymoon on Nantucket. In a sense, this chapter is the heart of the whole project, around which the book concept later developed. It all began a few days before Christmas 2017, when I was con-tacted by Ray Kramer, who had read and liked my Goodreads.com review of *The Fall of Valor.* Ray identified himself as the son of the man who had inspired the character of the Marine in Jackson's book, and told me that virtually the whole novel was a faithful account of his father's and Jackson's time on Nantucket. The exception, he told me, was the book's ending. Ray's story determined me to investigate the autobiographical basis of Jackson's book, but also how and why the novel came to have the ending that it did. Research into Jackson's papers at Dartmouth College, New Hampshire, revealed that *The Fall of Valor* was entirely and drastically reconceived three times prior to its publication. Initially, a happy ending of sorts was envisaged, but the process of writing about, and thereby fic-tionally remaking, his experience of same-sex desire on Nantucket, led Jackson to settle on a tragic ending. Mulling over this led me, eventually, to conceive the concept for this book.

In a move that aims at a critical queer recuperation of Jackson's novel, Chapter 3 will argue that, despite its tragic ending, it is a mistake to blame Jackson's choice of denouement on internalised homophobia. The chapter focuses on Jackson's biography as much as on his book, not only because the former illuminates the latter, but also because imaginative resistance can be seen to be at work as much in the novel as in Jackson's own life choices.

In Chapter 4 I turn to Gillian Freeman's largely forgotten 1961 best-seller, *The Leather Boys,* originally published under the pseudonym Eliot George. There are three main reasons why I chose Freeman's novel as my second case study, apart from being a fan of the book. The first is pragmatic. Having realised, through the study of Jackson's papers at Dartmouth, the extent to which archival research could enrich my project, I wished to select other case studies that afforded me the chance of carrying out such research. Freeman's papers are held at her alma mater, which – serendipitously – is also the institution where I have been based since 2010, the University of Reading.

Another reason for choosing *The Leather Boys* as my second case study is the author's identity as a heterosexual woman. This tickled my pre-existent research interest in female-authored creative production centring male same-sex bonds (see, e.g., Zanghellini, 2012). More importantly, it furnished a case study that would enable me to illustrate the ways in which normative orders biased against same-sex desire engender imaginative resistance to same-sex happy endings not just in queer people, but also in the heterosexual population around them, even sympathetic allies. A final reason for choosing *The Leather Boys* is that its focus on the bond between two young working-class men was ground-breaking in gay-themed fiction.

As I detail in Chapter 4, Freeman's book was adapted as a screenplay, preserved at the University of Reading. A film directed by Sidney Furie was based on the screenplay, though it significantly departs from it. The film was well-received and is generally well-regarded even by contemporary commentators, who praise its lack of homophobia. Nevertheless, I argue that the film is a profoundly heteronormative text, virtually impervious to the queer-affirmative outcome that – if, admittedly, it fails to come off in all three texts – the screenplay and, to a greater extent, the novel at least clearly gestured towards. I will offer an explanation for why, as the story made its transition through different media (novel, screenplay and film), its conclusion changed from the unrealised possibility of a same-sex happy ending to its radical impossibility.

My final case studies, in Chapter 5, are Patricia Highsmith's 1952 lesbian romance *The Price of Salt* (originally published under the pseudonym Claire Morgan), and her suspense novel *The Talented Mr Reply* (1955). Both have enjoyed a revival of interest – popular and academic – in the last two decades or so. *The Price of Salt* is widely touted as the first lesbian, and even homosexual, novel with a happy ending. This made it an obvious candidate for a case study in this project. As I began writing the chapter, I realised that the analysis could be enriched by a discussion of *The Talented Mr Ripley,* a popular work of mid-century suspense fiction whose queer content, unlike in Minghella's film adaptation, is not always acknowledged. Both books, I argue, contain same-sex happy endings – a real one in *The Price of Salt,* and a chimerical and perverse one in *The Talented Mr Ripley*. Through an analysis of select aspects of her biography, the chapter argues that it was Highsmith's psychic positioning at the edge of normality that made her less resistant to imagining and committing to paper same-sex happy endings – including the perverse one in *The Talented Mr Ripley*.

From imaginative resistance in fiction to queer imaginative resistance in the real world

The concluding chapter works out the normative and political implications of my study of queer imaginative resistance. The concept of queer imaginative resistance, extended from the case of authorial choices in fiction to the case of one's self-authorship, centres the ways in which (hetero)normative constraints make it hard for same-sex attracted people to imagine or commit to certain options that may be conducive to their well-being. In the conclusions, my arguments will be to the effect that, in doing so, the concept of queer imaginative resistance illuminates certain non-obvious harms caused by laws inimical to same-sex desire. In this sense, my argument strengthens the case for (at least some) global gay rights. Specifically, centring queer imaginative resistance helps us appreciate that the sizeable minority (more than one third) of countries worldwide that continues to criminalise same-sex intimacy negatively affects the well-being of queer people, even in contexts where these laws are rarely or never enforced. A majority of countries worldwide, albeit not criminalising gay sex, does not make provision for any form of same-sex relationship recognition. My arguments will be to the effect that the concept of queer imaginative resistance helps us appreciate how this stance too affects queer well-being. It does so through omission in ways that exceed the material consequence of not securing relationship-based rights.

The European Court of Human Rights has argued that 'the very *existence*' (emphasis added) of sodomy laws 'continuously and directly affects [gay people's] private life', and that fear that such laws will be enforced (even when they are not) is a harm in its own right (*Dudgeon v UK*). Similarly, the US Supreme Court has stated that 'the state cannot demean [gay people's] existence or control their destiny' through sodomy laws; that, even if such laws remain unenforced, 'stigma might remain'; and that criminalisation 'in and of itself is an invitation to subject homosexual persons to discrimination' (*Lawrence v Texas*). The Supreme Court has also argued – admittedly by deploying a heteronormative rhetoric that I want, for the present purposes, bracket – that being locked out of marriage stigmatises and demeans lesbians and gay men, who too 'may aspire to the transcendent purposes of marriage' (*Obergefell v Hodges*). These judicial pronouncements show an awareness – if, perhaps, a relatively dim one – of the fact that the harms of legal hostility to same-sex desire are not exhausted by the immediately tangible consequences that attend either the enforcement of sodomy laws, or the denial of 'the constellation of benefits that … States have linked to marriage' (*Obergefell v Hodges*).

Psychological work on LGBTQ well-being and so-called 'minority stress' (Meyer, 2003) goes a long way toward illuminating just how normative orders inimical to same-sex desire damage queers' quality of life. One limitation of this work, however, is that its focus is on mental health. This book complements this literature by providing – from the perspective of philosophy and cultural/literary criticism – an account of how normative orders hostile to same-sex desire interfere with queers' quality of life even when the interference does not produce the kind of pathological outcomes that psychologists are concerned with (suicide, substance abuse, self-harm, risky sex, etc).

This also has implications, as we will see in the conclusions, for some queer postcolonial literature that is critical of gay rights activism in non-Western contexts. Specifically, it brings into evidence some limits of this literature. Postcolonial queer critics rightly take issue with some of the practices associated with gay rights activism. But some (not all) of these critics overreach in two ways: both to the extent that they take issue with the very idea of gay rights, and to the extent that they romanticise forms of queer intimacy that flourish in the shadow of legal and social prohibition.

Same-sex happy endings in fiction and in the real world

The normative arguments just foreshadowed are predicated on a rather definite and even demanding conception of same-sex happy ending: for the purposes of my normative arguments, I take a same-sex happy ending to be one in which committed same-sex relationships stand a fair chance of flourishing. This is not, necessarily, the meaning of same-sex happy ending I have in mind when discussing the four novels I chose as case studies.

Let me illustrate by reference to three of my four case studies. For the leather boys of *The Leather Boys* – Dick and Reggie – the kind of flourishing that they look forward to, and which the tragic ending denies them, is to leave behind the aimlessness, tedium, false relationships, and small-mindedness of their current existence, in order to start a new life together as lovers. In the short term this was to be accomplished – until their plan is thwarted by tragedy – by their joining the merchant navy – where, conveniently, sex between men did not raise too many eyebrows. In the longer-term, if Dick and Reggie had managed to embark on the ship, much would have depended on their eventual destination, and the extent to which the society in which they settled carved – legally and socially – a space for same-sex relationships. Admittedly, in the early 1960s, the odds would not have been in the boys' favour.

For Grandin (the Professor) and Cliff (the Marine) in *The Fall of Valor,* a happy ending would have involved, conceivably, finding a way to manage their relationship in a way that did right by their pre-existing heterosexual bonds without requiring either the men's unhealthy denial of their same-sex attraction (as it effectively does for Cliff, who ends up nearly killing Grandin in a fit of homosexual panic), or their self-denial and self-repression in the interest of those pre-existing heterosexual bonds. Realistically, compromise of some sort would have been necessary, someone would have been hurt, and – this being, as we will see in Chapter 2, America on the verge of a war on homosexuals – the secrecy of any sexual affair between the two men would have had to be carefully guarded.

Finally, as Val McDermid (2010: vi) argues in the introduction to the Bloomsbury paperback edition of *The Price of Salt*, the novel's happy ending suggests that '[w]hatever lies in the future', the relationship between the book's female leads, Carol and Therese, 'will never be an unmixed blessing', for 'Carol pays a high price for her love'. This price is Carol having to give up both custody of and contact with her daughter. Though Highsmith does not sentimentally expatiate on the breaking up of the parent-child relationship, it is clear that this is a central element in the story. Indeed, this is just the price of salt, the price Carol has to pay in order to recover her relationship with Therese and hence restore salt – the savour of life – to their world. This much is apparent from the passage where – the two women having put an end (albeit, as it transpires, only a temporary one) to their affair – Therese wonders, 'how would the world come back to life? How would its salt come back'? (Highsmith, 2010: 278).

Thus, in these novels the actual happiness of the conceivable happy endings that fail to eventuate (in *The Fall of Valor* and *The Leather Boys*) or in the happy ending that does eventuate (in *The Price of Salt*) is considerably limited by factual possibilities (the state of society; the characters' past histories). Nonetheless, Dick and Reggie could still have made it to the ship unharmed; and Cliff could have turned down Grandin's pass without a display of quasi-homicidal violence. In other words, in either *The Fall of Valor* or *The Leather Boys,* neither the factual possibilities of the world in which the characters move about, nor the factual possibilities determined by their past histories explain authorial choices to end the story in tragedy; the authors' imaginative resistance does. So, strictly speaking, the imaginative resistance I discuss in respect of my case studies is less a resistance to a happy ending in which same-sex relationships flourish unimpeded by societal prejudice and real-life compromise, than a resistance to failing to conclude the story in tragedy and misery.

As we move, however, from thinking about authorial imaginative resistance to same-sex happy endings in fiction, towards a normatively-inflected philosophical treatment of imaginative resistance as experienced in the real world by queer people as authors of their lives, the meaning of same-sex happy ending usefully shifts. We no longer foreground a lack of tragic outcomes, but rightly demand positive outcomes – ones in which same-sex attracted people stand a fair chance of flourishing. Of course, normative orders inimical to same-sex desire are all too capable of marring queer lives and relationships with tragedy or misery. As I mentioned above, the literature on minority stress often foregrounds precisely these kinds of outcomes in queer lives. Through the concept of imaginative resistance we can, usefully, bring into focus less egregious ways in which (hetero) normative orders may cause queer lives to fail to flourish.

Same-sex desire, queer well-being and homonormativity

'Flourishing' is part of the vocabulary associated with philosophical conceptions of well-being. In everyday parlance, 'well-being' tends to refer to an individual's state, at any point in time, of physical and mental health, usually assumed to be accompanied by emotional satisfaction. From this perspective, for the professionals of well-being (doctors, psychologists, the wellness industry), the challenge is to work out and/or counsel strategies directed at preserving or restoring that physical and mental state. Philosophy, however, assigns a more technical meaning to the term 'well-being', foregrounding the idea of the quality of one's life as a whole. Within this broad concept, a variety of more specific philosophical conceptions of well-being exists. But virtually all of them, in raising the question of well-being, ask how well one's life went, how good or successful it was for the person leading it.

The political ideal of personal autonomy – namely, the idea that one should be the (part) author of one's life – is one of several conceptions of well-being, and one that has acquired particular prominence in modern societies (Raz, 1986: 369–370). In centring the ways in which (hetero)normative constraints limit queer practical agents' ability to bring off certain positive outcomes in their lives, my account of imaginative resistance presupposes precisely a conception of well-being as the autonomous life.

There is reason to believe that personal autonomy has always featured in the ways in which people have attempted to make their lives good: it is often an overstatement to theoretically insist on a radical discontinuity between an older pattern of 'structures of class, gender, religion, and family' providing people with 'pre-given life worlds and trajectories', and a contemporary pattern of people reflexively negotiating 'about their life projects' and being 'able to be architects of their own lives' (Duncan, 2011: 242–243). In any case, contemporary societies are organised in ways that make personal autonomy central to our lives: as an empirical fact, we simply cannot thrive unless we are successfully autonomous (Raz, 1986: 391–394). But we can only be successfully autonomous, and hence flourish, if we have an adequate range of worthwhile options to choose from (Raz, 1986: 378–381). Because goals, broadly defined to also include personal relationships, are constitutive of our well-being, our well-being depends on the value of the goals we pursue: success in goals that are not worthwhile does not add to our well-being (Raz, 1999: 322).

There are two main reasons why my arguments in this book assume an understanding of well-being along these lines. First, this conception of well-being is more plausible and attractive than other mainstream philosophical conceptions of well-being. It makes room for the pursuit of pleasure and for the satisfactions of our desires, but it does not overstate their importance, and eschews the paradoxical subjectivism associated with hedonistic and desire-based theories of well-being (according to which our quality of life is higher the more successful we are at satisfying our desires or maximising our pleasure, regardless of what our desires may be or what gives us pleasure). In centring personal autonomy, this understanding of well-being also avoids the excessive prescriptiveness and paternalism associated with so called 'objective lists' theories of well-being (according to which one's quality of life increases the more one realises certain objective goods).

Second, if it is a recommendation to anyone at all that an account of well-being happens to centre personal autonomy, surely it should be so for queers. The reason is obvious: around the world, same-sex attracted people continue to struggle for the freedom to determine the shape of their own sexual, intimate and relational lives against considerable social odds. Being able to rely on a general account of well-being that builds on an established legacy of intellectual reflection on these matters, and does so by reference to the ideal of personal autonomy, provides us with a shared vocabulary to articulate and make more intelligible our needs, interests and aspirations to ourselves, to one another and to non-queers.

Unsurprisingly (to me, but probably not to queer-theoretical thought that insists on necessary discontinuities between queer and mainstream epistemologies), some brands of queer theory clearly resonate with the understanding of well-being I have just sketched. Warner's (1999) reflections on sexual autonomy harmonise particularly well with it. This is especially apparent where Warner (1999: 4–5) rejects 'fuzzy' relativism, takes his distance from those who believe that 'all morality [is] merely a version of the same coercion', and distinguishes genuine morality from the 'moralism' and 'pseudo-morality' of traditionalists who reject benign sexual variance and refuse to accord 'ethical respect to the autonomy of others'. It is also clear where Warner (1999), albeit recognising that 'variation … is a precondition to autonomy' (12), stresses that it is not a good in itself, for the nature of variation – whether or not the options on offer are valuable – matters (7).

Now I want to return to the point I made above, to the effect that, for the purposes of my normative arguments in this book, I take a more demanding standard to determine the meaning of 'same-sex happy ending' than I do where I discuss same-sex happy endings in fiction. In fiction, the imaginative resistance that interests me is to a same-sex happy ending understood, minimally, as an ending that does not involve tragedy or misery. On the other hand, the queer imaginative resistance I have in mind when thinking about the real, non-fictional world, is to happy endings understood in both a more demanding and specific sense – namely, as a life in which the conditions exist for same-sex partnerships to flourish as committed (erotic-companionate) affairs.

I use the term 'committed' to point to seriousness and endurance over time. This need not necessarily involve sexual monogamy, though under certain conditions monogamy may demonstrate, and to that extent enhance, commitment. Similarly, commitment need not necessarily involve cohabitation, though, in a context in which many non-cohabiting partners understand their 'love/sexual relationships … as contingent, unresolved and fluid' (Roseneil, 2006) it seems clear that cohabitation culturally functions as a marker of commitment.

Of course, as with heterosexuals, all sorts of projects and relationships matter to queer lives: partnerships are only one of the things that people may care about. Yet, same-sex desire is a relational concept that points to intimate relations. So, what is both conceptually and politically salient when discussing, specifically, queer well-being and autonomy (rather than human well-being and personal autonomy generally) is the place that same-sex intimacy has within it. This explains why, in my conception of real-life same-sex happy endings (whose imaginability, I argue, our socio-legal worlds must secure), I foreground same-sex happy endings built around same-sex intimacy; but why, of the possible forms of intimacy that queers pursue, do I concentrate on committed partnerships?

The answer has to do with the nature of well-being. As we have seen, well-being is a function of succeeding in the pursuit of our autonomously chosen (worthwhile) goals and relationships. But not all desires for worthwhile things, relationships or activities are equally important to well-being. Since the philosophical concept of well-being captures the idea of how one's life goes *overall*, it is those desires that 'are integrated with central aspects of our lives' (Raz, 1999: 64), that is our *'comprehensive* goals and relationships', that matter to well-being, rather than desires that are more short-term, or transitory in nature (324, emphasis added). As Raz (1999: 325) argues, we may well 'have strong reasons to pursue intense pleasures, but unless they fit in with our life's goals and ambitions (as they do for Don Juan, and others), they do not affect our well-being'.

From this perspective, sex (including gay sex) may conceivably come to matter to well-being in different ways, as long as it is integrated with comprehensive goals, and as long as these are worthwhile. A successful career in sex work may be an example. Here, under certain conditions, sex instrumentally contributes to the sex worker's well-being. Other ways of integrating sex with comprehensive goals are conceivable, as for those who perfect hedonism into an art form – one that so to speak, takes all the casualness out of casual sex. But these cases may be relatively rare.[1] It seems that for most people sex comes to matter to their well-being in a different way: because it is integrated with central aspects of their lives by being embedded in some form of committed relationship, whether monogamous or polyamorous. Here, the contribution of sex to well-being is non-instrumental, as a constitutive part of a valuable form of life.

Many same-sex attracted people care about committed relationships, and aspire to them. For example, Bourne et al.'s (2013) quantitative study found that UK men who have sex with men identify sex within a relationship as constituting the ideal sex life, with monogamous relationships most commonly cited. If this response is added to the second most common response, namely sex with an emotional connection, they account for two thirds of respondents. Additionally, there is a positive correlation between being out and idealising both relationship formulation and emotional connection.

Bourne et al. (2013) acknowledge the possible effect of social desirability bias on these responses. Indeed, some queer literature is quick to dismiss or discredit at least some of these aspirations (particularly those for dyadic, committed relationships) as homonormative queers buying into heteronormative respectability, and being both rewarded (through same-sex relationship recognition and social approval) and co-opted by the mainstream for doing so. This critical move, however, is problematic.

Critiques of homonormativity obscure, to borrow from Roseneil et al. (2013: 186), the 'historical and ongoing incommensurability of heteronormativity and homonormativity as regulative and normative regimes', as well as the 'incompleteness' of processes of same-relationship recognition. Indeed, there is a much more complex relationship between heteronormativity and the regulation of same-sex desire than is conveyed by the flattening characterisation of committed, and even exclusive, same-sex relationships as homonormative. Calhoun (2002), for example, made a compelling case that the privileging of heterosexuality in the US has been contingent on the representation of lesbians and gay men as family outlaws – a point that, if generalised beyond the US context, seems consistent with the fact that decriminalisation of gay sex always precedes (often by decades and sometimes by centuries) same-sex relationship recognition. Even Foucault (2010, n.p.) suggested that what troubles people is less gay sex per se than the fact that 'individuals are beginning to love one another' – same-sex 'affection, tenderness, friendship, fidelity, camaraderie, and

---

1   How many of your sexual partners had skills that made you infer their *genuine* vocation for what could be called an *ars erotica*?

companionship, things that our rather sanitized society can't allow a place for without fearing the formation of new alliances and the tying together of unforeseen lines of force'.

In any case, value is experienced through and mediated by social forms. Thus, in societies where, say, sexual monogamy signifies respect for or commitment to one's partner, then monogamy constitutes one's partnership as a mutually respectful or committed one, thereby contributing to its value. This does not prevent one from having a consensual open or polyamorous relationship as valuable in its own right – 'the emotional work that helps people feel and understand their emotions, communicate without confrontation, and contain the difficult emotions of others' (Brunning, 2018: 513) being constitutive of the distinctive good that open or polyamorous relationships are. The point is, however, that because value is mediated through social forms, conformity between one's life choices and established social forms (as long as these are sound) is a benign way of having a good life – not always already suspect as a kind of capitulation to dominant social norms. After all, as Warner (1999: 43) notes it, we only have reason to reject the normative to the extent that 'the world's pseudo-morality is a phobic and inauthentic way of life'.

Dines's (2019: 123–126) intriguing discussion of UK queer novels published in the 1950s illustrates how an analysis centring homonormativity – albeit thought-provoking in its own right – may occlude other valuable hermeneutic moves. Although Dines (2019) does not expressly use the terminology of homonormativity, he invokes its logic to make sense of the texts he analyses. His argument is that UK queer fiction from this period shows a bourgeois reformist orientation, attempting as it does to cast a privatised and domesticated version of homosexuality as non-threatening and deserving of the de-criminalisation advocated in 1957 by the Wolfenden report, from whose recommendations it was propertied 'middle class men who stood to benefit most' (Dines, 2019: 125). However, for several reasons (the fact that domesticity does not make for compelling reading material; the fact that privatising homosexuality makes it in some way unrepresentable) such texts are haunted by the other they attempt to exclude, but on which they are reliant for sheer narrative interest – the disreputable queer congregating in gay bars or seeking pleasure in public conveniences (Dines, 2019: 127–138). But is this reading not ultimately dependent on the equation of sex in private (which is what the Wolfenden report recommended protection for) with sex specifically in one's privately owned space, as well as of the former with respectable sex (as if one could not have casual sex in private)? Is it not dependent on the elision between middle-class status and home ownership/respectability – when by the outbreak of WWII, for better or for worse, home ownership and the respectable lifestyle it conveyed had become working-class aspirations and achievements (Scott, 2008)? And is it not, finally, dependent on the conflation of sex in private with sex that thereby becomes inaccessible to an author's pen?

On reflection, it seems clear why queer British novels from the fifties should turn to the conflict between the aspiration for stable relationships and the allure of more unruly queer erotic spaces in order to build their narrative tension. For that tension is, even now, characteristic of gay life, and it is so for non-contingent reasons that were explored above: namely, the fact that, built as we are, we have strong reasons for seeking hedonic pleasure, coupled with the fact that hedonic pleasure contributes little to our quality of life unless it is integrated with our comprehensive goals. On this view, if these mid-century queer texts are interesting, it may be less because they fail at successful depictions of bourgeois same-sex domesticity (Dines, 2019: 138), than because their brief may have not been to paint an unsullied image of respectable queer life to begin with.

References

Bergman, D (2004) *The Violet Quill and the Making of Gay Culture* (New York: Columbia University Press).

Bourne, A et al. (2013) 'What Constitutes the Best Sex Life for Gay and Bisexual Men? Implications for HIV Prevention', *BMC Public Health*, vol 13, 1083.

Brunning, L (2018) 'The Distinctiveness of Polyamory', *Journal of Applied Philosophy*, vol 35(3), 513–531.

Calhoun, C (2002) *Feminism, the Family, and the Politics of the Closet: Lesbian and Gay Displacement* (Oxford: Oxford University Press).

D'Emilio, J (2014) *In a New Century. Essays on Queer History, Politics, and Community Life* (Madison, WI: University of Wisconsin Press).

Dines, M (2019) 'Is It a Queer Book?: Re-Reading the 1950s Homosexual Novel' in Bentley, N, Ferrebe, A and Hubble, N (eds) *The 1950s: A Decade of Modern British Fiction* (London: Bloomsbury).

Dudgeon v UK 4 EHRR 149 (1981).

Duncan, S (2011) 'The World We Have Made? Individualisation and Personal Life in the 1950s', *The Sociological Review*, vol 59(2), 242–265.

George, E (1961) *The Leather Boys* (London: Anthony Blond).

Foucault, M (2010) *'Friendship as a Way of Life' (John Johnston trans) Caring Labor: An Archive.* https://caringlabor.wordpress.com/2010/11/18/michel-foucault-friendship -as-a-way-of-life/, an interview with de Ceccaty, R, Danet, J, and le Bitoux, J originally published in *Gai Pied* (April 1981).

Highsmith, P (2010) 'Afterword' in Highsmith, P *Carol* (London: Bloomsbury) 309–311.

Highsmith, P (1955) *The Talented Mr Ripley* (New York: Coward-McCann).

Jackson, C (1946) *The Fall of Valor* (New York: Rinehart).

Lawrence v Texas 539 US 558 (2003).

McDermid, V (2010) 'Foreword' in Highsmith, P *Carol* (London: Bloomsbury) v–viii.

Meyer, IH (2003) 'Prejudice, Social Stress, and Mental Health in Lesbian, Gay, and Bisexual Populations: Conceptual Issues and Research Evidence', *Psychological Bulletin*, vol 129(5), 674–697.

Morgan, C (1952) *The Price of Salt* (New York: Coward-McCann).

Obergefell v Hodges 576 US 644 (2015).

Raz, J (1986) *The Morality of Freedom* (Oxford: Oxford University Press,).

Raz, J (1999) *Engaging Reason: On the Theory of Value and Action* (Oxford: Oxford University Press).

Roseneil, S (2006) 'On Not Living with a Partner: Unpicking Coupledom and Cohabitation', *Sociological Research Online*, vol 11(3), www.socresonline.org.uk/11/3/rose neil.html.

Roseneil, S et al. (2013) 'Changing Landscapes of Heteronormativity: The Regulation and Normalization of Same-Sex Sexualities in Europe', *Social Politics*, vol 20(2), 165–199.

Scott, P (2008) 'Marketing Mass Home Ownership and the Creation of the Modern Working-Class Consumer in Inter-War Britain', *Business History*, vol 50, 4–25.

Warner, M (1999) *The Trouble with Normal: Sex, Politics, and the Ethics of Queer Life* (New York: The Free Press).

Weeks, J (2012) 'Queer(y)ing the "Modern Homosexual"', *Journal of British Studies*, vol 52(3), 523–539.

Zanghellini, A (2012) 'Gay Intimacy, Yaoi and the Ethics of Care' in Davies, C and Robinson, K (eds) *Queer and Subjugated Knowledges: Generating Subversive Imaginaries* (Sharjah, UAE: Bentham) 192–211.

1 Imaginative resistance in and beyond fiction

Introduction

In this chapter, I examine 'imaginative resistance', a concept used in the philosophy of fiction. I then work out an expanded version of that concept. Gendler (2000: 79), who can be credited for drawing academic attention to it, describes imaginative resistance as a reader's 'failure to follow the author's lead in make-believing what the author wants to make fictional'. This definition draws attention to the connection between issues of imaginability and issues of fictionality. Fictionality raises the question of when authors are able to make something true in fiction (or 'fictional'), while imaginability is about what we are able to make-believe.

I will argue that imaginative resistance is not only experienced by readers of fiction, but that it also governs the narrative outcomes that authors of fiction feel able to bring off in their work. Furthermore, imaginative resistance is experienced by practical agents, that is, people faced with the task of making decisions in the real world. Imaginative resistance, I will argue, limits the range of outcomes that practical agents feel they can bring off in their own lives. In so doing, imaginative resistance may have an effect on well-being, understood as successful life authorship – that is, success in being the author of one's life.

The first half of the chapter critically engages the analytical philosophical literature on imaginative resistance in order to clarify the contours of the concept. In the second part of the chapter, I summon insights from hermeneutics and phenomenology to extend the concept of imaginative resistance so as to cover authors' experience of writing fiction and practical agents' experience of self-authorship. In addressing imaginative resistance as experienced by authors of fiction and practical agents' self-authorship, I will discuss, specifically, the question of heteronormative constraints on the imagination. In order to draw with the necessary precision the contours of the concepts at the heart of this project, this chapter is written in the philosophical register. Albeit dependent on the conclusions reached this chapter, the analysis of the case studies themselves – in Chapters 3, 4 and 5 – will switch to a literary-critical register more readily accessible to non-philosophers.

DOI: 10.4324/9781003188797-2

What is it to imagine?

Imaginability raises the question of the circumstances under which we are able to successfully conjure up something in the imagination, or make-believe it. But what is it to make-believe a fictional world? Black and Barnes (2017: 71), in their fairly recent discussion of imaginative resistance, refer to it variously as readers' unwillingness or inability 'to imagine', 'buy into', or 'enter into' certain fictional worlds. Clearly, these verbs are not synonymous: the first points to a basic failure to represent the relevant thing in one's own mind at all; the second to a failure to believe or be convinced by the thing that we do represent; and the third to a failure to be transported. I think that to 'imagine', for the purposes of imaginative resistance, is best conceived as the second of these things – a failure to be convinced of something.

A number of authors (Liao et al., 2014: 347; Sauchelli, 2019: 166) account for imaginative resistance in terms of a failure to be transported by, or immersed in, a story: on this view, when readers experience imaginative resistance, they pop out of a fictional bubble. For Nanay (2010: 594–595), this happens when readers become preoccupied with what the author might have meant or intended, for '[o]nce our attention is drawn to the author, it is drawn away from the world of fiction' (592). But there are reasons to doubt such transportation/absorption-driven accounts of imaginative resistance. First, though commercial fiction perhaps invariably aims at transporting the reader, it is unclear that all literary fiction does. Secondly, and accordingly, it is unclear that imaginative resistance is best characterised as a reader's attention being temporarily diverted from the fiction to its author. Authors sometimes, even in realist fiction, self-consciously replace fictional narrators, regularly reminding the reader (for example in addressing her directly) that the narrative is no more than a literary artefact. In these circumstances, the author's deliberate intrusion does not necessarily cause imaginative resistance, despite the fact that readers' attention is drawn away from the fiction and to the author. This suggests that imaginative resistance is not usefully thought of as the opposite of transportation.

Nor is it useful to reduce imaginative resistance to a failure to represent something in the imagination at all. For we can represent something to ourselves, or intend it as an object of imagination, without make-believing it. Gendler (2000: 80–81) argues that this is what commonly happens when we are asked to *suppose* something. In mere hypothetical supposition, we are not being asked to commit ourselves to the content of what we are invited to picture; accordingly, we experience no resistance in supposing anything at all at someone's mere say-so. It is difficulty in make-believe-type imagining, not in supposition-type imagining, that matters when we experience imaginative resistance. After all, fiction demands of readers that they do more than just suppose; and it is the failure in this demand's uptake that imaginative resistance designates. For the purposes of imaginative resistance, therefore, to imagine is to represent something in our mind, but to do so in a particular way, one that involves a certain commitment on the reader's part. This is consistent with

Matravers' (2003) claim that imaginative resistance involves the withdrawal of our *assent* from what the narrator is asking us to represent.

What elicits imaginative resistance?

Gendler (2000: 56) argues that imaginative resistance gives rise to 'the puzzle of explaining our comparative difficulty in imagining fictional worlds that we take to be morally deviant'. The puzzle of imaginative resistance, thus, draws attention to a disparity in the way we imaginatively treat morally deviant fictional worlds and factually deviant ones, such as those found in science fiction. While imaginative resistance may also occur in respect of factually deviant worlds,[1] it is generally conceded that resistance is stronger vis-à-vis fictional claims that we take to be *morally* false (Driver, 2008: 303–304).

Matravers (2003) explains the disparity in our imaginative treatment of morally deviant and factually deviant worlds by drawing on the idea of readers' assent. Matravers (2003: 99) argues that the salient distinction is between (purported) truths in respect of which fictional narrators are and are not in an epistemologically privileged position: we assent to the former kinds of truths, but not to the latter (unless we antecedently happen to agree with them). Specifically, Matravers (2003: 99) argues that a fictional narrator's authority only extends to that in respect of which she is in an 'epistemologically privileged' position by virtue of having it (fictionally) witnessed it, so that her 'testimony' is 'sufficient for belief'. This condition does not obtain in respect of a fictional narrator's assertion that something is a moral truth, or other types of assertions such as that a certain joke is funny, or that something is a good reason for something else (Matravers, 2003: 99).

These are all examples of evaluative claims: it might be tempting to conclude, therefore, that fictional narrators' authority extends to assertions of non-evaluative fact, whether or not they are false in the real world, but not to moral assertions, as well as some other kinds of evaluative assertions. But it seems clear that fictional narrators also lack authority in respect of certain assertions of non-evaluative fact. These include not only those involving patent mistakes or logical impossibilities,[2] but also claims that violate what we deem to be psychological truths, leading to our complaint that characters are not believable or credible.

Interestingly, if we want to engage with a fictional world we *have no choice but* to take a (reliable) fictional narrator's word for a character behaving, speaking, feeling, or thinking in a certain way. That is, engaging in the practice of reading fiction presupposes that we accept that (reliable) fictional narrators

---

1 Thus, in the interest of imaginatively engaging with a fictional world, readers may edit out of a story claims that they know to be factually inaccurate.

2 For example, the narrator of *La Recherche* makes Cottard die, only to forget and make him re-appear a few pages after killing him off. Readers cannot assent to, or make-believe, both claims – that the doctor dies and that he did not. Here, imaginative resistance to the factual claim of Cottard's death is a pre-condition to imaginative engagement with the subsequent factual claim that he is alive, and with the story as whole.

are in a privileged epistemological standing in respect of all of a characters' actions or mind states, even those that strike us as improbable. Yet, while we must needs assent to the fictional narrator's report that the characters felt this or did that, if those feelings or deeds strike us as unlikely, there is likely to be a breakdown of our goodwill in respect of the story *as the author's creative product*. That is, we may well be required to give our assent to the characters' actions or states of mind at the say-so of the fictional narrator, but there is a second-order type of assent that we withdraw from the story, leading to the infelicity of the fictional project as a whole.

I think this case – the case of a fiction violating psychological truths – calls for a broader understanding of imaginative resistance. Imaginative resistance cannot be reduced to readers' inability to assent to a fictional narrator's sayings in respect of which the narrator has no privileged epistemological standing: rather, it occurs whenever our second-order assent to the author's work of fiction is withdrawn. This tends to occur not only when we are presented with morally deviant fictional worlds, but also psychologically deviant ones.

More specifically, we tend to experience imaginative resistance in at least two cases: first, when a (reliable) fictional narrator makes, expressly or implicitly, evaluative claims (whether moral, aesthetic, etc) that conflict with norms we are committed to; and secondly, in respect of the fictional narrator's non-evaluative factual claims (whether explicit or implicit) if they conflict with our beliefs about psychological truths.

Imaginability and fictionality

It is now a standard move in the literature on imaginative resistance (Mahtani, 2012: 416) to distinguish the 'imaginability puzzle: why are … people unwilling or unable to engage in a prompted imaginative activity?' (the typical case being a morally deviant fictional world) from the 'fictionality puzzle: why … mere authorial say-so is insufficient to make it the case that something is true in a story?' (Liao et al., 2014: 342). Most accounts of imaginative resistance explain the fictionality puzzle in terms of imaginability (Stueber, 2011: 158). It cannot be ruled out, these accounts concede, that it is possible to make true in fiction what cannot be imagined; yet, they insist, when it comes to false moral claims, their non-imaginability does explain the difficulty of making them true in fiction (Mahtani, 2012: 416).

For Mahtani (2012: 427–428) this move is ill-conceived:[3] she argues, rather, that a moral principle is true in fiction by virtue of being automatically imported into it by a reader who believes it to be true, and there is nothing an author can do to make a moral principle true in their fiction if it conflicts with the principle the reader has imported. This explanation, however, proves too

3   This is, according to Mahtani (2012), because part of imagining something is to imagine experiencing it, and there is no imaginative perspective from which 'bare' moral principles can be experienced. It would follow that when moral principles are true in fiction they cannot be so because they are successfully imagined.

much: it seems to preclude a fictional story from changing the reader's mind about what moral principles hold true. This is inconsistent with the hermeneutic insight that although readers will project their pre-judgements onto texts, the text's recalcitrance will normally result in readers partially shifting their horizons (Gadamer, 2013).

We might as well concede that authors can and sometimes do change our beliefs about the truth of a moral principle. What they cannot change is its actual truth-value (whether in the real world or in fiction). All readers import into fiction what they purport to be a moral truth. Most readers are competent knowers of basic moral truths, so the moral principles that they import into fiction (say: torturing someone for fun is wrong, feeding the starving is good) are actually true. If such readers are then confronted with a false moral claim, they will tend to experience imaginative resistance. In this case, not only is it *impossible* for the author to change the truth value of whatever principle is imported into the fiction by the reader, but she will also find it *hard* to change the reader's *beliefs* about its truth value. The reader will then tend to not follow the author's lead in make-believing the prompted imaginative activity. This is the classic case of imaginative resistance.

Therefore, on the view I propose, imaginative resistance theorists who think that the non-imaginability of false moral claims explains the difficulty of making them true in fiction get the relationship between imaginability and fictionality exactly the wrong way round. It is because moral non-truths cannot be made true in fiction that discerning readers will find themselves hard-put (not necessarily incapable) to make-believe them, not vice-versa.

To put it another way, the fictionality puzzle (why certain claims but not others fail to be true in fiction) is not about anyone's imaginative resistance: it is about what, as matter of fact, holds true in fiction. Imaginability is about what we succeed in make-believing, or fail to make-believe, holds true in a fiction; but fictionality is about what *actually* holds true in it. Furthermore, the puzzle of fictionality is not a puzzle: the truth-value of moral (and psychological) claims in fiction simply tracks their truth-value in the real world. Such claims are true in fiction if, *mutatis mutandis*, they would be true in the real world.

Practical reason, fictionality and the alignment principle

I argued that an author cannot change the actual truth value of moral principles. I will call this the alignment principle, to suggest a necessary alignment between the truth value of moral principles in the real and fictional worlds. The alignment principle is a structural feature of fiction as a valuable human practice, because the point of fiction lies, at least partly, in our imaginative engagement with a world that remains meaningful to us from the point of view of practical agency.[4]

---

4   Fiction that makes a point of toying with nonsense and the absurd is the exception that confirms the rule: its success lies precisely in the reader identifying the absurd and nonsensical for what they are, which implicitly ratifies the norms of logic, purposiveness, and meaningfulness violated in this kind of fiction.

Since an appreciation of the good (that is of values, whether moral or otherwise) is central to structures of meaning, and since practical agency means meaningfully orienting ourselves in the world in light of the good, then, for a work of fiction to speak to us, it must needs to speak to the good. This is because practical agency is an 'inexpungible', 'constitutive' feature of human experience (Radin and Michelman, 1991: 1058). While we welcome (unless we are dogmatically-minded readers unable to genuinely experience the value of fiction) authors opening our eyes to what we were otherwise blind to, including moral truths (Nussbaum, 2003), we cannot grant authors of fiction the authority to switch the actual truth value of human goods and normative principles. That would be tantamount to depriving fiction of its central value – its significance to us as always already practical agents.

Because the valuable exceeds the morally valuable, and all goods, not just moral ones, are relevant to practical agency, one would expect that we also cannot grant authors authority to switch the truth value of all evaluative claims, not just moral ones. As it happens, all the examples of claims that imaginative resistance theorists typically adduce to show that resistance is also experienced in respect of non-moral claims are evaluative ones. Such examples include fictional claims to the effect that a joke is funny, or a poem good, or that something is a good reason for something else (Matravers, 2003: 99), or that something is beautiful (Black and Barnes, 2017: 71).[5]

That the value of fiction cannot be prised apart from its ability to speak to our practical thought explains not only why readers cannot grant authors the authority to bring about a misalignment between what values and evaluative principles (moral or otherwise) actually hold true in fiction and in the real world. It also explains why we do not grant authors the authority to switch the truth value of psychological truths. This is because the workings of the human mind are just the medium through which we orient our practical thought towards the good in the world.

Imaginability and the principle of putative alignment

I argued that the alignment principle is a structural feature of fiction as a valuable practice (where its value centrally rests on its ability to speak to our practical thought): readers cannot grant authors the authority to bring about a mis-alignment between what values and principles (moral or otherwise) actually hold true in fiction and in the real world.

Imaginative resistance itself, however, is less about fictionality than imaginability. Yet, although the alignment principle explains the conditions of fictionality

5   These are all evaluative statements that invoke an implicit validity claim of legitimacy (Habermas, 1979: 55). That validity claim is vindicated only if the norms of beauty, humour, logic, artistic merit, etc that purport to legitimate the statement soundly orient our practical thinking towards the relevant value or good (beauty, humour, etc) and are correctly applied to the relevant thing (a joke, a poem, etc).

(rather than imaginability) of both evaluative claims and psychological ones, it must have something to do with imaginative resistance. This is because evaluative claims and psychological ones are, as we know, just the kind of claims that may trigger imaginative resistance.

It is, I propose, a modified version of the alignment principle that accounts for imaginative resistance. I call this the principle of putative alignment. The alignment principle states that readers cannot grant authors the authority to bring about a misalignment between what evaluative (and psychological) claims actually hold true in fiction and in the real world. According to the principle of putative alignment, on the other hand, readers are resistant to assenting to a misalignment between what evaluative (and psychological) claims the author purports (successfully or unsuccessfully) to make true in fiction and those the readers *believe* (rightly or wrongly) to hold true in the real world. That is, we typically experience imaginative resistance simply by virtue of a conflict between what we *hold* to be true and what we are being asked to make-believe holds true, regardless of where the actual truth of the matter lies.

The connection between the alignment principle (which spells out the conditions of fictionality) and the principle of putative alignment (which accounts for imaginative resistance, that is, the ease of imaginability of certain claims) lies in this. When a reader experiences resistance, she is sufficiently convinced of the truth of her normative and psychological beliefs that she *believes* (rightly or wrongly) that there is a failure of fictionality. That is, she believes (rightly or wrongly) that the alignment principle is not satisfied. Thus, it is because we are committed to the alignment principle that authors may fail to convince us to make-believe something to be (normatively or psychologically) true that we do not believe holds true. Yet that failure to make-believe (our imaginative resistance) occurs in accordance with the putative alignment principle, not with the alignment principle itself (for we may be wrong in our beliefs of what holds and does not hold true).

If the reason why we experience imaginative resistance were the fact that we do not want authors to challenge our beliefs (whether right or wrong), none of us could believe in the transformative power of fiction. Yet many of us do, and with good reason. Ultimately, therefore, the principle of putative alignment *predicts when* we are likely to experience resistance; but it is our commitment to the alignment principle that *explains* our imaginative resistance, even in cases when the author happens to be right in wanting to make a principle true and we are wrong in thinking the principle false.[6]

6   One might expect things to be different for readers who are genuinely committed to amorality (that is, who do not believe in the good and the bad), for value conventionalists who reduce value (including moral values) to whatever social conventions any given society might find itself committed to, and for sceptics who have freed themselves from normative commitment (see Nussbaum, 1993). It might be supposed that such readers will have no objection to authors switching the truth value of moral and other evaluative claims. Because such readers can be expected not to care for the alignment principle they would have no *reason* for experiencing imaginative resistance. In fact, Todd (2009: 195–197) seems to have in mind such

Phenomenology helps us see why the principle of putative alignment better predicts the occurrence of imaginative resistance than the alignment principle itself. Phenomenology argues that humans are motivated by a desire to invest their life with meaning: our sense of self is dependent on and embedded in inter-subjectively validated semantic structures (Rubin, 1998: 1719–1724). Since these structures revolve around appreciations of the good, including the moral good, it is no wonder that we do not grant writers the option of toying with our normative universe as we *believe* it to be, rather than as it is. I suggested that in many cases readers are competent knowers of moral truth: when they are, the alignment principle and the putative alignment principle yield the same predictions in respect of imaginative resistance. But when readers are mistaken in their normative commitments (as they are when, for example, they have embraced or internalised homophobia), then it is consistent with phenomenology that it will be the putative alignment principle, rather than the alignment principle, that predicts the cases that will trigger imaginative resistance. For it is the normative beliefs we actually happen to hold (rather than those that correctly hold) that are bound up with our sense of identity and meaning.

Thus, as empirical, rather than reasonable, agents, it is the desire to hold on to our moral beliefs – regardless of how sound their grounds are – that matters, simply because it causes us anxiety to let go of them. Such desire will generally be unconscious and give rise to defence mechanisms when we are confronted with challenges to our moral beliefs. Denial is a well-recognised unconscious coping mechanism, whereby we block out anxiety-inducing features of the real

readers when arguing that there is no genuine puzzle of imaginative resistance, but only: a) readers with different pre-theoretical (psychological, moral, aesthetic, meta-ethical, etc) commitments, which make them more or less willing, and on occasion unable, to imagine certain things claimed in fiction; and b) concepts that have conventionally inbuilt certain evaluative judgements, which make it harder for an author successfully to deploy them in ways that violate those judgments, without however absolutely precluding such successful use. None of this, however, proves that there is no genuine puzzle of imaginative resistance. First, because it is only in very rare cases that people genuinely lack normative commitment. As I showed elsewhere (Zanghellini, 2020: 541), despite what people may profess, normative commitment tends to come back to haunt them: many fewer people do not believe in the good than there are people who believe they don't. This means that the central case of a text's readership is a normatively committed reader, for whom the problem of imaginative resistance will therefore present itself full-fledged. Secondly, even for those people who actually are the self-professed relativists, skeptics, etc that they fancy themselves to be, other factors tend to orient them towards habits of thought or conduct (Fish, 1989: 242–243) which, even without genuine normative commitment, commit them to collective structures of meaning. So, even if for these categories of readers it does not make sense to speak of their not granting authors the authority to switch the actual truth value of evaluative claims, one may expect that they would not grant authors, or only grant them reluctantly, the authority to make evaluative claims that conflict with whatever is most centrally integrated into the structures of meaning that the readers have come to rely on in their lives.

world (Freud, 2018). Imaginative resistance, in some cases, may well be understood as the equivalent – in respect of a reader's relationship to a fictional world – of a practical agent's denial in the real world.

Thus, phenomenology has explanatory power in respect of the puzzle of imaginative resistance, illuminating, specifically, the claim that many of us 'cannot go along with moral claims we take to be false, because that would seem to involve a rejection of something we care very much about' (Driver, 2008: 304). The reason why non-moral evaluative claims also have the capacity to trigger imaginative resistance is that all of one's normative attitudes (both moral and non-moral ones) are generally constitutive of identity. This is because, as I argued, all human values (not just the moral good) are relevant to practical thought; and because our identities are, first and foremost, those of *acting* individuals, that is practical agents (Zanghellini and Sato, 2020). The more centrally integrated certain normative commitments or attitudes are with our sense of self, the more it can be expected that we will experience imaginative resistance when confronted with claims that conflict either with those commitments, or with the conclusions generated by those attitudes. Thus, the more I think of myself as having a good sense of humour, the more likely it is that I will experience imaginative resistance to a fictional claim that a lame joke is hilariously funny.

Making phenomenological sense of the puzzle of imaginative resistance

Phenomenology also enriches the explanation I provided for the puzzle of imaginative resistance – the puzzle, that is, of why fictional moral (and other evaluative) claims, when they conflict with a reader's own, tend to elicit imaginative resistance in a way in which factually deviant fictional worlds do not. Evaluative statements – because of their relevance to practical thought and our subjective constitution as, first and foremost, practical agents – have implications for meaning and identity in ways that other kinds of claims do not. The criterion of validity for evaluative statements is legitimacy (Habermas, 1979: 55) and legitimacy means justifiability in light of relevant goods (or values). Such goods (ethical, aesthetic, etc) are not only what practical reason is oriented towards, but also what we utilise to invest life with meaning. So the stakes are high when we are being asked to buy into statements that expressly or implicitly invoke these goods in ways that we reject. Analogous reasons account for why falsifying psychological truths (something authors tend to do inadvertently rather than deliberately) also tends to elicit imaginative resistance. Our appreciation of psychological truths too is bound up with our (self-reflection on how we exercise) practical reason, and so with our sense of self as practical agents seeking to invest our lives with meaning.

This analysis is consistent with Stokes' (2006: 400) point that mental activities in which we imagine a different set of values to be true from those we actually hold are 'egocentric in nature': they commit our sense of self in a way in which prescriptions to imagine different descriptive facts about the world do not (Stokes, 2006: 400–401). The problem, a phenomenology-based account of imaginative resistance would suggest, is not just with having to imagine being the kind of person who values what we do not: it is that the very prompt to do so may be destabilising to our sense of self.

Stueber (2011: 174) argues that we try to make sense of moral statements different from ours in terms of their providing others – those who hold such statements to be true – with reasons for action. It is this, in turn, that 'requires us to reenact [the other's] very thoughts in our own minds by feeding our cognitive system with the necessary pretend-beliefs and by being able to quarantine our own beliefs and commitments from the simulation'. The imaginative resistance we may experience when being prescribed normative views different from those we hold will vary depending on how successful we are at 'quarantining' (Stueber, 2011: 174–175) or backgrounding our actual values, and/or on their 'strength' (Stokes, 2006: 404). Phenomenology suggests that both the 'strength' of our values and beliefs, and our ease at backgrounding them depend on how centrally integrated they are with our sense of self. It also draws attention to the fact that the constraints that our value-system places on our imagination are social in nature, not simply a matter of individual idiosyncrasies – a fact rarely discussed in the literature on imaginative resistance. Phenomenology tells us that meaning sediments as a result of inter-subjective processes (Rubin, 1998): thus, the values we come to hold as true, which act as constraints accounting for the puzzle of imaginative resistance in accordance with the principle of putative alignment, are collectively validated.

In those cases in which the imaginative activity prescribed to us does not involve values (conjured up by evaluative claims) but non-evaluative facts, our degree of imaginative resistance will also depend on how centrally integrated our commitment to certain non-evaluative facts is with our sense of self. However, it seems likely that it is commitment to certain values or normative beliefs that accounts for the fact that our commitment to certain non-evaluative facts may be inextricably bound up with our sense of self. Thus, a flat-earther may refuse to imaginatively engage with a fiction prescribing to imagine the non-evaluative fact of a round Earth because they believe the Bible teaches the Earth is flat; and they cannot imagine being the kind of person who rejects Biblical teachings, which are central to their own sense of self and their exercise of practical reason. If I am right, then, even when we experience imaginative resistance in connection to descriptive, non-evaluative factual claims, this too may be due, ultimately, to the implications of the prescribed imagining for our practical reason.

Gender, same-sex desire, and imaginative constraints

Peterson (2019: 74) argues that a useful account of imaginative resistance will make (imaginative) constraints central to it. He goes on to classify constraints into architectural (roughly, ones related to the ways in which our cognition is structured) and non-architectural, which are normative in nature (Peterson, 2019: 75). It will be apparent that the former are context-independent, and the latter context-dependent. Some non-architectural constraints have to do with genre conventions: readers may experience imaginative resistance if a text fails to meet genre expectations that track genre conventions (Liao et al., 2014: 345–346). Thus, sentences that trigger resistance in realist fiction might not necessarily do so in the context of surrealist fiction (Nanay, 2010). Other non-architectural constraints are those relating to a reader's own values and normative commitments (Peterson, 2019: 75). It is this latter kind of normative constraints that Gendler's (2005) original account of imaginative resistance centred; and it is these constraints that matter for the purposes of my own argument in this book.

Peterson (2019: 75) follows Clavel-Vazquez (2018) in labelling non-architectural constraints that consist in a reader's values and normative commitments as 'appreciator's interpretive horizons'. Clavel-Vazquez (2018), specifically, has utilised the concept of 'interpretive horizons' to describe the specific constraint on readers' imagination that accounts for imaginative resistance to 'rough heroines'. Clavel-Vazquez's (2018: 204) account expands the concept of imaginative resistance to embrace what she calls the 'affective puzzle', namely, resistance to a text's prescription to take on not so much a morally deviant viewpoint, as an 'ethically inappropriate' affective response. Rough heroines are the female counterpart of 'rough heroes', characters who are 'deeply morally flawed', but who command, often successfully, readers' allegiance (Clavel-Vazquez, 2018: 202). This happens via a mechanism whereby the readers' overall assessments are unconsciously contaminated by their approbation of other qualities the rough hero possesses (Clavel-Vazquez, 2018: 205), which leads readers 'to bracket their moral appraisals' (206). This mechanism, however, is much more difficult for a narrative to set in motion in respect of rough heroines; for rough heroines' badness is misaligned with the gender norms and gendered expectations that constitute readers' interpretive horizons, in a way in which rough heroes' is not (Clavel-Vazquez, 2018: 207–209).

Clavel-Vazquez's (2018) analysis of affective response to rough heroines shifts the focus away from what has so far been the paradigmatic case in scholarship on imaginative resistance – namely, the case of readers with sound moral beliefs resisting a fiction's morally unsound claims. Rather, her focus is on the regulatory regime of gender. This shift is interesting for two reasons. First, gender exceeds the moral dimension, in the sense that gender-based prescriptions appeal to both moral and non-moral (e.g. aesthetic) values. Secondly, because gender-based prescriptions are more often than not normatively unsound rather than sound, to the extent that they constrain readers, they tend to bring into evidence the distance between the normatively regulated beliefs people happen to hold and those that actually hold true.

The normative constraints/interpretive horizons that concern me in this book function like the regulatory regime of gender in both these key aspects. That is, they generate both moral and aesthetic prescriptions, and they articulate unsound rather than sound beliefs. These normative constraints are those associated with the psycho-social regulation of same-sex desire (including its legal regulation), when it takes the form of heteronormativity, homophobia and heterosexism. As regulatory regimes, heteronormativity, homophobia and heterosexism structure people's appreciation of the good, and particularly what counts as good interpersonal relationships, legitimate forms of intimacy and desire, genuine family relationships, and valuable forms of life. These are all goods that tend to be centrally integrated with people's sense of their personal identity, and they feature prominently within their conceptions or intuitions of what it is to lead a meaningful life. As such, heteronormativity, homophobia and heterosexism are precisely the kinds of normative constraints that, phenomenologically, are both capable and likely to trigger imaginative resistance in accordance with the principle of putative alignment.

The understanding of each of these terms – heteronormativity, homophobia and heterosexism – is somewhat contested. Some useful definitions, by those who pioneered the use of these terms, are as follows. Homophobia is the kind of prejudice rooted in 'the dread of being in close quarters with homosexuals – and in the case of homosexuals themselves, self-loathing' (Weinberg, 1972: 4). Heterosexism is 'a belief in the inherent superiority of one pattern of loving over all others' (Lorde, 1993: 9). Heteronormativity is 'heterosexual culture's exclusive ability to interpret itself as society … as the elemental form of human association, as the very model of intergender relations, as the indivisible basis of all community' (Warner, 1993: xxi).

Albeit the most recently coined, heteronormativity is the broadest and most fundamental of the three concepts, in the sense that while widespread homophobia and/or heterosexist institutions, where they exist, will accompany heteronormativity, heteronormativity can exist in the absence of the others. Likewise, heterosexism can exist in the absence of widespread homophobia. Heteronormativity and heterosexism are also broader than homophobia because they posit normative (couple-based, cis-, etc) heterosexuality as superior (as in heterosexism) or paradigmatic (as in heteronormativity) not just in relation to same-sex desire, but other forms of intimacy too, such as those involving trans partners, polyamorous relationships, etc. Both heterosexism and heteronormativity, additionally, tend to carry with them the connotation of their being problems that are systemic in nature, in a way in which homophobia does not have to be (but sometimes is). This is perhaps because homophobia's more virulent nature makes it psychologically and morally worthy of note even where it occurs on an episodical basis, while heterosexism and heteronormativity seem to matter, ultimately, to the extent that they have relatively widespread social consequences.

Not just heteronormativity and heterosexism (for example through family and immigration laws), but homophobia itself (through such legal categories as sodomy and buggery) have a long history of being embedded in Western law. The relationship tends to be mutually constitutive: laws are homophobic, heterosexist and/or heteronormative because society is, and vice-versa. Law constitutes and reinforces (but may also, through law reform, de-authorise) heterosexism, heteronormativity and homophobia. It does so to the extent that it is an authoritative discourse that makes claims to truth (Smart, 1989) and shapes social meanings, value judgements and identities, particularly, though not exclusively, through the criminal/non-criminal dichotomy (Merry, 2000: 262). Hence, law is implicated in structuring the normative commitments that may trigger imaginative resistance in readers who are confronted with fictional treatments of same-sex desire that challenge the homophobic, heteronormative, or heterosexist structures of their societies.

Imaginative resistance beyond readers' imagination

The concept of interpretive horizon invoked by Clavel-Vazquez (2018) is borrowed from Gadamer (2013), where it stands for the baggage of tradition-ratified values and pre-judgments that each reader brings to any interpretive encounter with a text. Interpretive horizons both enable and constrain interpretation. They enable it because they are constituted by broader, collectively validated structures of meaning – what Gadamer (2013) calls 'tradition'. This provides the common ground between readers and texts: texts have their own horizons too, derived from the same tradition as the reader's own horizon, and consisting in the outcomes of the tradition-enabled interpretive practices to which texts have been subjected. For the very same reason that they enable interpretation, horizons also, necessarily, constrain interpretation; but they do so fluidly. This is because interpretation is the fusion of the reader's and text's horizons (Gadamer, 2013: 317, 386) both of which shift with each new interpretive encounter. A reader projects her horizon's 'prejudices' (her theoretical and normative commitments that precede the encounter with the text) onto the text, but the text's carrying its own horizon means that it puts up some resistance, giving rise to a process of revision and mutual adjustment between the reader's and text's horizons (Eskridge, 1990: 620–624). From this perspective, imaginative resistance can be seen to occur when a reader's prejudices are (rightly or wrongly) resistant to change, or to the degree of change necessary for her to find a common ground with the text.

The hermeneutic process described by Gadamer (2013) is not confined to texts of a particular kind (indeed, it is not confined to written texts at all: it also encompasses, for instance, interpretive encounters with works of art). Since hermeneutics is, at its most fundamental level, about what makes understanding possible, it seems clear that it is always implicated in communicative acts – not just when a recipient needs to make sense of such acts, but from the very moment the originator of the communicative act conceives the act and proceeds to deliver it to the world. Specifically, the originator's interpretive horizons will enable and constrain the communicative acts by determining, among other things, the range of contents it can carry. In the context of fiction, I want to argue that, therefore, imaginative resistance is not an experience peculiar to readers, that is to the recipients of the communicative act. Because any author, inevitably, has her own horizon, she will also experience imaginative resistance, in the sense of a resistance to make-believing (and committing to paper) what she *could* make fictional, if what she could make fictional conflicts with her own normative commitments.

If, in accordance with the alignment principle, what is normatively true in fiction must be capable of being true, *mutatis mutandis*, in the real world, then an author *could* make fictional the claims that homophobia is wrong, heterosexism damaging, and heteronormativity misguided (for these moral propositions are true in the real world). There are many reasons, however, why an author might choose not to make a claim of that kind. For example, she might not want to *spell out* that claim because she thinks, probably rightly, that fiction that preaches is bad fiction. But she might even choose not to make that claim indirectly – as she could do, say, by drawing attention to the dogmatic or irrational nature of characters who hold homophobic views – because, for example, it may not fit the story, or narrative voice. To the extent that there is no conflict between the claim that the author could make fictional and the (aesthetic) value judgements that lead her not to make that claim, these are not examples of authorial imaginative resistance. For analogous reasons, cases in which an author fails to make something normatively true in fiction because it conflicts with the normative commitments that the author ascribes to publishers, or to the general reading public, are also not genuine cases of an author's imaginative resistance. Rather, they are pragmatically-driven choices.

Genuine cases of an author's imaginative resistance are those where, in accordance with the alignment principle, she could make a normative claim (such as 'homophobia is wrong') true in fiction, but she fails to do so because it conflicts with the normative commitments that are constitutive of *her own* horizon. More interesting are cases where the conflict giving rise to imaginative infelicities is less stark: I have in mind, specifically, not the case where an author fails to make a certain normative claim, but where she feels that a certain narrative choice or outcome is precluded to her on *normative* grounds. The lack of same-sex happy endings in mid-century queer fiction fits this case.

The constatives that make up a story's ending are – more so than other fictional constative claims – especially likely to be dictated by normatively-inflected choices. Authors, particularly contemporary ones, may be very deliberate (for good aesthetic reasons) in trying to avoid reducing their story to a parable with a clear moral teaching. But the fact that the value of fiction is dependent on its ability successfully to speak to us as practical agents, together with the fact that moral reasons are of central significance to practical reason, explains why no-one bats an eyelid at using, as matter of course, the expression 'the moral of the story'. And it is a story's ending – as the culmination of the narrative – that delivers the story's moral. Thus, though the claim that Jack and Jack lived happily ever after, or at least a narrative outcome in which Jack and Jack are spared tragedy, is a statement of non-evaluative facts, an author's failure to use it as a way of wrapping up her story is as likely as not to be normatively inflected. In other words, it may be a case of imaginative resistance.[7]

---

7   Recall, here, what I argued in respect of imaginative resistance to non-evaluative claims, such as the claim that the earth is round: ultimately, it is commitment to certain normative beliefs (rather than to purely non-evaluative, theoretical ones) that accounts for why people may experience imaginative resistance even to such non-evaluative claims.

If, therefore, certain narrative outcomes in mid-century queer fiction are due to imaginative resistance, what are the normative constraints that engendered such resistance? It may be too crude, in many cases, to ascribe a story's tragic endings to the author's internalised homophobia. Texts of mid-century queer fiction were often, though not always, penned by queer writers themselves: it seems unlikely that many of them had a *dread* of queer people. In any case, the texts themselves often convey no such dread (though sometimes they do). Heteronormativity and, to a lesser extent, heterosexism are more likely candidates for explaining the majority of mid-century's queer fiction tragic endings. Here it is important to recall that, as I argued, heterosexism and heteronormativity, as regulatory regimes, generate not only moral prescriptions, but aesthetic ones too. An author (or reader) may, therefore, have resisted a same-sex happy ending on aesthetic rather than moral grounds. That is, an author's commitment to heteronormativity or heterosexism may be unconscious or unreflective enough that, although she might – with perfect sincerity – disclaim a commitment to the 'superiority of one pattern of loving' (Lorde, 1993: 9), or the view that heterosexual culture is 'the very model of intergender relations' (Warner, 1993: xxi), she might still be aesthetically drawn to narrative outcomes that are consistent with those views.

There is, of course, no simple relationship between a same-sex tragic ending and an author's heteronormative commitments. A same-sex tragic ending might, in *some* cases, be part of a narrative strategy directed at eliciting sympathy for queer characters, by conveying in an especially powerful way the evaluative claim that homophobia or heterosexism are unjust. Even in these cases, such authorial intentions do not rule out that the lack of happy ending may also be due to heteronormativity. In other words, a tragic ending may be overdetermined in complex ways. After all, the collectively validated semantic structures on which we draw to shore up our sense of identity, and to invest our lives with meaning, are not necessarily seamless, internally coherent webs. Thus, an anti-homophobic intent may co-exist alongside other determinants, such as an author's imaginative resistance to narrative outcomes that challenge heteronormativity, if only on the aesthetic plane.

Imaginative resistance beyond fiction

Although we have seen that they are not the only normative factors that have an effect on imaginative resistance (genre conventions being another), those normative constraints that consist in a reader's value-commitments are of particular interest – partly because they raise questions that are significant to branches of philosophy beyond the philosophy of fiction. It is these normative constraints that Stueber (2011: 159) has implicitly in mind where he argues that the imaginability puzzle transcends 'philosophical aesthetics', forcing on us the question of how we relate to the worldviews of those coming from different cultural backgrounds.

But how we relate to the other and her worldviews is only one of the 'real-world' problems that the imaginability puzzle confront us with. Another one addresses questions that have to do, broadly, with how we relate to ourselves and our own life. In this book, specifically, I tie the imaginability puzzle with the problem of an agent's self-awareness and practical reason. My question is: how do our normative commitments (interpretive horizons) constrain our sense of self as practical agents and, specifically, the options towards which we orient ourselves as authors of our own lives?

Just like the puzzle of readers' imaginative resistance in the fictional context has a real-world equivalent in the problem of how and why we may fail to relate to the worldviews of the other, so the problem of the non-imaginability of certain options one could choose as one scripts one's own life echoes, in the real world, the problem of authorial imaginative resistance in the fictional context. It is not by coincidence, I think, that Raz (1986: 369) describes the political ideal of personal autonomy precisely in terms of being '(part) author of [one's] own life'. The concept of authorship here provides a convenient link between the fictional context and the real world. It enables us to appreciate why it is not far-fetched to think of the real-life problem in the selfsame terms as the fictional problem – that is, in terms of imaginative resistance. This claim is particularly plausible if we accept, as I think we should, that imagination plays a crucial role in decision-making, particularly, it seems, when it comes to our non-routine decisions or decisions with long-term effects (Nanay, 2016).

Given the centrality of the ideal of personal autonomy to contemporary concep-tions of human well-being (Raz, 1986: 393), the application of the concept of authorship to describe one's agency in determining one's life course is especially apt. On the one hand, the concept draws attention to life's narrative structure – the fact, that is, that 'we equate life with the stories that we tell about it' (Ricoeur, 1991: 195). Just like the story an author of fiction has created remains open to interpretation, including her own re-interpretations as a reader of her own work, so our life's authorship is an ongoing process where the meaning of the choices we have made is redefined retrospectively through their interaction with subsequent choices, and the overall narrative into which we integrate them as we pause to take stock. On the other hand, far from overemphasising self-determination, the idea of being the author of one's own life also carries with it the useful connotation of acting within constraints. For, as I argued in the previous section, the paradigmatic case of author-ship (that of the fiction writer) is no less subject to normative constraints than the central case of readership (that of a normatively-committed reader) is.

We have seen above that, in the domain of fiction, constraints that account for imaginative resistance and that are not dependent on the deep structure of human cognition, are normative in nature, ranging from genre conventions to readers' and authors' interpretive horizons. In the real world, as in fiction, imaginative constraints are also normative in nature.[8] And, as in fiction, their

---

8   Material constraints – in the sense of lack of material resources, when it comes either to fiction or scripting one's life – restrict opportunities rather than directly the imagination as such. Lacking pen and paper, or a computer, or schooling, may prevent me from writing, not imagining. Similarly, lacking the means to leave a small and relatively isolated community might prevent me from finding a same-sex partner, not dreaming about one. There is a way in which severe lack of material

source is less the individual herself, than collective processes of meaning-making. At the same time, in committing to or internalising certain norms or regulatory regimes such as heteronormativity, and in taking them as action-guiding, the individual participates in the processes through which norms and normative orders are collectively validated and reinforced.

To pose the question of the imaginability puzzle in the context of the real, rather than fictional, world, and to do so not in respect of individuals faced with the task of imaginatively connecting with the worldviews of unfamiliar others, but in respect of practical agents as authors of their own lives, therefore, is to ask: how do normative commitments, whether conscious or unconscious, engender imaginative resistance in respect of the options we may pursue, the kind of life we can have, and the outcomes we can hope for?

Psychological literature has identified a greater incidence of mental disorders in lesbians, gay men and bisexuals than heterosexuals, and has accounted for it through the concept of minority stress, whereby mental health problems are both due to a social environment structured by prejudice and mediated by various stress processes, including internalised homophobia (Meyer, 2003). This is entirely consistent with the conception of well-being I have described in the Introduction. One's attitude towards oneself and one's life is important to one's well-being: being besieged by self-doubt or self-hatred (or feeling alienated from one's goals, even if worthwhile) diminishes one's quality of life and one's well-being (Raz, 1999: 306; Raz 1986: 382–383). Yet, the concept of imaginative resistance, applied, as I am proposing, to same-sex attracted practical agents in their capacity as authors of their lives, goes beyond this psychological approach. For it encourages us to consider how and why we can fail to flourish in ways that fall short of mental health disorders, and even when we do not suffer, necessarily, from internalised homophobia. The idea that the approach I am proposing gestures towards is perhaps more germane to a notion increasingly popular in 'positive psychology', as well as non-academic 'wellness' discourses – the idea of so-called 'self-permission'. The concept remains academically 'under-investigated in an empirical setting', but it can be taken to point to 'the degree to which a person allows themselves to attend to personal well-being and to lead a fulfilling life' (Løvestam, 2019: 22).

Same-sex happy endings and the good life

The imaginative resistance that interests me in the novels I analyse in this book is resistance to a same-sex happy ending. It interests me not only in its own right, but because interrogating the imaginative resistance authors experience in the process of fiction-writing has implications for our understanding of the imaginative resistance people experience in the real world, as authors of their own lives. Since, unlike most works of fiction, the process of self-authorship is

resources may also shackle the imagination, but considering these complexities is beyond the scope of my current analysis.

ongoing (until an end is put to it by events generally out of the author's control), the object of imaginative failure in the real world is less a happy ending than the good life. Indeed, there is a straightforward analogy here between fictional happy endings and the real world's good life, for after all a paradigmatic happy ending is just that: the promise of a good life.

I will not discuss those concepts – happy endings and the good life – in the abstract, but I am going to close this chapter by elaborating on them in relation to the particular set of problems they pose in the context of mid-century queer fiction and contemporary queer lives. Let me start with happy endings. The dearth of happy endings in queer-themed work dating from the middle of the twentieth century is doubly remarkable, perhaps, if we consider that much same-sex themed fiction revolves, by definition, around self-discovery, desire, love, and relationships. After all, these self-same themes are also central to a very specific genre of heterosexual fiction – romance – where happy endings are almost *de rigueur*. Interestingly, in the context of romance fiction, a lack of happy ending is perhaps often (not invariably) *ipso facto* also a tragic ending: a tale of shattered hopes, emotional wounds, the best years of one's life misspent, though in mid-century queer fiction these outcomes may be compounded by despair, suicide, violence, etc.

It is customary to account for early and mid-century same-sex themed fiction's tragic endings as products of writers' internalised homophobia. I have already explained that internalised heteronormativity or heterosexism seem more likely candidates to me. Additionally, I have noted that tragic endings may be serviceable to anti-homophobic goals – drawing attention to 'the plight of the homosexual', etc. It is also fair to say that literary fiction (and hence 'serious' writing) is not known for favouring unreconstructed happy endings, though it is obviously not incompatible with them.[9] Thus, the general dearth of happy endings in mid-century queer fiction may be due to different reasons in different texts, and may well be over-determined in the same text. An author's internalised heteronormativity may go hand-in-hand with imaginative constraints having to do with genre conventions, which commit her to the normatively regulated idea of 'serious writing'.

Critics endowed with a queer-theoretical sensibility might well challenge the assumption that underlie this project: namely, that there is something problematic, or regrettable, about the way in which mid-century queer fiction

9   An unreconstructed happy ending is possibly one of the very criteria (though neither a sufficient, nor a necessary one) we use to judge whether a novel is literary or commercial – something that has to do with the way in which high-brow fiction, by the twentieth century, came to define itself as being about the treatment of 'serious' themes, rather than providing readers with enjoyment or pleasurable feelings. I know that in the context of contemporary same-sex-themed fiction, when an author makes a point of marketing herself as committed to happy endings, my immediate expectation is that the novels she writes will fall in the category of commercial, rather than literary or upmarket, fiction. In some cases – notably, contemporary female-authored M/M romance – happy endings are virtually a genre convention.

systematically eschewed conventional happy endings. Such critics, for whom authentic queerness may be synonymous with a counter-normative impulse, might well choose to read the kinds of texts I am interested in against the grain. They might thus be able to find new, perhaps covert, possibilities for queer being and queer belonging in the very ways in which the texts resist what might be a conventional same-sex happy ending. They might, perhaps, find in such texts echoes of the kind of counternormativity that, for example, the fiction of Genet expressly celebrates.

As I argued, however, the value of fiction is dependent at least in part on how successfully it speaks to our practical reason. This does not mean that fiction needs to be morally edifying. It does mean, however, that it should be able to speak intelligibly about human goods in ways that are consistent with their truth-value in the real world (and a choice of ending may well – though it does not have to – play a role in how successfully a work of fiction manages to speak to the good). It follows that the value of Genet's work is (partly) dependent on illuminating moral truth by indirection, not in its being taken at face value as ratifying an inversion of the good. Such inversion would not be a genuine, hence interesting, alternative to the kind of good life gestured towards (only to remain ultimately unattainable) in the more mainstream kinds of texts that I centre in this book.

Broadly speaking, a good life is one in which an individual succeeds in realising her autonomously chosen, valuable comprehensive goals, which include the pursuit of meaningful personal relationships (Raz, 1999: 64). The particular shape that human goods, including forms of human relationships, concretely take in any society is partly dependent on collectively validated social forms (Raz, 1986: 398). Because of this, the kind of queer imaginative resistance to the good life that concerns me in this book is less a failure to imagine radically different forms of intimacy, relationality, or, indeed, unattached forms of queer existence, than imaginative resistance to forms of human flourishing described in the introduction as same-sex committed relationships. These are not only the valuable forms of life that have traditionally been made impossible or unnecessarily difficult to pursue for same-sex attracted people in the real world, but also those that tend to preoccupy the characters of mid-century queer novels, and which, by the end of the story, tend to remain elusive to them.

Conclusions

When, as readers of fiction, we experience imaginative resistance we withdraw our assent from the fictional world the author has created because we cannot bring ourselves to make-believe certain of its features. Evaluative (including moral) claims, when they conflict with normative beliefs we are committed to, are particularly liable to elicit our imaginative resistance, though non-evaluative factual claims may do too, particularly if they conflict with readers' beliefs about psychological truths.

The truth-value of moral (and psychological) claims in fiction simply tracks their truth-value in the real world. Such claims are true in fiction if, *mutatis mutandis*, they would be true in the real world. An author cannot change the actual truth value of moral principles because the point of fiction lies, at least partly, in readers imaginatively engaging with a world that remains meaningful to us from the point of view of practical agency. An appreciation of the good is central to structures of meaning, and practical agency means meaningfully orienting ourselves in the world in light of the good; thus, for a work of fiction to speak to us, it must need speak to the good. In sum, moral non-truths cannot be made true in fiction because fiction is a purposive activity governed by practical reason.[10]

In this sense, Nanay (2010: 587) is right in claiming that the fictionality puzzle (the question of what makes something true in fiction) is, unlike the imaginability puzzle (the question of what we are able to imagine) 'not really about us' (as readers). For what is true in fiction is a function of what makes something true in the real world, and of certain structural features of the social practice of fiction. These features, in turn, are a function of the responsiveness of both practical reason and meaning to the good, rather than being dependent on the beliefs of any contingent community of readers, writers, publishers, critics, etc.

That the value of fiction cannot be prised apart from its ability to speak to our practical thought explains why readers cannot grant authors not only the authority to bring about a misalignment between what values and principles (moral or otherwise) actually hold true in fiction and in the real world, but also the authority to switch the truth value of psychological truths. This is because the workings of the human mind is just the medium through which we orient our practical thought towards the good in the world

We experience imaginative resistance *because* we do not grant authors the authority to bring about a misalignment between what evaluative (and psychological) claims actually hold true in fiction and in the real world. However, because we believe, rightly or wrongly, in the correctness of our *beliefs* about moral and other goods and principles, we tend to experience imaginative resistance *when* authors would have us make-believe something to be normatively (or psychologically) true that we do not *believe* holds true (regardless of where the truth of the matter actually lies).

Humans are motivated by a desire to invest their life with meaning, as our sense of self is dependent on inter-subjectively validated structures of meaning. These structures revolve around appreciations of the good, including the moral

10 Suppose, for example, that the entire community of people involved in the practice of fiction when Forster wrote *Maurice* had a chance to read it, and they all believed same-sex desire to be always wrong. That consensus would not make Forster's sympathetic treatment of same-sex desire incapable of being true in fiction, because it is not people's beliefs that determine the actual truth value of the goodness of same-sex desire: rather, this depends on the kind of thing that same-sex desire is and/or the consequences that it has or may have.

good. This explains why our imagination withholds from writers the option of toying with our normative universe as we *believe* it to be, rather than as it is.

Moral and other evaluative claims that conflict with our normative commitments tend to elicit imaginative resistance because our normative commitments are central to our practical thought and to our subjective constitution as, first and foremost, practical agents. Thus moral and other evaluative claims often have implications for meaning and identity in ways that many purely factual claims do not. That is, the stakes are high when we are being asked to buy into statements that expressly or implicitly invoke moral, aesthetic, and other goods in ways that we reject: this is because appreciations of such goods are just what guides our practical reason, and what we utilise to invest life with meaning. Analogous reasons account for why falsifying psychological truths tends to elicit imaginative resistance: our appreciation of psychological truths too is bound up with our practical reason, and so with our sense of self as practical agents. More broadly, in those cases in which the imaginative activity prescribed to us involves non-evaluative facts, our degree of imaginative resistance will also depend on how centrally integrated with our sense of self is our commitment to conflicting non-evaluative factual beliefs. When commitment to certain non-evaluative factual beliefs is inextricably bound up with our sense of self, this is itself likely to be a result of our commitment to certain normative beliefs (as in the case of religious beliefs prescribing commitment to the − in itself non-evaluative − fact of the flatness of the Earth).

The normative beliefs or commitments that may lead us to experience imaginative resistance are those that imbue our world with meaning. Meaning sediments as a result of inter-subjective processes: thus, the values we come to hold as true, which act as imaginative constraints accounting for the puzzle of imaginative resistance, are collectively validated. Such constraints are normative in nature. The normative constraints that concern me in this book are those associated with heteronormativy, homophobia and heterosexism.

Heteronormativy, homophobia and heterosexism structure people's appreciation of what counts as good interpersonal relationships, legitimate forms of intimacy and desire, genuine family relationships, and valuable forms of life. These are all goods that tend to be centrally integrated with people's sense of their personal identity, and they loom large in their conceptions the good life. Thus, heteronormativy, homophobia and heterosexism are precisely the kinds of normative commitments that can constrain a reader's imagination. To the extent that law is built on heteronormativity, it is implicated in triggering imaginative resistance in readers who are confronted with fictional treatments of same-sex desire that are misaligned with their own heteronormative beliefs.

The normative beliefs readers are committed to are part of their interpretive horizon. But everyone has their horizon − not just readers, but also authors. Therefore, imaginative resistance is not an experience peculiar to readers. Authors will also experience difficulty in make-believing (and hence committing to paper) what they *could* make fictional, if this lies beyond their own interpretive horizon. Of particular interesting to this book are cases where an author feels that a certain narrative choice or outcome (rather than a normative claim *per se*) is precluded to her on normative grounds. The lack of same-sex happy endings in mid-century queer fiction fits this case. A fictional outcome in which same-sex attracted characters live happily ever after, or at least are spared tragedy, is likely to be normatively inflected even if the outcome itself is no more than a statement of non-evaluative fact, of what happened. Indeed, a story's ending – as the culmination of the narrative – is especially likely to be dictated by normatively-inflected choices.

While in some cases queer authors of mid-century queer fiction may have been self-loathing, it seems that more frequently their choice to end the story in tragedy was due to heteronormativity or heterosexism, rather than internalised homophobia. Since heterosexism and heteronormativity, as regulatory regimes, generate not only moral prescriptions, but aesthetic ones too, some authors of mid-century queer-themed novels may have imaginatively resisted a same-sex happy ending on aesthetic rather than moral grounds. Because the semantic structures on which we draw to invest our lives with meaning are not necessarily internally coherent webs, a tragic ending may also be overdetermined in complex ways.

The imaginative resistance that interests me in the following chapters is authorial resistance to a same-sex happy ending. It interests me in its own right, but also because the problem of authorial imaginative resistance in the fictional context has a real-world parallel in the non-imaginability of certain options for a practical agent involved in the process of scripting her own life. The concept of imaginative resistance, then, illuminates not just the constraints on the imagination of authors of (queer) fiction, but also the real-life problem of one's (queer) self-authorship. Self-authorship here describes one's agency in determining one's life course, and draws attention to life's narrative structure. As in fiction, imaginative constraints in the real world are also normative in nature, and their source is less the individual herself, than collective processes of meaning-making. Since, unlike most works of fiction, the process of self-authorship is ongoing, the object of imaginative infelicities in the real world is less a happy ending than the good life. An advantage of applying the concept of imaginative resistance to same-sex attracted practical agents in their capacity as authors of their own lives is that it brings into focus how and why we can fail to flourish in ways that fall short of those described in the psychological literature on mental health disorders.

References

Black, JE and Barnes, JL (2017) 'Measuring the Unimaginable: Imaginative Resistance to Fiction and Related Constructs', *Personality and Individual Differences*, vol 111, 71–79.

Clavel-Vazquez, A (2018) 'Sugar and Spice, and Everything Nice: What Rough Heroines Tell Us about Imaginative Resistance', *The Journal of Aesthetics and Art Criticism*, vol 76(2), 201–212.

Driver, J (2008) 'Imaginative Resistance and Psychological Necessity', *Social Philosophy and Policy*, vol 25(1), 301–313.

Eskridge, WN, Jr (1990) 'Gadamer/Statutory Interpretation', *Columbia Law Review*, vol 90, 609–681.

Fish, S (1989) 'Anti-Professionalism' in *Doing What Comes Naturally: Change, Rhetoric and the Practice of Theory in Literary and Legal Studies* (Durham and London: Duke University Press) 215–246.

Freud, A (2018) *The Ego and Mechanisms of Defence* (Abingdon, UK and New York: Routledge).

Gadamer, HG (2013) *Truth and Method*, Weinsheimer, J and Marshall, DG (trans), (London: Bloomsbury, revised 2nd edition).

Gendler, TS (2000) 'The Puzzle of Imaginative Resistance', *Journal of Philosophy*, vol 97(2), 55–81.

Habermas, J (1979) *Communication and the Evolution of Society*, McCarthy, T (trans), (Boston: Beacon).

Liao, S, Strohminger, N and Sripada, CS (2014) 'Empirically Investigating Imaginative Resistance', *British Journal of Aesthetics*, vol 54(3), 339–355.

Lorde, A (1993) 'There Is no Hierarchy of Oppressions' in Cleavers, R and Myers, P (eds) *A Certain Terror: Heterosexism, Militarism, Violence, and Change* (Chicago: Great Lakes Regional Office of the American Friends Service Committee).

Løvestam, CK (2019) 'Self-Permission and Well-Being: Self-Permission as a "Key" to Flourishing in Therapy and Positive Interventions'. Master of Applied Positive Psychology (MAPP) Capstone Projects 164. https://repository.upenn.edu/mapp_capstone/164.

Mahtani, A (2012) 'Imaginative Resistance without Conflict', *Philosophical Studies*, vol 158(3), 415–429.

Matravers, D (2003) 'Fictional Assent and the (So-Called) "Puzzle of Imaginative Resistance"' in Kieran, M and Lopes, DM (eds) *Imagination, Philosophy, and the Arts.* (London: Routledge) 91–106.

Merry, SE (2000) *Colonizing Hawai'i: The Cultural Power of Law* (Princeton: Princeton University Press).

Meyer, IH (2003) 'Prejudice, Social Stress, and Mental Health in Lesbian, Gay, and Bisexual Populations: Conceptual Issues and Research Evidence', *Psychological Bulletin*, 129 (5) 674–697.

Nanay, B (2010) 'Imaginative Resistance and Conversational Implicature', *The Philosophical Quarterly*, vol 60(240), 586–600.

Nanay, B (2016) 'The Role of Imagination in Decision-Making', *Mind & Language*, vol 31(1), 127–143.

Nussbaum, M (1993) 'Skepticism about Practical Reason in Literature And the Law Commentary', *Harvard Law Review*, vol 107, 714–744.

Nussbaum, M (2003) 'Cultivating Humanity in Legal Education', *University of Chicago Law Review*, vol 70, 267–279.

Peterson, E (2019) 'Imaginative Resistance and Variation', *British Journal of Aesthetics*. vol 59(1), 67–80.

Radin, MJ and Frank Michelman, F (1991) 'Pragmatist and Poststructuralist Critical Legal. Practice', *University of Pennsylvania Law Review*, vol 139, 1019–1058.

Raz, J (1986) *The Morality of Freedom* (Oxford: Oxford University Press).

Raz, J (1999) *Engaging Reason: On the Theory of Value and Action* (Oxford: Oxford University Press).

Ricoeur, P (1991) 'Narrative identity' in Wood, D (ed.) *On Paul Ricoeur: Narrative and Interpretation* (London and New York: Routledge).

Rubin, EL (1998) 'Putting Rational Actors in Their Place: Economics and Phenomenology', *Vanderbilt Law Review*, vol 51(6), 1705–1727.

Sauchelli, A (2019) 'On the Study of Imaginative Resistance', *Analytic Philosophy*, vol 60(2),164–178.

Smart, C (1989) *Feminism and the Power of Law* (London: Routledge).

Stokes, DR (2006) 'The Evaluative Character of Imaginative Resistance', *The British Journal of Aesthetics*, vol 46(4), 387–405.

Stueber, KR (2011) 'Imagination, Empathy, and Moral Deliberation: The Case of Imaginative Resistance', *Southern Journal of Philosophy*, vol 49(s1) 156–180.

Todd, CS (2009) 'Imaginability, Morality, and Fictional Truth: Dissolving the Puzzle of "Imaginative Resistance"', *Philosophical Studies*, vol 43(2), 187–211.

Warner, M (1993) 'Introduction' in Warner M (ed.) *Fear of a Queer Planet: Queer Politics and Social Theory* (Minneapolis: University of Minnesota Press) 7–31.

Weinberg, G (1972) *Society and the Healthy Homosexual* (New York: St Martin's Press).

Zanghellini, A (2020) 'Antihumanism in Queer Theory', *Sexualities*, vol 23(4), 530–548.

Zanghellini, A and Sato, M (2020) 'A Critical Recuperation of Watsuji's *Rinrigaku*', *Philosophia*, https://doi.org/10.1007/s11406-020-00296-1.

2 Same sex desire in Britain and the United States in the postwar years

Introduction

The Anglo-American novels I discuss in the following chapters date from a period spanning the immediate aftermath of World War II (WWII) through to the years leading up to the sexual revolution of the 1960s. A review of historical findings provides evidence of considerable debate over, and regulation of, same-sex desire on both sides of the Atlantic during this period. An appreciation of these regulatory practices and discourses will bring home the ideological and normative constraints at work on the authors of the queer novels I analyse in subsequent chapters – constraints that, in accordance with what I argued in the second part of chapter one, help explain these authors' imaginative resistance to same-sex happy endings. My review of historical literature begins with the war years, as the regulatory practices surrounding same-sex desire in the period we are concerned with were partly a reaction to, and shaped by, the treatment of homosexuality during wartime.

The United States

There is general agreement that in both Britain and the US, WWII provided probably unprecedented opportunities for same-sex desire to be enacted and even validated, in ways impossible during the interwar or postwar years. The treatment of homosexuality in the US armed forces during WWII has been comprehensively researched by Bérubé (2010). The US Military had had no policy or procedures in place to exclude homosexuals *qua* homosexuals from the armed forces during World War I (WWI). Rather, to the extent that sodomy was a criminal offence, its occurrence among servicemen was liable to criminal prosecution, resulting in a court-martial and sentencing to several years of hard labour and dishonourable discharge (Bérubé, 2010: 129). After the war, however, the incidence of mental illness among WWI veterans convinced military authorities – given, also, the costs of providing psychiatric care – that it was advisable to prevent those deemed psychologically unsuited to service from joining the armed forces in the first place. As a result, psychiatric screening standards to that effect were introduced during the interwar years, though

DOI: 10.4324/9781003188797-3

never seriously implemented (Bérubé, 2010: 13–14). In the early forties, psychiatrists – partly motivated by a desire to increase the social influence of their profession – pushed for updating such standards (which used the outmoded vocabulary of degeneration) and for establishing a full-blown screening process (Bérubé, 2010: 9, 13, 14). While some of the leading figures among these psychiatrists were homosexuals who opposed homosexuality being included among the psychiatric conditions that should disqualify one from serving, military authorities were more easily swayed by those who did recommend treating homosexuality as a psychiatric disturbance that made one unfit for service (Bérubé, 2010: 10–11).

Excluding homosexual male recruits, thus, became the Military's official policy during WWII. Conversely, the lack of criminalisation of female same-sex sexual activity and the social invisibility of female same-sex desire meant that any policy concerning the rejection of lesbian recruits was belated, with little time to implement before the end of the war (Bérubé, 2010: 28–32). In practice, however, those in charge of assessing recruits often did not turn away same-sex attracted men either. This is because they disagreed with the policy, or because they had to meet recruitment targets, or because they were embarrassed to pursue an investigation into potential recruits' sexuality, or because they were mindful of the social consequences (ostracism, unemployment, etc.) that a recruit rejected on the ground of homosexuality might incur; or, finally, because the recruits themselves were eager to serve and concealed their homosexuality (Bérubé, 2010: 20–27). The effect of the policy, however, was to make homosexuality itself, understood as a pathological mental condition – as distinct from the (criminalised) same-sex sexual activity to which it could give rise – an object of preoccupation and censure in the Military (Bérubé, 2010: 33).

Homosexual men and women joined the US armed forces in such numbers that the Military could neither afford to ignore them nor to purge them *en masse* (Bérubé, 2010: 34). An array of responses was employed to manage trainees' homosexuality, sometimes deferring to the views of psychiatric consultants, who went some way toward normalising the idea of situational homosexuality in the armed forces (Bérubé, 2010: 45–46). These responses included unofficial practices, such as assigning homosexual trainees to tasks deemed suitable to their psychological makeup (Bérubé, 2010: 57); semi-official ones, such as the publication of a handbook encouraging soldiers to sublimate their same-sex desire, reassuring them that it was a by-product of their gender-segregated environment, and implicitly recommending tolerance of servicemen who kept their sexual life private (49, 51); and official ones, such as educational lectures (46), or the Women Armed Corps' advice to channel trainees' female same-sex desire into hero-worship beneficial to the war effort (50).

Then, in 1944, came a formal policy change concocted by psychiatric consultants working in cooperation with military authorities (Bérubé, 2010: 131): only cases of non-consensual sodomy, or sodomy with minors, would be prosecuted and result in dishonourable discharges (137). Homosexuals – male or female – who were deemed redeemable (typically, though not exclusively, young men and women supposed to engage in situational homosexuality) would be rehabilitated and retained (137, 142). On the other hand, irredeemable, confirmed homosexuals and lesbians would be discharged without trial – whether or not they had performed same-sex sexual acts (142, 146–147) – with the kind of 'undesirable' (rather than dishonourable) discharge hitherto reserved for the mentally ill (139). Often this would be after many months of forcible confinement in hospitals' psychiatric wards (148). This treatment, distinguishing between young redeemable homosexuals and confirmed homosexuals, was also now officially reserved to lesbian women in the armed forces (142). In practice, some sympathetic psychiatrists in charge of assessing servicemen technically due for undesirable discharges sometimes managed to conceal their patients' sexual orientation and retain them in the service or secure for them honourable discharges (166). Officers, however, could be ruthless, adopting practices designed to humiliate and coerce personnel into confessing their homosexuality so as to proceed with their discharge (203–204). An undesirable discharge meant, among other things, that veterans so discharged were not deemed by the Veterans Administration entitled to veteran benefits. This is despite the fact that the relevant law excluded from those benefits only those discharged under 'dishonourable conditions' – an expression that should have been understood to cover only dishonourable discharges, which, unlike undesirable discharges, were effected following due process procedures in a court martial (Walters, 2004: 15).

In any case, the employment of the criminal law as a means of dealing with homosexuals was reduced as a result of the new discharge policy. The reach of the Military's management of homosexuality, however, increased via the deployment of medical discourses, reinforcing the pathologisation of lesbians and gay men (Bérubé, 2010: 148). At the same time, the confinement of large numbers of gay men in US military hospitals resulted in a considerable number of psychiatric studies (152), some of which challenged the crudest medical stereotypes and misconceptions, and recommended a more sensitive treatment of homosexuality in the armed forces (169–174).

Despite a move away from prosecuting adult consensual same-sex sexual activity, there is evidence of outbursts of gay witch-hunts (though their frequency is difficult to establish), resulting in confining gay servicemen in special makeshift 'queer stockades' or 'pink cells' under armed guard, often without trial, sometimes for months (Bérubé, 2010: 213–216). The US Military's growing preoccupation with homosexuality in the armed forces also resulted in increased surveillance of servicemen's sexual activity while on leave. The vice-control powers of the military police, originally granted with a view to curbing heterosexual prostitution and the spread of venereal disease, were now employed to target same-sex sexual activity, particularly by clamping down on venues where such activity occurred (Bérubé, 2010: 120–121), or making them out of bounds for servicemen (Faderman and Timmons, 2006: 73).

Yet, simply by extricating young men and women from their tightly controlled family environments and releasing them on leave in large numbers in urban environments, the war multiplied their opportunities for engaging in same-sex sexual activity (Bérubé, 2010: 126; Faderman and Timmons, 2006: 72; Walters, 2004: 20). A combination of factors played a role in precipitating this state of affairs. These include recruits' and civilians' wartime urge to take chances in a climate of precariousness about one's immediate future (Bérubé, 2010: 98); the crowded conditions in servicemen's hotels and similar establishments, which encouraged promiscuity (109); the relocation of gay bars towards city centres, where servicemen and servicewomen would spend their short leave (113); and the increasing specialisation of these venues, as they reorganised following a crackdown at the hands of the military police (124–126). Thus, the war also had a more enduring effect on gay civilian life, prompting it to shift from a model organised around 'stable private networks' towards more transient patterns of interpersonal engagement in the context of 'public commercial environments' (126).

Meanwhile, gay servicemen and women developed their own survival and fitting-in strategies, such as avoiding physical contact during the first months of service (Bérubé, 2010: 38–39), exploiting the buddy system to insulate their relationships from suspicion (187–188), capitalising on the tendency to credit butch women with authoritative leadership (56), and exploiting the benevolent tolerance afforded to effeminate men by straight personnel as long as they fulfilled expected social roles, such as entertainer (52–54). Forms of entertainment affording some gay men tolerance or popularity included GIs' all male shows incorporating drag routines (67–68). These were organised with the blessing of military authorities, who saw the shows' potential for boosting troops' morale (97).

As the war effort progressed, the need for manpower prompted a relaxation of the Military's anti-homosexual stance. Officially, this included, among other things, the re-induction of gay ex-servicemen with undesirable discharges but no proven commission of in-service same-sex sexual acts, as well as the War Department's recognition that environmental factors (namely, the exposure of men serving overseas to different moral codes) might understandably lead to 'unnatural practices' (Bérubé, 2010: 180). Unofficially, it meant anything from turning a blind eye to homosexuality if it meant retaining valuable military personnel (180), through officers protecting flamboyant gay soldiers who performed well (184), to servicemen's camaraderie transcending sexual divisions (186, 198).

The military authorities' mellowing of their anti-homosexual policies and practices was paralleled by servicemen's own liberalisation of attitudes towards same-sex desire as they were thrown into gender-segregated, high-risk environments and came to rely on each other for physical and emotional support. This led to heterosexually-identified personnel becoming involved in same-sex intimate relationships providing for both romantic and sexual comfort (Bérubé, 2010: 188–189). In other cases, heterosexual servicemen turned to same-sex intimacy simply because they could, for sexual relief and experimentation: certain locales had become notorious as gay cruising grounds in the armed forces, and homosexual sexual partners could be found even in the districts frequented by men in search of straight sex (192–194).

For many lesbians and gay men, when the war ended it was business as usual – going back into the closet, self-denial, and trying to fit in with the expectation that they marry heterosexually. But for others, their wartime experiences profoundly altered their sense of self and of life options, so much so that Bérubé (2010: 257) claims that they 'were the first generation of gay men and women to experience … rapid, dramatic, and widespread changes in their lives as homosexuals'.

On the one hand, the comparative affirmation of their sexuality during service (through meeting other same-sex attracted soldiers, discovering gay bars and gay cruising in the cities, and being accepted by other servicemen living through similar hardships, regardless of sexuality) emboldened gay veterans to resist, upon their return to civilian life, the social pressures to hide or repress their sexuality. On the other hand the armed forces' apparatus to identify, manage or discharge *homosexual* servicemen (as distinct from servicemen engaging in same-sex sexual acts) also had a number of unexpected effects: it made it impossible for some homosexual soldiers to go back into the closet, and it gave others a vocabulary and conceptual framework to elaborate a sense of their own sexual identity (Bérubé, 2010: 256). A few gay veterans set up gay support organisations, such as the Veterans' Benevolent Association; and many more took steps at least to improve their own private lives, for example by coming out to their families, or by falling in with the broader population's postwar pattern of relocation to the suburbs, but doing so in order to share a quiet life with same-sex lovers (Bérubé, 2011: 54). Others left their hometowns for cities such as Los Angeles (Faderman and Timmons, 2006: 72–74) or San Francisco (Bérubé, 2011: 54), where opportunities to meet like-minded people and lead less conventional lives were greater (Bérubé, 2010: 243–252).

Indeed, in major cities such as LA even before the end of the war a sizeable queer population had enabled some homosexuals to create support networks – in one documented case, a network embedded in the context of a self-managed small lesbian neighbourhood (Faderman and Timmons, 2006: 105–106). The further, postwar influx of gay people to cities – which the local press was sometimes the first to decry – was instrumentalised for political gain by both incumbents of and candidates for political office. The latter accused the former to be soft on deviates, and arrests of lesbians and gay men and revocation of licenses to queer bars dramatically increased at convenient times, such as shortly before or after local elections (Bérubé, 2011: 54–60; Faderman and Timmons, 2006: 76).

While gay bars proliferated around the country in the postwar years, they did so in a context of repressive regulation and police crackdowns. San Francisco's police force had its own special squad targeting sexual deviance (Bérubé, 2011: 54–60), and undercover officers of Los Angeles Police Department's (LAPD) vice squad were known not only to respond to, but also initiate invitations to sexual activity, leading to arrest of gay men via so-called 'entrapment' (Faderman and Timmons, 2006: 78–80). In Chicago same-sex dancing and cross-dressing (which at the time was associated with homosexuality) were illegal, and plainclothes police officers saw that no same-sex physical contact occurred

(D'Emilio, 2014: 139, 162, 166). The same activities in LA could lead to a bar being closed down; and by the mid-fifties even the comparative tolerance that the LPDA had extended, in the forties, to lesbian establishments – which by now had diversified to include working class bars patronised by butch-femme couplings – disappeared, under cultural pressures to enforce conformity to gender roles. This also led to targeting gender-nonconforming lesbians on the street across all major American cities (Faderman and Timmons, 2006: 83–97).

In short, while gay bars played a vital function in enabling patrons to meet with like-minded people, they were hardly a haven of sexual liberation (D'Emilio, 2014: 166–167). The California Supreme Court did hold, in 1951, that a bar could not be shut down simply because homosexuals – who had a First Amendment right to freedom of association – socialised there; but it also sanctioned the practice of arresting lesbians and gay men engaging in public displays of affection in these venues, by declaring that manifestations of sexual desire could be legitimately regulated (but failing to note that the police did not enforce any such regulations against heterosexuals, Walters, 2004: 21). On the other hand, gay bathhouses with an exclusively gay male clientele (which also first emerged in this period) appear to have been often tolerated better than bars, because of their more discrete and elite nature (Bérubé, 2011: 70–71).

It has been argued that the postwar years are poorly understood in American political and cultural life 'because they were so unstable', with many forces – both progressive and reactionary – 'at work in unprecedented ways' (Bergman, 2004: 44). Consistent with this assessment, the postwar years – albeit hailing a re-elaboration of traditional family values, as well as collective anti-homosexual hysteria finding expression in the so-called 'lavender scare' (Johnson, 2004) – also saw the emergence of a recognisable gay political movement and gay press (Bérubé, 2010: 270–273).

Indeed, Bergman (2004: 44) claims that until 1953 there was a veritable 'flowering of homosexual expression' in the US. *Vice Versa,* for example, was a short-lived, limited circulation lesbian magazine, which appeared in LA in the 1940s (Faderman and Timmons, 2006: 106–108). Lesbian pulp was perhaps the most visible and profitable form of same-sex themed printed work in the 1950s (see Keller, 2005: 387, 402–403). Although most lesbian-themed paperbacks were often written by straight men for heterosexual erotic titillation, both Keller (2005: 390) and D'Emilio (2014: 147–148) note that a number of lesbian authors did turn to the genre and were thereby able to write stories that, albeit constrained by genre conventions, better resonated with a female same-sex attracted readership.

Most lesbians and gay men living in the fifties did not engage in political mobilisation to assert their rights – whether through fear of the consequences, internalisation of discourses on homosexuality that impaired their sense of self-worth, or pessimism about the prospects of change (Walters, 2004: 22). The Mattachine Society, however – founded in Los Angeles in 1950 – was propelled to notoriety in 1952, when it organised a campaign in support of one of its members, Dale Jennings, who had been set up for criminal prosecution by a police officer posing as a sexual partner. After Jennings' acquittal, Mattachine's membership grew exponentially (White, 2009: 19–27; Walters, 2004: 23).

Mattachine failed, however, to attract many lesbians, whose gendered socialisation alienated them from political activism, and whose survival strategies involved (particularly for middle-class lesbians) the creation of private support networks or companionable communities coupled with a quest for not drawing attention to themselves. While the first US lesbian organisation, Daughters of Bilitis, was, like Mattachine, founded in the fifties, it was intended, at its inception, less as a political organisation than a social one. Even when practices of consciousness-raising gave the organisation a political valence, this did not translate into public political activism, and the organisation's goals remained ill-defined (Faderman and Timmons, 2006: 126–131). After its first year Daughters of Bilitis did issue a statement of educational and research purposes, but both the organisation's membership and the circulation of its magazine, *the Ladder,* remained small (Walters, 2004: 11, 25).

Mattachine members (including Jennings himself) launched, under the aegis of ONE Inc, the magazine ONE, whose goal was to analyse homosexuality scientifically, historically, and critically, and to promote social integration for homosexuals (White, 2009: 33ff). In both Mattachine and ONE, tensions existed between culturalists, who saw homosexuals as a discrete minority with a distinctive culture and championed the right to self-expression and to be different, and assimilationists, who downplayed differences between heterosexuals and homosexuals, and sought to secure homosexuals the right to privacy and to participate in mainstream society (White, 2009: 28–29, 38–43; Walters, 2004: 24). Mattachine also saw infighting quickly arise between its original founders, who were political radicals influenced by Marxism, and its expanded membership. The latter, in the context of a national climate all-too-inclined to equate homosexuality with treason and communism, insisted on the need for the society to be politically neutral (White, 2009: 44–45). It has also been claimed that Mattachine was, on the whole, hostile to 'queens', and did not open its ranks to them out of fear that they would discredit the movement (Faderman and Timmons, 2006: 113–114).

ONE Inc's achievements were considerable. The magazine's circulation sold about 5,000 copies per month in several US states (Faderman and Timmons, 2006: 116). In 1955 ONE managed to set up an Institute for Homophile Studies, an educational project directed at promoting unbiased scholarly research into homosexuality (White, 2009: 73–74; Faderman and Timmons, 2006: 120–121), as well as a volunteer-run 'Division of Social Services', offering support and advice to gay people and their families (Faderman and Timmons, 2006: 122).

Yet, all this occurred against a background of undiminished, and in many ways intensified, coercive institutional practices against homosexuality in the postwar years.[1] The heterosexual nuclear family and traditional gender roles

---

1   The exception to this is that in the *immediate* aftermath of the war, military authorities showed themselves receptive to arguments about the injustice of denying veteran benefits to gay soldiers with undesirable discharges. These arguments were championed by black civil rights advocates, who argued that undesirable discharges were unfairly used not only against homosexuals, but also black soldiers who had challenged their dismal living conditions during service. Accordingly, the authorities

were pervasively idealised and promoted, as a reaction to the social upheaval wrought by the war. This was accompanied by anti-homosexual moral panics stirred up by the press; and much 'psy' discourse on homosexuality took a homophobic turn (Bérubé, 2010: 258; Walters 2014: 9–10). In 1952, Congress enacted a reform of immigration law that legitimised the exclusion of 'psychopathic' personalities, including homosexuals. In the first draft of the law, homosexuals had been expressly singled out alongside psychopaths for exclusion, but the drafter was later satisfied that homosexuality was already covered by the concept of psychopathic personality – an approach that the Immigration and Naturalization Service indeed proceeded to take, with the blessing of the Supreme Court, in *Boutilier v Immigration and Naturalization Service* (Walters, 2004: 16). This reform to federal immigration law was preceded by twenty-one states enacting so-called 'sex psychopaths laws' between 1947 and 1951, legalising the indefinite detention of homosexuals in mental asylums, requiring their registration as sex offenders with the police upon their release, and contributing to stigmatising them as degenerate, deviant and child molesters. Arrests for consensual sodomy, public indecency, patronising gay bars and cross-dressing increased (Bérubé, 2010: 258–259).

Arrests of gay men during bar raids or as a result of entrapment, often followed by exposure in the press, typically led to job loss, as well as loss of insurance and credit. Social ostracism, suicide, or cutting one's social ties and seeking anonymity through relocation were not uncommon consequences (Walters, 2004: 10–11). Gay men convicted of sodomy might on occasion be incarcerated for long terms, if a judge felt an example should be made of them (as in the case of some offenders of high professional or social status). Some states had particularly punitive laws. In California, the law was reformed in 1945, so that a second conviction for sodomy meant automatic life imprisonment. Sodomy laws and societal homophobia also made socially privileged gay men vulnerable to blackmail, including by organised crime and rogue police officers. There is also anecdotal evidence of electro-shock therapy and lobotomies performed on non-consenting lesbians and gay men, sometimes as a result of their being arrested and referred for psychiatric evaluation (Walters, 2004: 17–18).

It is no wonder that – despite oral history evidence of opportunities for homosexuals to socialise both in private and, in some locales such as LA beaches, publicly (Walters, 2004: 21–22) – many lesbians and gay men declared that living in the closet was *de rigueur* in the fifties, even in urban environments. Fears of exposure ran high even for lesbians, whose sexual activities were not in themselves unlawful. Passing strategies involved the practice of 'lavender couplings', where a gay man and a lesbian would pretend to date each other (Faderman and Timmons, 2006: 99–100).

(notably the Navy) allowed appeals by gay veterans and upgraded their discharges, though by 1947 hardliners prevailed (Bérubé, 2010: 229–243).

After the war, the Department of Defense (taking its lead from a new 1949 Navy directive) also rationalised its approach to homosexuality in a more punitive direction. Officials started systematically indoctrinating all new recruits into homophobia by delivering lectures on the homosexual threat to all recruits; and the discharge rate for homosexuals from 1946 and throughout the fifties was three times as high as during the war, save for plummeting again in the Navy during the Korean war, when securing manpower took a backseat to enforcing anti-homosexual policy (Bérubé, 2010: 260–264).

The Military's wartime and postwar anti-homosexual policies also paved the way for the lavender scare of the 1950s, when cold-war anxieties about enemies of the state concentrated on the figure of the homosexual public employee as a security threat. Homosexuals' general deviance, it was argued, predisposed them to Communism, and their liability to blackmail might well result in release of classified information (Johnson, 2004). Indeed, military intelligence officers testified to the security threat posed by homosexuals at the hearings of the Senate subcommittee investigating homosexuals in employment with the government, especially Department of State (Bérubé, 2010: 264–267). Republicans, out of office for two decades, and catching on to the potential benefits of politically instrumentalising homosexuality as a security threat (Walters, 2004: 14), claimed that homosexuals were overrepresented in the New Deal administration (Johnson, 2004: 84–89). The subcommittee's hearings and findings prompted an immediate and dramatic rise in the dismissal of homosexual government employees (Johnson, 2004: 73, 98). Between 1950 and 1952, three times as many Department of State employees were dismissed as those who lost their jobs for 'more straightforward security concerns' (Office of the Historian, 2011: 128–129).

This anti-homosexual witch-hunt culminated in President Eisenhower's executive order that sexual perverts must be neither hired nor retained in federal employment, including the workforce of companies with government contracts (Bérubé, 2010: 269). More than 800 gay or lesbian employees resigned or were dismissed in the two years that followed, in part thanks to the concerted efforts of the FBI and local police forces, which compiled lists of names following arrests, and passed them on to the Civil Service Commission. Some public universities were also affected (Walters, 2004: 14). Even the American Civil Liberties Union played its part, conceding that an inquiry into homosexuality was pertinent to security clearances, and defending the constitutionality of sodomy laws (Walters, 2004: 11). Bureaucratic agencies' efforts to exclude lesbians and gay men from federal employment 'persisted long after the political issue … died down', until a formal policy change in 1975 (Lewis, 1997: 387). This followed Court rulings such as *Norton v Macy*, in which the federal Circuit Court of Appeals for the District of Columbia cautiously held that a civil servant's homosexuality was not, without more, a legitimate ground for dismissal (Walters, 2004: 13).

At the very time the lavender scare was in full swing, Donald Webster Corey published his plea for justice in his 1951 book *The Homosexual in America* (Bérubé, 2010: 259–260). Not long afterwards, starting from the mid-fifties,

Evelyn Hooker published her psychological research, concluding that male homosexuality was not a mental illness and that gay men were as well-adjusted as their heterosexual counterparts (Faderman and Timmons, 2006: 124–125). But it is Alfred Kinsey's 1948 report, perhaps, that captured America's collective imagination the most: with its findings that 50 percent of adult males acknowledged being sexually attracted to other males on occasion, that 37 percent had sexual contact with another male leading to orgasm, and that homosexuals tended to have a vigorous sexual life and high levels of male sexual hormones, Kinsey's work radically challenged the widely held view that homosexuality was a pathological condition afflicting a minority of men deficient in virility (Tripp, 2002: 13–16). The Kinsey report has also been credited with enabling a genre of queer novels in the immediate postwar years which eschewed the rigid categorisation of characters into homosexual and heterosexuals, and rather relied on a conceptualisation of sexual orientation as a continuous, sliding scale (Bergman, 2004: 47).

Despite the importance and progressive impetus animating the Kinsey report and Corey's *The Homosexual in America,* it is difficult to gauge their concrete effects in the lives of gay Americans. The Kinsey report, for example, by insisting that there was no reliable way to attempt to spot homosexuals by their outward appearance or manners, might have increased social paranoia about the gay threat lurking in the midst of respectable America. And Corey's book, making a case for considering homosexuals a persecuted minority, might have added to the discourse that made self-acceptance and coming out so difficult for many gay teenagers in the fifties (Walters, 2004: 8–9).

In any case, the reason why these studies were ground-breaking is that they challenged the general orthodoxy about homosexuality in mid-century America – an orthodoxy that fully legitimised the othering of homosexuals as pathological, criminal, and disloyal. As Walters (2004: 12) puts it,

> The postwar campaign against homosexuals was stunning both in its scope and callousness.… [E]very major political institution was implicated.… The most insidious actions happened quietly, often blandly and bureaucratically, in exchanges of information amongst government agencies and in their administrative rulings, in the drafting of legislation, in legal outcomes, in the disregarding of acts of violence and intimidation, and of course, in the arrests of persons guilty of simply wanting to explore their own sexuality and meet basic social needs.

Britain

Cook (2014: 6) argues that although throughout much of the twentieth century sex between males was criminalised in Britain and homosexuality feared, London at least 'was (and was seen to be) equivocally accommodating of men who were "that way"'. In the first half of the century, there was no typical life experience, lifestyle, or living arrangements for same-sex attracted men: they could live alone, with other men, share a home with wives, reside either in the city or the country, and enjoy varying levels of material comfort (Cook, 2014: 77).

Circulation of knowledge about same-sex desire increased in British society in the interwar years, largely through the vehicle of the popular press, which promoted an association between same-sex desire and gender inversion. Except for reports of arrests or trials for same-sex sexual activities in the press, same-sex desire was rarely directly discussed in its own right; rather, it was largely addressed in a coded way through representations of mannish women and effeminate men. By the start of WWII, this association between gender inversion and same-sex desire had become consolidated in the popular imagination, at the very time when male effeminacy and female mannishness were becoming less and less the norm in the lives of queer men and women. This was partly as a result of queers increasingly policing – in a quest for acquiring respectability and maintaining anonymity – their own and other queers' gender presentation. This led to a decline in the numbers of (typically working-class) queans, who had traditionally been a fixture of urban environments (Vickers, 2013: 30–33).

British medical boards screening recruits to fight in WWII were on the lookout for general signs of psychiatric disorders, but it appears that homosexuality was not officially identified as a reason unfitting one for service. In some cases – notably Quentin Crisp's – a board rejected a potential recruit admitting to homosexuality in the context of a particularly egregious camp gender performance. Otherwise, the need for manpower, the way in which same-sex desire – if uncoupled from effeminacy – was generally understood purely in terms of (criminal) acts rather than as a psychological identity, and the lack of an official stance on excluding homosexuals from service resulted in most same-sex attracted men joining the war effort (Vickers, 2013: 36–45).

As in the US, British queer servicemen during WWII were afforded an opportunity to socialise with other queers in ways that might not have been possible or easy to replicate in their hometowns. They could also find the army's homosociality congenial, and even conducive to same-sex intimacy, particularly in the form of mutual masturbation with partners who might or might not identify as primarily same-sex attracted (Vickers, 2013: 55–56).

Again, as in the US, vast numbers of servicemen and women on leave changed the patterns of social and sexual life in Britain, particularly its cities. Bill Thorneycroft recalled that wartime

> was the heyday in picking people up so easily – in crowded trains, in the blackout – but it was always just the one off ... people never spoke in those days at all ... if you did try to speak, they always ran away.
>
> (Thorneycroft, Weeks, and Sreeves, 1988: 95)

London, in particular, became known for its thriving same-sex male sexual scene (Dickinson, 2015: 40), with, in the words of a US gay veteran, 'large number of servicemen of all nations and ranks cruising each other in Piccadilly and Leicester Square' (Bérubé, 2010: 250). This is corroborated by the testimony of a Canadian soldier stationed in London for six months, who expressed himself in almost identical terms (Dickinson, 2015: 40).

Blacked out, regularly flooded with British soldiers, as well as servicemen from the Commonwealth and the US, and largely emptied of women and children (who had sought refuge in rural areas), the capital witnessed a veritable flourishing of same-sex sexual intimacy – in bars, clubs, hotels, hostels, parks and lavatories. The Ritz became famous for attracting queers; the Union Jack hostel was notorious for allowing sex between servicemen; certain West End streets were well-known as prime cruising spots. With a drastically diminished police force (for their manpower had been claimed by the army), queer sex could go on largely untroubled by the prospect of vigorous enforcement of laws against gross indecency, or the Park Regulations Act. The defence regulations passed pursuant to the Emergency Powers (Defence) Act 1939 and Emergency Powers (Defence) Act 1940 did allow the military police to shut down bars or clubs where same-sex sexual activity occurred; and some foreign armed forces put pressure on the Metropolitan Police to prosecute landlords allowing 'disorderly conduct'. But there is little evidence that even such powers were widely used. There is also anecdotal evidence that enforcement of laws was somewhat disparate – working-class, cross-dressing, effeminate queers being more vulnerable to being targeted than uniformed servicemen (Vickers, 2013: 76–81).

Oral testimony suggests that, as for US servicemen, being faced with common hardships and sharing a common goal tended to have a levelling effect on British soldiers in service: consequently, sexual preference and gender presentation, like one's class, did not necessarily act as barriers to soldiers' reciprocal acceptance (Dickinson, 2015: 41). While the press went on a rampage against decadent and effete queers who had eschewed service, and ridiculed and conflated pacifism and queerness, openly effeminate servicemen were often tolerated in the armed forces as 'good fellows'. This was especially the case when the need to prove themselves made queer soldiers heedless of danger in action; or when they could fulfil the role of joker or even semi-professional entertainer in servicemen's theatricals; or when the vulnerability projected by their gender presentation triggered other soldiers' protectiveness. Masculine homosexual servicemen might be looked upon with more suspicion, being presumed to be 'shit stabbers' (sexual predators who took an insertive role during sex), but rank could insulate same-sex attracted officers, even predatory ones, from opprobrium – much turning on a specific unit's moral code (Vickers, 2013: 85–98).

Pragmatic considerations – particularly the use that the armed forces could make of men caught offending – dictated how officers responded to sexual acts between servicemen during the war. Male offenders could be prosecuted in both military and civil courts, for both buggery and lesser offences such as gross indecency or indecent exposure; and convictions could carry heavy penalties, including life imprisonment for buggery. But courts martial were a means of last resort. In practice only the most egregious offenders or those deemed incorrigible tended to be disciplined and discharged (Vickers, 2013: 104–144). This approach was formalised in a 1950 War Office document to the effect that confirmed homosexuals unlikely to be rehabilitated should be removed from the army (Dickinson, 2015: 43).

Same-sex sexual activity between servicemen was often tolerated by officers as a necessary outlet in the absence of opportunities for servicemen to have sex with women who could be trusted to be free from venereal disease. Indeed, it could be embedded within relationships between officers and their batmen in the army and RAF, or between new recruits and their mentors ('wingers'), or those providing them with peer support ('oppos'), in the Navy. The relatively widespread occurrence of sex between men in the armed forces during WWII was also facilitated by the well-established, pre-war practice of sexual activity between queers and 'normal' men. This had typically taken the form of working-class men financially benefitting from playing the insertive role (which allowed them to keep their masculinity and 'normalcy' intact) with middle or upper-class queer partners. The conditions of war created a new rationale for such intimacy between queers and non-queers to continue, while also divorcing it from its financial dimensions. These forms of intimacy were often carefully managed so as to avoid displays of affection that could call into question the heterosexual orientation of the non-queer partner; queers themselves, in order to fit in with the heteronormative requirements of ideal servicemen, commonly pretended to a sexual and romantic interest in the other sex. Same-sex intimacy between queers and non-queers largely disappeared, however, in the postwar period, with the removal of the conditions that had contingently enabled it to flourish during wartime, and with the progressive entrenchment of more rigid sexual identities (Vickers, 2013: 57–65).

In the aftermath of the war, efforts at national reconstruction targeted not only material damage, but also the precarious state in which socially and politically salient categories – prime among them British masculinity – had been left by the social and moral upheaval wrought during the war years. Dickinson (2015: 47) notes that 'anxieties regarding homosexual corruption of society regularly surfaced in the many post-war debates regarding the perceived decline in moral standards in the UK'. The point was neatly made, as early as 1954, by Kenneth Soddy (physician at the Department of Psychological Medicine at University College London Hospital). Waters (2015: 195) quotes him as having written: 'In settled times, homosexuality does not greatly trouble the community. But social disturbance – and particularly a war – is apt to cause variations in social and sexual practices which engender attacks of acute public anxiety'. Such anxieties were exacerbated by the Kinsey report, whose non-minoritising understanding of homosexuality made its way to the UK (Dickinson, 2015: 49–50). It is in this context that Government propaganda emphasising family values, (Dickinson, 2015: 47), or the Archbishop of Canterbury advocating a rejection or 'war time morality' (Cook, 2014: 174), should be understood.

The postwar years have become associated with the image of 'lonely and sad' homosexuals, but Cook (2014: 76) argues that queer men could be reasonably well-integrated in society if, for example, a sympathetic heterosexual network and their own social capital acted as a buffer. Oral history confirms the existence of groups of queer men socialising in public venues and private parties in both Edinburgh and London during the 1950s, but also the fact that such groups were not necessarily accessible, or their existence known, to many other gay men. In Thorneycroft' experience, these groups tended to be composed primarily of 'clerks and shop assistants', with the occasional manual worker; they formed following 'casual pick-ups'; they were largely apolitical and tended to treat homosexuality as a fact of life without discussing it; and its members took great care to cultivate a 'straight image outside the ghetto' (Thorneycroft, Weeks, and Sreeves, 1988: 95).

Individual experiences could vary widely. Many queer Britons experienced the 1950s as a particularly difficult time, with families unwilling or unable to accept them, and frightening experiences with the law (Cook, 2014: 160, 166, 174). The public aspects of London's queer life were toned down (Dickinson, 2015: 49). At the same time, others found that their families of origin and their city-dwelling heterosexual neighbours might envelope their sexuality in a knowing but benevolent silence (Cook, 2014: 155, 158–160) – one that allowed for a degree of social integration, while suiting both the pre-coming out culture of the times and the value placed on discretion and propriety by the postwar generation (170). London could offer particularly supportive environments, with complicit landladies and relatively inclusive neighbourhoods (160). For a short time after the war, sex between queers and heterosexually-identifying males continued – no longer in the form of relationships between comrades in arms, but rather between Britons and Afro-Caribbean immigrants in areas like Notting Hill: 'This was a transitional period in British sexual cultures when it was still just possible to sleep with men and women and have a claim to "normality"' (161).

That period, Smith (2015: 7) argues, continued for longer in the North of England, where same-sex sexual contact between working-class men had, traditionally, not been taken to impugn the participants' normality, and had not been systematically targeted by the police. But it came to an end in the late fifties, following, among other things, 'the increased visibility of men with a clear sexuality' (Smith, 2015: 3). Yet, it is difficult to generalise. Gay rights pioneer Allan Horsfall (1988: 11) spoke of 'the overall bleakness of small-town gay life in the early fifties'. He declared that it was precisely in places such as 'the small mining and weaving towns of industrial Lancashire', where he was raised by his publican grandparents, 'that the pressure for social and legal conformity bore down most heavily on homosexuals' (Horsfall, 1988: 10).

Class-differentiated same-sex relationships appear to have become less common than before the war, and some queer men gravitated towards more symmetrical, companionate, domestic relationships, apparently responding to the prevalent relationship standards of the 1950s, as well as to new economic opportunities that did not exist before the war (Cook, 2014: 157, 159). The pedestrian nature of these bonds enabled sharing a common ground with, and hence a degree of integration within, the local broader heterosexual society (Cook, 2014: 158). It did not necessarily, however, protect queers from police interference. Indeed, it appears that in certain rural towns it was common practice for the police to target private homes (Horsfall, 1988: 11). The Metropolitan police more frequently targeted casual sexual contact in public places, but it too was known for also searching homes. Additionally, the aspiration towards domestic same-sex coupledom remained out of reach for many, who would lose professional status if they openly lived with a same-sex partner, or who found the prospect of self-justification in the face of family and neighbours' inquisitiveness or ostracism an insurmountable obstacle. However, it was precisely this, new more clearly emerging, distinction between public and privatised homosexuality that gave impetus to homosexual law reform – notably in the form of the 1957 Wolfenden Report, which made a case for decriminalising consensual sex between men in private (Cook, 2014: 166–169).

Wolfenden was not alone in advocating reform of the laws on same-sex sexual activity in the 1950s: so did the Homosexual Law Reform Society, a report commissioned by the Church of England Moral Welfare Council, and the popular 1953 novel *The Heart in Exile* (Cook, 2014: 174; Lewis, 2016: 6). Sociologist Michael Schofield, criminologist Gerrit Theodore Kempe, and psychiatrist Donald J West also published scholarly work in Britain arguing for understanding, tolerance and/or law reform (Waters, 2015: 199–206). Later, the pro-reform torch was carried by none less than Oxford's Professor of Jurisprudence LHA Hart (1963), in a famous written exchange with Lord Devlin (1965). In short, just like not all homosexual Britons were prosecuted, victimised, or felt oppressed in the postwar years, so the dominant negative discourse on homosexuality did not go unchallenged, either in the scientific or popular literatures.

While more recent qualitative scholarship, as surveyed above, has taken care to add nuance to an otherwise unidimensional account of the postwar years as a time of relentless oppression, it would be nonetheless distorting to downplay the considerable degree of repression against same-sex attracted Britons in the 1950s. Duncan's (2011 246) re-analysis of data – including 'representative survey, first hand accounts and ethnography' (247) – from two empirical studies on personal life in Britain, dating from 1949 and 1950, is instructive. Although the studies' material on homosexuality is not necessarily representative, Duncan (2011: 249) concludes that there appears to have been a general 'climate of incomprehension, rejection and hostility ... common to all classes, age groups, and genders'. This led to two main choices for both male and female homosexuals: either some form of sub-cultural queer separatism, or 'private suppression', including in egregious forms, such as a young man's statement that he would probably undergo castration if he found himself unable to control his exclusively homosexual impulses (Duncan, 2011: 250).

Significantly, after a relative lull in prosecutions for same-sex sexual activities during the war, the postwar years saw a more activist law enforcement stance being resumed (Houlbrook, 2005: 34–37; Lewis, 2016: 5), with the police engaged in practices equivalent to what we have seen going under the name of 'entrapment' in the US (Dickinson, 2015: 51). Crackdowns were facilitated by the existence of no less than eight separate male same-sex sexual offences in English law. Between them, they covered more or less any imaginable form of sexual contact (or attempted contact) between males: sodomy, attempted sodomy, assault with intent to commit sodomy, indecent assault, gross indecency, procuring gross indecency, attempting to procure gross indecency, and persistent soliciting (Lewis, 2016: 17–18, 23–24).

Prosecutions for indecent assault were mainly used to target men interfering with boys (Lewis, 2016: 23–24), while the bulk of prosecutions involving adult males were for gross indecency, typically used against two men mutually masturbating in public urinals (Lewis, 2016: 18–19, 25). In London, half of those prosecutions followed arrests by plainclothes policemen. Law enforcers claimed before the Wolfenden Committee that such plainclothes officers 'were not specially employed for this purpose', only immediately to concede that '[s]ometimes, however, a particular lavatory becomes notorious … and special attention has to be given to it' (Lewis, 2016: 25). The police also had other means at its disposal to harass troublesome queers – notably by taking action (in London under the Metropolitan Police Act 1839) against licensees who allowed groups of homosexual men to patronise their public house or other venue, and engage in 'indecent or disorderly conduct … extremely offensive to ordinary chance customers' (Lewis, 2016: 29). Similar – and even more draconian – powers were used or abused against gay bars in Northern English cities (Horsfall, 1988: 10).

Cross-dressing was taken as one of the tell-tale signs of homosexual perversion, leading to police harassment and, sometimes, arrest. Not surprisingly, many queers living through the postwar years felt persecuted, and feared being incarcerated (Dickinson, 2015: 52). Yet, because law enforcement varied so widely between different police forces, and even within the same force between one Chief Constable and the next, the danger 'was impossible to quantify' (Horsfall, 1988: 11).

The evidence provided by Metropolitan Police Chief Butcher to the Wolfenden Committee is probably fairly indicative of the mindset of many law enforcers at the time. Butcher drew a distinction between professional male prostitutes – who are in it for the money and are the lowest kind of criminal (lacking as they do the initiative and intelligence to pursue more distinguished criminal careers) – and genuine homosexuals. The latter were described by Butcher as bitches in heat, aroused by the chase and the scent of public urinals, to the point of becoming oblivious to the very obvious identity of plainclothes officers, and thereby becoming easy targets for arrest (Lewis, 2016: 30–32).

Many commentators took the rise in prosecutions as a worrisome sign that homosexuality was spreading (Lewis, 2016: 5; Waters, 2015: 197). This concern was voiced expressly in the press, which in the postwar years, and especially the fifties, began to discuss homosexuality more frequently, and in less coded terms. This ranged from the vitriol typical of tabloids to more measured, often scientifically-informed, contributions in more respectable broadsheet outlets – which, nonetheless, tended to cast homosexuality as a problem to be tackled (Dickinson, 2015: 53–56; Lewis, 2016, 5; Waters, 2015: 196).

Many of the criminal prosecutions for same-sex sexual activity in the postwar years are attributable to 'low-level decision-making in a small number of Metropolitan Police districts and among certain provincial forces' rather than an orchestrated national campaign (Lewis, 2016: 5; see also Horsfall, 1988: 11). Nonetheless, as I have argued in detail elsewhere (*contra* Higgins, 1996), it is not inappropriate to speak, at this time in British history, of an anti-homosexual witch-hunt trading on ideas of homosexuals' political disloyalty, and taking its cue from the US lavender scare. This was sparked by the defection to Russia in 1951 of Foreign Office staff member Guy Burgess and diplomat Donald Maclean, who had acted as spies for the Soviets. After the suspected spies' disappearance, the British Foreign Office informally consulted with the US Department of State, which – it will be remembered – was at the centre of the 'scandal' of homosexuality in the government in the US. In 1952, so-called 'positive vetting', involving investigations into the character and personal life of British civil servants, was introduced. In 1953 a joint Home Office/Scotland Yard mission to the US was organised, with a view to their being briefed on homosexuality by the FBI. The same year, the Home Secretary met with magistrates to discuss their role in enforcing the law against homosexual offences. Finally, in 1954 the exemplary conviction for homosexual offences of a peer of the realm – Lord Montagu – was secured, with the government carefully managing the trial's publicity (Zanghellini, 2015: 163–169). A preoccupation with homosexuality as posing a security risk, and more broadly as being implicated in all manner of deviousness and corruption also emerges (although by no means unchallenged) in strident contributions to be found in the Parliamentary debates from 1954 to 1958 (Zanghellini, 2015: 173–178).

The public framing of homosexuality both as an identity (Gleeson, 2007) and as a medical condition was also in ascendance during this period and into the 1960s (Dickinson, 2015: 61). Starting from the 1950s, a number of British cities established clinics administering varying forms of treatments for homosexuality, though they 'did not seem to become mainstream within UK mental services' (King, Smith and Bartlett, 2004: 3). Often, framing homosexuality as a mental health issue went hand-in-hand with a 'compassionate' stance advocating for decriminalisation. Yet, there was nothing compassionate about the electrical and chemical variants of aversion therapy that were used to try to convert queers to heterosexuality – requiring the patient's exposure to arousing material while being administered either electric shocks or drugs that induced nausea and vomiting (Dickinson, 2015: 64–65).

The Government's decision to charge the Wolfenden committee, originally set up to look into prostitution, with the additional task to investigate homosexuality is not really surprising in the context of a postwar decade in which same-sex desire had attracted increasing attention as a moral, political, legal and medical problem (partly, but not exclusively, through the State's own changing priorities and discourses). While the Wolfenden report of 1957 went down in history as a progressive document for recommending the decriminalisation of sex in private between consenting adult males, the initial impetus for it was less a liberal political impulse, than the desire to find a way of successfully managing the problem of homosexuality (Zanghellini, 2015: 168; Lewis, 2016: 6).

It is also worth noting that Wolfenden's recommendation, albeit politically significant, had limited practical reach: law enforcers testified before the Committee that prosecutions for same-sex sexual activity occurring between adults in private were rare (Lewis, 2016: 18–19). Even the recommendation's symbolic value, though far from negligible, should not be overstated: for the Wolfenden report did not displace (indeed part of the case for law reform relied on) the view that homosexuality was a pathological condition harmful to those who practiced it (Zanghellini, 2015: 185). Indeed, setting at 21 of the age of consent for same-sex sexual activity in private was intended to prevent younger men – particularly those aged 18–21, and undergoing national service – from falling prey to 'corruption' (Lewis, 2016: 17).

Hundreds of witnesses gave evidence to the Committee, variously portraying homosexuality as either an offence susceptible to control by the criminal law, or a medical/psychological problem (Lewis, 2016: 9). Prosecutors and police officers tended to favour the former account of homosexuality, which legitimised a more punitive response, while the opinion of magistrates, lawyers and prison officials – taken as whole – was more ambivalent. Whether pro or anti-reform, however, Lewis (2016: 14) notes that most contributions made use of 'a conventional language of horror and disgust'.

The government did not follow up on Wolfenden's recommendations for a decade, and then only after intensive lobbying by the Homosexual Law Reform Society and the Albany Trust. Scotland and Northern Ireland would have to wait until the 1980s (Roseneil et al., 2013: 175). Horsfall (1988: 15) catalogued the strategies commonly used throughout the fifties and sixties to forestall progress on the reform by preventing it even from being debated within a political party. These included the claims that homosexual law reform was not a political matter, but one of individual conscience; that it was a non-party matter cutting across party lines; that championing reform would alienate voters; and that it was not a matter to be discussed in the presence of women.

The Wolfenden report, the laws whose reform it recommended, and the practices of the police enforcing them, all concerned exclusively male homosexuality. Indeed, Derry (2020: 221) has argued that the Wolfenden report deliberately neglected lesbianism, so as not to have to consider the principle of equality as a more radical ground for law reform than privacy. As she puts it, the report 'presented a novel tactic for achieving the repression of male homosexuality: its silencing in the public domain through limited toleration in the private. Lesbianism, already similarly silenced, need not be discussed' (Derry, 2020: 221).

Even much popular and medical discourse on homosexuality – to the extent that it fed into and off an account of homosexuality as a crimino-legal problem – was gay male-centred in the 1950s. Dines (2018: 131), for example, notes that there is a lack of novels that treat primarily of lesbian desire and experience during the 1950s, and ascribes this less to the publishing industry being male-dominated, than to the lack of crimino-legal salience of lesbian desire.

Oram (2012: 48–49) points out that during this period – in addition to a confused psychiatric discourse on female same-sex desire – the media did touch upon lesbianism, if rather tangentially, particularly in popular press reports on crime or divorce cases (as a wife's lesbian relationship could justify divorce on the ground of 'cruelty'). From an analysis of these texts Oram (2012: 53–54) reconstructs a discourse on lesbianism that is internally heterogeneous, with elements that connect female same-sex desire to legal and psychological deviance, and others that portray it as embedded within (and threatening) families and everyday relationships, with a blurred line between female friend-ships and lesbian relationships. At the same time, these popular press reports relocated representations of lesbian desire away from the Continent, Bohemia and the elite, where pre-war popular discourses had placed it, and towards the British 'lower middle class or respectable working class' (Oram, 2012: 54).

The relatively inconspicuous presence of lesbianism in British public discourses on homosexuality in the fifties is matched by the less sustained attention afforded to it by social scientific research during the same period (Waters, 2015: 189). This contrasts with the nascent but serious literature on male homosexuality as a social phenomenon (Waters, 2015: 189–190, 199–201). Lesbians also enjoyed a less developed socio-cultural infrastructure compared to male homosexuals. Although the 'postwar period … brought the emergence of coherent and extended [lesbian] networks that achieved the sizeable ideological leap of extending beyond urban centres', this appears to be largely a 1960s phenomenon, accompanying the increase in number of lesbian bars and the founding of the first British lesbian magazine, *Arena Three* (Murphy, 2013: 165).

Obscenity laws and queer fiction in the postwar years

As this review of historical literature shows, the pressures of heteronormativity, in both their legal and non-legal dimensions, were severe in both Britain and America during the postwar years. It is this that makes mid-century queer fiction a particularly promising case study for the purposes of deepening and broadening my central hypothesis in this book: that heteronormativity engenders imagina-tive resistance to happy same-sex outcomes, both in fiction and in projects of self-authorship in the real world.

Might there be, however, a simpler explanation for the tragic endings char-acteristic of mid-century Anglo-American queer novels? Might these have been due simply to authors' and publishers' adjusting the content of their outputs in an attempt not to be charged under the obscenity laws? Whilst it cannot be ruled out that this explanation may account for the treatment of same-sex desire in *some* mid-century queer fiction, it does not actually fit the particular texts I have selected as my case studies in the chapters that follow.

Charles Jackson's *The Fall of Valor* was published in 1946 – a time when censorship of queer fiction on obscenity grounds had not yet been systematically mobilised in the US. So, the novel's tragic ending cannot be convincingly ascribed to a calculated attempt on Jackson's part not to fall afoul of obscenity laws. Consistent with this, my archival research, whose findings are presented in Chapter 3, indicates that the possibility of censorship was never treated as a consideration relevant to the choice of ending by either Jackson or his publisher. Indeed, Patricia Highsmith's *The Price of Salt* (1952) shows that as late as the early fifties it was still possible for a US queer novel to have an unmistakably happy ending without thereby being targeted as obscene. Shortly thereafter, however, US authorities did start responding to the proliferation of queer fiction by deploying federal obscenity laws and postal department regulations against publishers of gay novels. Greenberg, a mainstream press that had been publishing queer fiction immediately prior to the great depression, and then again after the war, was found guilty on obscenity charges in 1953. This stymied not only Greenberg's but also other US publishers' queer output (Bergman, 2004: 47–50). Even more significant than official prosecutions, however, was 'the mass suppression of books through secret lists distributed by private or public authorities to book dealers or distributors threatening prosecution unless the books [were] removed from circulation' (Lockhart and McClure, 1954: 395). Depictions of homosexuality were one of several reasons why a book would be singled out as obscene by either private organisations, such as the National Organization for Decent Literature, or public officials (Lockhart and McClure, 1954: 308).

Then, in 1958, ONE Inc won a legal battle (albeit not before it reached the Supreme Court) against the US Postmaster, who, on the basis of the Comstock Act 1873, had refused to distribute ONE publications on the ground of their purported obscenity. The ruling in *ONE, Inc v Olesen* is taken to have opened the way to homosexual advocacy in the US (White, 2009: 76–78, 83–85; Faderman and Timmons, 2006: 117–120). The Court's decision consisted of one sentence citing a recent precedent (*Roth v Unites States*) that had set a new obscenity standard, which ONE did not meet. The clear implication was that merely dealing with homosexuality did not make a publication automatically obscene (Walters, 2004: 18).

Highsmith's *The Talented Mr Ripley* (1955) does date from the period (1953–1958), when publishers or distributors of queer work were vulnerable to prosecutions and convictions for obscenity, or to be threatened with prosecution, merely because they published gay-themed work and/or afforded it sympathetic treatment. But, as I will argue, *The Talented Mr Ripley* subverts the happy ending/tragic ending dichotomy. Both *The Price of Salt* and *The Talented Mr Ripley,* therefore, illustrate Highsmith's distinctive capacity to *transcend* heteronormative constraints, rather than these constraints generating authorial imaginative resistance to same-sex happy endings. So, the question of the effect of restrictive obscenity laws on Highsmith's most famous book, *The Talented Mr Ripley,* is moot.

As to Freeman's *The Leather Boys,* it was published in 1961, when more restrictive approaches to UK obscenity law had started being relaxed. A new Obscene Publications Act had been enacted in 1959, with the aim of liberalising the law, including by introducing a 'public good' defence. This, among other things, would allow an otherwise obscene work to escape criminalisation if it had sufficient literary merit (Rowbottom, 2018). The defence was successfully argued the following year, 1960, in *R v Penguin Books,* in which the publisher was acquitted of obscenity charges for publishing *Lady Chatterley's Lover.* The ruling is widely reputed to have 'introduced the age of permissiveness into England' (Cohen, 2016: 222).

Thus, imputing the tragic ending of Freeman's novel to the state of obscenity law at the time it was published is no more convincing than making that move in respect of Jackson's book: the latter was published before US authorities started tightening their approach to obscenity laws, and the former after UK authorities had relaxed theirs. In neither case was the law of obscenity, at the relevant times, so settled as to rule out the publication of queer-themed work with a happy ending; and it certainly did not require the tragic endings that conclude both novels.

Conclusions

Seeing the 1950s – sandwiched as they are between the war years and the gay and women's liberation movement – purely as the triumph of middle-class, heteronormative family values obscures the ways in which queer life and culture managed to thrive in the shadow of repression and censure (Bauer and Cook, 2012: 2, 7). It is safe to say, however, that in both the UK and the US the years comprising the sixth decade of the twentieth century were marked by intense preoccupation with same-sex desire in both institutional and non-institutional domains – including the popular press, psychiatry, the law, and politics. The historical literature reviewed in this chapter reveals that these years witnessed a departure from the comparative permissiveness that had characterised the war years, as well as from the more liberal attitudes that we have come to associate with the late sixties. Mid-century queer fiction does not appear, on the whole, to have participated in the most virulently homophobic aspects of the governance of same-sex desire in either postwar Britain or the US. Its tendency to favour tragic endings, however, cannot be meaningfully divorced from the pervasively heteronormative, heterosexist, and indeed homophobic, institutional and discursive structures discussed in this chapter. The case studies in the next three chapters give texture to my claim that mid-century same-sex tragic endings were, at least in part, a function of authors' imaginative resistance to fictional outcomes that challenged – politically, ethically and/or aesthetically – the normative constraints generated by those structures.

References

Bergman, D (2004) *The Violet Hour: The Violet Quill and the Making of Gay Culture* (New York: Columbia University Press).

Bauer, H and Cook, M (2012) 'Introduction' in Bauer, H and Cook, M (eds) *Queer 1950s: Rethinking Sexuality in the Postwar Years* (Basingstoke, UK: Palgrave Macmillan).

Bérubé, A (2010) *Coming Out under Fire: the History of Gay Men and Women in World War II* (Chapel Hill, NC: University of North Carolina Press).

Bérubé, A (2011) *My Desire for History: Essays in Gay, Community, and Labour History* (Chapel Hill, NC: University of North Carolina Press).

Boutilier v Immigration and Naturalization Service 387 US 118 (1967).

Cohen N (2016) 'Love, Story, Law – From the Scarlet Letter to Freedom and Privacy', *Law & Literature*, vol 28(2), 209–231.

Comstock Act 1873 (US).

Cook, M (2014) *Queer Domesticities: Homosexuality and Home Life in Twentieth-Century London* (Basingstoke, UK: Palgrave Macmillan).

D'Emilio, J (2014) *In a New Century: Essays on Queer History, Politics, and Community Life* (Madison, WI: University of Wisconsin Press).

Derry, C (2020) *Lesbianism and the Criminal Law: Three Centuries of Legal Regulation in England and Wales* (London: Palgrave Macmillan).

Devlin, P (1965) *The Enforcement of Morals* (Oxford: Oxford University Press).

Dickinson, Y (2015) *'Curing Queers': Mental Nurses and Their Patients, 1935–1974* (Manchester: Manchester University Press)

Dines, M (2018) '"Is it a Queer Book?": Re-Reading the 1950s Homosexual Novel' in Bentley, N, Ferrebe, A and Hubble, N (eds) *The 1950s: A Decade of Contemporary British Fiction* (London: Bloomsbury)

Duncan, S (2011) 'The World We Have Made? Individualisation and Personal Life in the 1950s', *The Sociological Review*, vol 59(2), 242–265.

Emergency Powers (Defence) Act 1939 (UK).

Emergency Powers (Defence) Act 1940 (UK).

Faderman, L and Timmons, S (2006) *Gay LA: A History of Sexual Outlaws, Power Politics, and Lipstick Lesbians* (New York: Basic Books).

[Freeman, G] George, E (1961) *The Leather Boys* (London: Anthony Blond).

Gleeson, K (2007) 'Discipline, Punishment and the Homosexual in Law', *Liverpool Law Review*, vol 28, 327–347.

Hart, HLA (1963) *Law, Liberty, and Morality* (Stanford: Stanford University Press).

Higgins, P (1996) *Heterosexual Dictatorship: Male Homosexuality in Postwar Britain* (London: Fourth Estate).

[Highsmith, P] Morgan, C (1952) *The Price of Salt* (New York: Coward-McCann).

Highsmith, P (1955) *The Talented Mr Ripley* (New York: Coward-McCann).

Horsfall, A (1988) 'Battling for Wolfenden' in Cant, B and Hemmings, S (eds) *Radical Records: Thirty Years of Lesbian and Gay History 1957–1987* (London and New York: Routledge) 10–21.

Houlbrook, M (2005) *Queer London: Perils and Pleasures in the Sexual Metropolis, 1918–1957* (Chicago: University of Chicago Press).

Jackson, C (1946) *The Fall of Valor* (New York: Rinehart).

Johnson, DK (2004) *The Lavender Scare: The Cold War Persecution of Gays and Lesbians in the Federal Government* (Chicago: University of Chicago Press).

Keller, Y (2005) '"Was it Right to Love Her Brother's Wife so Passionately?": Lesbian Pulp Novels and US Lesbian Identity, 1950–1965' *American Quarterly*, vol 57(2), 385–410.

King, M, Smith, G and Bartlett, A (2004) 'Treatments of Homosexuality in Britain since the 1950s – An Oral History: The Experience of Professionals' *BMJ*, doi:10.1156/bmj.37984.496725.EE.

Lewis, B (ed.) (2016) *Wolfenden's Witnesses: Homosexuality in Postwar Britain* (Basingstoke, UK: Palgrave Macmillan).

Lewis, GB (1997) 'Lifting the Ban on Gays in the Civil Service: Federal policy toward Gay and Lesbian Employees since the Cold War', *Public Administration Review*, vol 57(5), 387–395.

Lockhart, WB and McClure, R (1954) 'Literature, the Law of Obscenity and the Constitution', *Minnesota Law Review*, vol 38(4), 295–395.

Metropolitan Police Act 1839 (UK).

Murphy, AT (2013) '"I Conformed; I Got Married. It Seemed Like a Good Idea at the Time": Domesticity in Postwar Lesbian Oral History' in Lewis, B (ed.) *British Queer History: New Approaches and Perspectives* (Manchester: Manchester University Press,) 165–187.

Norton v Macy 417 F2d 1161 (DC Cir 1969).

Obscene Publications Act 1959 (UK).

Office of the Historian (2011) *History of the Bureau of Diplomatic Security in the United States Department of State* (US Department of State).

One, Inc v Olesen 355 US 371 (1958).

Oram, A (2012) 'Love "Off the Rails" or "Over the Teacups"? Lesbian Desire and Female Sexualities in the 1950s British Popular Press' in Bauer, H and Cook, M (eds) *Queer 1950s: Rethinking Sexuality in the Postwar Years* (Basingstoke, UK: Palgrave Macmillan, 2012) 41–57.

R v Penguin Books [1961] Crim LR 176.

Roseneil, S et al. (2013) 'Changing Landscapes of Heternormativity: The Regulation and Normalization of Same-Sex Sexualities in Europe, *Social Politics: International Studies in Gender, State and Society*, vol 20(2), 165–199.

Roth v Unites States 354 US 476 (1957).

Rowbottom, J (2018) 'The Transformation of Obscenity Law', *Information & Communications Technology Law*, vol 27(1), 4–29.

Smith, H (2015) *Masculinity, Class and Same-Sex Desire in Industrial England, 1895–1957* (Basingstoke, UK: Palgrave Macmillan).

Thorneycroft, B, Weeks, J and Sreeves, M (1988) 'The Liberation of Affection' in Cant, B and Hemmings, S (eds) *Radical Records: Thirty Years of Lesbian and Gay History 1957–1987* (London and New York: Routledge) 95–103.

Tripp, CA (2002) 'Alfred C Kinsey (1894–1956)' in Bullough, VL (ed.) *Before Stonewall: Activists for Gay and Lesbian Rights in Historical Context* (New York: Harrington Park Press) 13–23.

Vickers, E (2013) *Queen and Country: Same-Sex Desire in the British Armed Forces, 1935–1943* (Manchester: Manchester University Press).

Walters, F (2004) *Law and the Gay Rights Story: The Long Search for Equal Justice in a Divided Democracy* (New Brunswick, NJ and London: Rutgers University Press).

Waters, C (2015) 'The Homosexual as a Social Being in Britain, 1945–1968' in Lewis, B (ed.) *British Queer History: New Approaches and Perspectives* (Manchester: Manchester University Press) 188–218.

White, CT (2009) *Pre-Gay L.A.: A Social History of the Movement for Homosexual Rights* (Urbana, IL and Chicago: University of Illinois Press).

Zanghellini, A (2015) *The Sexual Constitution of Political Authority: The Trials of Same-Sex Desire* (Abingdon, UK: Routledge).

3 Charles Jackson's *The Fall of Valor* (1946)

Introduction

In his introduction to the Valancourt Books edition of Charles Jackson's 1946 gay novel *The Fall of Valor* (TFOV), Bronski (2016: vii) mentions that the book is partly autobiographical. In this chapter, among other things, I will discuss new and fascinating evidence that shows this to be something of an understatement. Understanding the extent to which the novel is rooted in its author's biography is a matter of intrinsic interest for everyone who cares about queer literary history. But it is also part of a broader attempt, hazarded here, to bring extrinsic evidence to bear on the interpretation of Jackson's work, with a view, particularly, to establishing the author's intention in respect of TFOV. This is not because I think author's intent theory is the one correct approach to textual interpretation. It is due, rather, to author's intent having been invoked against Jackson, to argue that TFOV is not a gay novel properly-so-called, that it is homophobic, and that it does not merit inclusion in the queer canon (Crowley, 2006: 262, 266, 267). I will try to show that these conclusions about the merits of TFOV are dubious even accepting the premise from which they stem – namely, that authorial intention matters to textual interpretation.

Setting the record straight is important. For all its groundbreaking qualities (Bronski, 2016: vi), TFOV has remained understudied. Caserio (1997: 185), a decade before Crowley's (2006) dismissal of TFOV as homophobic, had found the novel politically astute. More recently, Bronski (2016: vii) has praised 'Jackson's genius' in placing the novel's love triangle 'in the dead center of the war's crisis of masculinity and death'; and Schwartz (2017) has argued that TFOV foregrounds no less than 'the key question in gay life'. But Bronski's (2016) and Schwartz's (2017) positive critical assessments appear in short pieces, published in non-academic outlets. Meanwhile, the lengthiest academic study of Jackson's work, while noting the 'courage' it took for Jackson to openly address homosexuality in 1946, found TFOV to suffer from 'vagueness and lack of conviction' (Connelly, 2001: 104, 105). And Crowley's (2006) uncompromisingly negative assessment has had a critical influence on the major piece of research on Jackson to date: at the end of his biography of Jackson, Bailey (2013: 433) thanks Crowley for sharing with him 'his excellent scholarship'.

DOI: 10.4324/9781003188797-4

Unsuprisingly, Bailey (2013: 246) rates TFOV 'dreary'. He even chides Jackson for choosing to make his protagonist 'a proper tragic hero' expressing desire 'in terms of the Classical' (Bailey, 2013: 222–223). Only at first blush might these judgements appear purely aesthetic rather than queer-political (despite the fact that Bailey, who is married to a woman, does not appear to identify as gay). For Bailey (2013) blames the aesthetic shortcomings of TFOV on politically dubious choices. Specifically, Bailey (2013: 222–223) thinks that the book's 'cardboard cast' of 'flat' characters and its unhappy choice of 'objective' narrative viewpoint are due to Jackson's attempt to address a general readership, who expected to see homosexual transgressions punished. It follows that if 'a generation of gay men' found the book appealing, it must be because they had little choice, and were 'glad to read about their dilemma in whatever terms' (Bailey, 2013: 225). Crowley's (2006), Bailey's (2013) and other negative assessments demand a response, and I set out to provide one in this chapter.

Without the novel's tragic ending, there would be much less, or no, contention over the (queer) value of TFOV. Defending the novel against the charge of internalised homophobia, however, is not the only reason for my detailed discussion, in this chapter, of TFOV's different drafts, and the way in which it finally settled on a tragic ending. The main reason why I analyse the permutations the novel went through is to substantiate, through illustration, my claim that normative orders hostile to same-sex desire engender queer resistance to make-believing happy endings. This resistance, as the case of Jackson and TFOV illustrates, may be at play as much when authoring a queer novel, as when a queer practical agent acts – in line with the political ideal of personal autonomy – as 'author of his life' (Raz, 1986: 369).

Autobiography in *The Fall of Valor*

In July 1943, Charles Jackson and his wife Rhoda went on vacation on Nantucket, a small Massachusetts island famed for its historic architectural heritage. This experience was to inspire the plot of TFOV, Jackson's second novel. TFOV tells the story of a university professor, John Grandin, who is finally starting to reap the professional rewards of years of hard work. He lives in New York with his wife Ethel and their two boys, but Grandin has been more preoccupied with his research than uxorial duties in recent years. The Grandins arrange a trip to Nantucket in order to rekindle the languishing flame of their marital rapport. On the ferry ride to the island they are befriended by a pair of newly-weds, the Haumans: Billie Hauman happens to be a former student of Grandin's, while Cliff, her husband, is a Marine injured in Guadalcanal. The two couples go on to spend much of the holiday together. The vacation fails to lead to the marital reconciliation both Grandin and Ethel desire, partly because Grandin becomes aware of his attraction to the handsome and athletic Cliff. Ethel catches on to this when she discovers Cliff's cap among her husband's personal effects. While Grandin protests (truthfully) that nothing has happened and nothing need happen to upset their marriage, Ethel cuts her holiday short, and joins their children at her own parents'. As the holiday comes to an end a few days later, Grandin, who is due to teach summer school, returns to their flat in New York. He exchanged contact details with the Haumans before parting, and the morning on the first day of teaching he receives a telephone call from Cliff, who is coming to town and suggests their meeting up. Later, in his New York flat, Grandin makes a pass at Cliff, who responds by seizing a pair of fire-tongs and striking Grandin on the head; the professor collapses on the floor. In the meantime Ethel has had time to think things through, and realises that in loving her husband she loves him for the kind of man he is, including the sensibility and vulnerabilities that make him same-sex attracted. She writes a letter to her husband in the new-found certainty that indeed he has been and will be faithful to her, and prepares to return to him. Cliff's strike was not fatal. Grandin, aching and bleeding, comes round as Ethel's letter is slipped under the flat's entrance door. He then knows that, in light of the turn of events, he lost everything that is of meaning to him: the love of his wife, his children, his career, and his self-respect.

Students of Jackson know that the novel was inspired by Jackson's encounter with a Marine on his holiday on Nantucket in 1943. Bailey (2013: 168) was also able to name him: Vince Kramer. But that is more or less as far as knowledge about the autobiographical basis of TFOV has, so far, gone.

In December 2017, I received a private message about my short Goodreads. com review of TFOV. It turned out to be from one of Vince Kramer's sons, Ray. I was able to meet Ray face to face in August 2018. In recent years, Ray has developed an interest in history, and he wants the story of how his parents inspired TFOV to be recorded before it is lost forever. Our interview, largely unstructured, takes place outdoors, over lunch, in Pearl Street, Lower Manhattan. Though personable, Ray is a self-confessed introvert (taking in this, he tells me, after his mother). He is a tall, handsome man, probably in his sixties. I know his father's looks from a picture Ray shared with me by email, when Captain Kramer was a young man honeymooning on Nantucket. The Ray I meet in 2018 could be the father of the twenty-five-year-old Vince of 1943: the resemblance is uncanny.

TFOV was never discussed at Ray's home during Vince's lifetime; only vague references were occasionally made to a 'college professor' writing a book about the Kramers.[1] Indeed, it looks like Vince Kramer preferred that his children should not develop an interest in Jackson's literary output, lest it should lead them to TFOV. 'Ah, why d'ya read that crap?' he said to one of his sons when he caught him reading one of Jackson's books, probably *The Lost Weekend*.

---

1   Since Ray's mother first met Jackson while studying on one of his courses, before he had his first novel published, the Kramers would naturally think of him as the college professor who wrote novels, rather than the novelist who occasionally did some teaching.

It is from his mother Barbara, before she passed away, that Ray learnt about Charles Jackson and TFOV. Barbara Kramer had been a student of Jackson's, just like her fictional counterpart, Billie Hauman, is a student of Grandin's. Ray tells me it must have been a night course, during the war, while she was working in public relations for Eastern Aircraft (a Division of General Motors making combat planes for the Navy). I expect Ray's mother took her course at New York University, as we know that Jackson in 1942 was teaching there (Bailey 2013: 120).

Ray wrote down some brief notes after speaking to her. According to one of these, Jackson 'fell in love with dad' on Nantucket. 'Dad', that is, Vince Kramer, was born in 1918. As with Cliff Hauman in TFOV, Vince's mother died when he was a boy. Just like Cliff is very attached to his 'daddy', so Vince was very close to his 'pop': Ray tells me that, much to his mother's bewilderment, when Vince – like Cliff in TFOV – was recuperating (after being injured in Guadalcanal) at a naval hospital in California, the first person he phoned was his father, not her, his fiancé. Vince's father was a working-class immigrant from Holland, who became a successful businessman, but had limited education. Vince himself – who, like Cliff, was already a Captain by the time of his Nantucket honeymoon – was 'smart' and eventually 'advanced to the rank of Colonel'.

Barbara Kramer majored in journalism at Rutgers, mirroring Billie's aspirations to become a writer in TFOV. But her career prospects were cut short by her husband's decision to stay in the Military,[2] which meant the family relocated almost on a yearly basis throughout the fifties. Her background was more 'genteel' than Vince's: her mother was daughter to a Newport-based architect, and her father a banker. It was Barbara's father who first informed the Kramers about TFOV after reading a review in the New York Times: 'They wrote a book about you', he told his daughter over the phone.

Ray tells me how, whenever he reads TFOV, he finds 'thing after thing' that is 'accurate', and how Jackson 'went into meticulous detail to report the dates, but [also] all the facts' about his parents and their Nantucket experience with the Jacksons. Cliff's background in TFOV is indeed a perfect match of Vince's Dutch, working class origins, and his rapid advancement through the military ranks. The class differences between Ray's parents also have their counterpart in the book: at one point Billie confesses to Ethel that Cliff 'isn't very well bred, you know.... They live in the wrong part of town' (Jackson, 2016: 112–113).

Vince Kramer was very outgoing and gregarious 'with people that he liked', and had a 'large circle of friends and admirers'. To illustrate, Ray shows me a picture of Vince's friend in 'Australia or New Zealand', where he was evacuated after Guadalcanal. It recalls to my mind one of the final scenes in TFOV: Cliff mentions to Grandin his 'pal Walt', and the fun they had in Melbourne, where neither of them 'ever laid a dame on leave that we didn't do it together' (Jackson, 2016: 219). Ray also shows me a picture of his father dining together

2   As Vince said in one of his letters, it would have been hard to find other forms of employment after the war.

with another member of military personnel, as well as their host, who had taken them to an upmarket Hollywood restaurant. This picture dates from the time when Vince was recuperating in California, before his wedding and honeymoon on Nantucket. This, in turn, brings to my mind the racy stories Cliff tells Grandin about his time in California, where it transpires that, in contrast to what Billie had been led to believe, his wounds had not kept him bed-bound (Jackson, 2016: 220).

There are also a few places, however, in which the book departs from the truth of Vince's life. In a scene in TFOV, the Grandins are invited to a military ball by Cliff; in reality, it had been Jackson who had had the Kramers admitted to the yacht club on Nantucket. Ray also says that Vince's war injuries were incurred during a spell of Japanese shelling, not, as with Cliff, as a result of an ambush in the jungle. Vince's injuries also did not match Cliff's 'ten broken ribs, all his teeth rammed down his throat, his whole face cut open to his jaw, a fractured skull and a concussion of the brain' (Jackson, 2016: 104). Indeed, though Vince, like his fictional counterpart, had 'false teeth', they were due to a football accident, not the war. Interestingly, however, Ray tells me his father 'never accepted a purple heart', which I, later realise, seems to reflect the view Cliff takes of his own war injuries: 'I'm not a hero ... it was my own darn fault' (Jackson, 2016: 104).

I ask Ray if he knows whether Vince gave Jackson his cap – the episode of Cliff giving it to Grandin being key in the book, for it precipitates the Grandins' separation. But Ray does not know. He also does not remember his father constantly breaking things like Cliff (something that, in the novel, prefigures Cliff's wrecking Grandin's life); Ray thinks that is just Jackson trying to show 'the big, brutish [soldier]'. Indeed, physical appearance is another matter in which Cliff and Vince are not exactly alike. Both were tall and athletic, ex-football players. But, whereas Cliff is a Michelangelesque Titan 'faintly inclined to fat' – for all that 'the excess weight' merely adds to his 'heroic physique' – (Jackson, 2016: 97), the Vince of Nantucket, 1943, has a perfectly lean, muscled build (Figure 3.1). It turns out, as Ray tells me, that his father had been suffering from dengue fever, and at the time of his honeymoon on Nantucket was at his slimmest ever. The true build of Vince Kramer at the time of Nantucket is, however, mirrored in the original concept for the novel, as outlined in one of Jackson's letters, where Cliff's figure is described, in unmistakably phallic terms, as 'solid strong tight hard upright strictly-for-business' ([PCJ1]).

TFOV's description of the Grandins and Haumans on the beach on Nantucket bears striking similarities to a picture Ray shared with me shortly after we made email contact, giving a clue to Jackson's almost obsessive urge to record every least detail of his experience (Figure 3.1). Ethel, like Rhoda in the picture, wears 'a black bathing suit' that 'fitted her tight, without ruffle of frill, and made her figure look straight and firm' (Jackson, 2016: 95). Billie, like Barbara Kramer, wears a custom-made 'ultrafeminine bathing dress of white satin lastex', which 'strikingly set[s] off her figure and beauty', with a 'short white skirt' that flips 'about her wide hips' (Jackson, 2016: 95, 98). The novel does

Figure 3.1 From the left: Barbara Kramer, Charles and Rhoda Jackson, and Captain
          Vincent Kramer. Nantucket, 1943
Source: Courtesy of Ray Kramer

not expatiate in the same way on what Grandin and Cliff are wearing on the beach, but in the first detailed outline that Jackson sent to his publisher, Grandin's and Cliff's outfits are a close match to Jackson's and Vince Kramer's in this picture. Grandin wears 'old loose gabardine shorts', while Cliff dons 'faded khaki coloured shorts, very brief, very tight. His build and figure are certainly ... most striking, even beautiful ... He is very tanned. His blond rather curly hair is bleached on top' ([PCJ1]).

When the Grandins first meet the Haumans on the boat to Nantucket, there is an awkward moment where Grandin realises Billie was one of his students, but cannot recall her name; nor could he during the entire semester (Jackson, 2016: 48). This, too, is true to fact: Ray tells me how it 'stuck' with his mother that Jackson could never remember her name. The incident is used in the book to indicate that Billie had made no impression on Grandin, and is the first element in a relatively unsympathetic portrayal of Cliff's wife, who is depicted as somewhat conventional, overly preoccupied with trifles, unwilling to develop an adequate awareness of war and its tragedy, even crude in the homophobic remarks she makes about a fellow guest at the hotel. These aspects of Billie's personality, however, tend to be filtered through Grandin's eyes, which – possibly like Jackson's own appraisal of Vince's wife – are unreliable: infatuated as he is with Cliff, Grandin views Billie, at least subconsciously, as competition, judging her ungenerously. Yet, TFOV is, in many respects, so faithful an account of the Jacksons' and Kramers' vacation on Nantucket that, understandably, Barbara Kramer resented 'some of the things that were written in the book'. Jackson did worry about the book's effect on the Kramers. One of the exceedingly scant references to them to be found in his archive, is in a 1945 letter to his agent, Bernice Baumgarten: 'The only thing that worries me is the Kramers; but the thing to do is forget about them until later: do the book first and do a fine job' ([PCJ2]). Jackson does not specify the nature of his concerns, but having tailored the story so closely to the truth of his experience on Nantucket, he must have worried that the Kramers would read TFOV as a true record of Jackson's feelings about them.

It was on Nantucket that Jackson received news that Farrar & Rinehart wanted to publish what would prove itself his fantastically successful debut novel, *The Lost Weekend* ([PCJ3]). Ray's mother pointedly remarked to her son that Jackson showed *The Lost Weekend*'s draft to her husband, 'not to *her*' – his former student, and a lover of books. Not that Vince Kramer lacked intellectual qualities of his own. Ray tells me his father 'could speak at a high level'. Indeed, Ray tells me that according to his mother 'what he [Vince] … I don't think the word "attracted", but… what *drew* him to Charlie [Jackson] was that Charlie was very intellectual'. With him, Vince could engage in discussions he did not necessarily have an opportunity to have when he went 'out to drink with his buddies'. Ray continues: 'I think that's what he saw … you know, if you want to call it "relationship", but the friendship that they had was … this guy's a professor'. In TFOV, Jackson makes reference to Cliff's attempts at engaging Grandin in conversation about books, but intellectual exchange is the last thing the professor seeks from the Marine, erotically invested as Grandin is in casting the other man in the role of man of action, bearer of martial values, vessel of physical prowess.

It is not so much research ethics considerations that make me take a roundabout route to asking Ray if Vince Kramer's interest in Jackson was coloured by erotic attraction. It is the gay man's instinctive habit of treading gingerly when hypothetically imputing same-sex desire to a straight man – at least when doing so to his face; or, in this case, his son's face. So, I tell Ray that the book makes it obvious that the relationship between Grandin and Cliff was not driven only by Grandin's same-sex desire, but also by Cliff's being 'a guys' guy who thrived in the company of men'. Ray interrupts me: 'I think that's exactly it', and it is clear that he means that this describes Jackson and Vince's relationship, too. I go on to explain the idea of a continuum between homosexuality and homosociality, and how homosocial relations may themselves be erotically charged (Sedgwick, 1985). Finally, I pluck the courage to ask Ray if he ever got the sense that something like this might have been going on with his father. 'My dad had literally hundreds of male friends, and many of them close friends', he replies. He tells me of how these friendships often continued until his death, of how Vince was admired, and of how 'one guy sees it one way, the other guys sees it another way, you know what I mean?' He is very definite in telling me his father was not gay. Earlier, when referring to a scene – which obviously Ray assumed to be autobiographical, like so many others – in which, at Cliff's instigation, the two men change into swimming costumes separately from their wives (rather than each couple doing so apart from the other), Ray told me: 'With the getting dressed, you know, things like that, you know, you're in the Marines, you do that all the time, cos, you know, that's the way it is, you don't think about that'. Now he reinforces the point: 'In no way he was a homosexual'. Yet, he continues, while warning me not 'to take this the wrong way', Vince Kramer 'was also a free thinker'. Ray explains that one thing he has 'never reconciled' is that when his parents were first dating, they went to a drag show club in New York, the Howdy Club. 'I guess he just found it interesting', he explains, and adds: 'It was a side of my dad I never knew'. Later Ray refers to it again: 'At least early on he was, you know, I'd say that going to [the Howdy Club in] New York it's just kind of like … but I wouldn't interpret that as … but I just found it.… My mum couldn't figure it out!'

Ray tells me that in his view TFOV is about 'the torment of a guy who has a crush' on another man, when there is no possibility for anything to happen: 'You know, you're married, he's married…' The theme of an impossible love makes it hard for Ray to see how the book could have ended other than in tragedy. He tells me about *Great Expectations*: the novel's (heterosexual) relationship across class lines does not end well, though Dickens wrote a 'second ending' in which the heroine and hero get together. But 'people did not want to see that happen … because it wasn't satisfying and maybe – I don't know – with Charlie [giving a happy ending to TFOV] maybe that wouldn't have been satisfying either'. Ray is very clear, in any case, that the tragic ending is not autobiographical: the book, said his mother, was 'pretty accurate', but the ending was 'made up'.

That Vince Kramer never gave Charles Jackson a beating upon returning from Nantucket is confirmed not only, as we will see, by the history of TFOV's drafts, but also by circumstantial evidence, which shows that Jackson made an effort to keep in touch with Vince for at least a couple of years after the holiday. Specifically, by early 1945, it looks like he had lost touch with Vince, but was trying to locate him. In a letter addressed to Buck Lielenthal, a Marine friend of his, Jackson asks: 'Tell me if, by any remote chance, you've ever run into a Marine captain by the name of Vincent Kramer.… He was wounded during the Guadalcanal campaign (there I go, spilling the beans) but has lately been returned to active service and is once again somewhere in the Pacific' ([PCJ4]).[3] I learn from Ray that at the time his father was in China, charged with rescuing pilots if a plane was shot down. In the summer of the same year, Jackson, by then deeply immersed in redrafting TFOV, declined to go, upon invitation from the Marine Corps Headquarters, 'on a two months

---

3   Previously in the same letter Jackson had outlined TFOV (then in draft form) for Buck's benefit; his reference to 'spilling the beans' ([PCJ4]) is clearly Jackson's way of acknowledging that he has just given away the autobiographical basis of the novel by identifying Vince Kramer as the real-life model for the fictional Cliff – both being Marine Captains injured at Guadalcanal. From the tenor of Jackson's letter to Lielenthal, it sounds like they might have been like-minded, sexually speaking, or at least that Lielenthal was openly tolerant of homosexual relationships.

trip to the Pacific fronts as a guest combat-correspondent' ([PCJ5]). Knowing that Jackson had been trying to locate Vince Kramer makes me wonder at the exact meaning of Jackson's confession that 'having missed the trip is something I'll always regret', and that 'there is nothing I'd rather do in this world' ([PCJ5]).

Eventually – either later in 1945, or 1946 – Jackson did see Vince Kramer again: Ray tells me that his father 'came to Brooklyn to have some dental work done' and he 'stopped to visit him'. Jackson's address book provides evidence of the continuity of the friendship around this time. The New Jersey address and telephone number of 'Capt. Vincent Kramer' is noted in it, with the rank later crossed out in pencil and amended to 'Major' (Ray tells me the rank change occurred in the spring of 1945), and the address updated to that of a NY military base ([PCJ6]). Afterwards, Jackson and Vince lost touch with each other again. Because of Vince's job in the Navy, the Kramers moved continuously throughout the fifties, but there are no further updates to Vince's address and his rank in Jackson's address book.

Clearly, the experience on Nantucket left a mark on Jackson. In 1946 he was regretting being unable to return to the island for a visit ([PCJ7]); in 1951 he used a windfall to book another holiday there ([PCJ8]); and in 1948, five years after the trip and two years after the publication of TFOV, he wrote to Rhoda from Los Angeles: 'Lying on the beach this noon … I had only to close my eyes to smell the suntan oil of Sconset and feel your presence with me and the presence, too, of the Haydens and the Kramers' ([PCJ9]). Writing of Nantucket to his wife must have been a way for Jackson to reassure himself of the reality of that experience at a time when he felt it slipping away into the mists of the past; drafting and redrafting TFOV had staunched the passage of time for three years, but by 1948 Jackson had put the book truly and well behind him. In any case, Jackson could not make it too obvious to Rhoda that, five years on, he was still pining over Vince Kramer; hence his studiedly casual mention of the Kramers, almost as an afterthought, after the Haydens (who had inspired secondary characters in the book).

In 1962, the year before the writer turned sixty, the Jacksons moved from Connecticut to New Jersey. The move was prompted by the relocation of the Yale's Center for Alcoholic Studies, at which Rhoda was employed, to the New Brunswick campus of Rutgers University. In October 1964, Jackson started teaching a course in 'Enjoying Good Literature' at the University [PCJ10]. It was all by accident: he had got to chat with someone at the 'info Department', whose husband turned out to be the Director of Continuing Education (Bailey 2013: 374). As it happens, 1964 was also the year Vince Kramer was appointed alumni secretary at Rutgers, a post he would hold for twenty-seven years after retiring from the military. Ray tells me that his father and Jackson 'might have met at the Rutgers Faculty Board'. It is the least definite segment of our conversation. At home, a few months after my interview with Ray, I consult the one-page photocopy he gave me of the notes he scribbled after discussing TFOV with his mother, prior to her death. Eventually, at the bottom of the page, I manage to decipher: 'Rutgers, 2nd or 3rd year as RAS

[Rutgers Alumni Secretary]. Saw him at Club. Buy lunch'. It is true, then: two decades after Nantucket, the men were serendipitously reunited.

Putting together Ray's information and Jackson's timeline in New Brunswik, the encounter between Jackson and Vince Kramer at Rutgers must have occurred at some point in 1965. We cannot know if seeing Vince one last time contributed to setting in motion everything that followed, but by the autumn of that year Jackson had separated from Rhoda (after twenty-seven years of marriage), and left New Brunswick for Manhattan. A lengthy dry spell from substance addiction had dried up Jackson's artistic vein since the early fifties ([PCJ11])). Now, in Manhattan, he resumed both his substance abuse and his writing; published a new book; came out of the closet; and eventually committed suicide (Bailey, 2013: 379–420).

A few short months before dying, in 1968, Jackson wrote a letter to Rhoda. In telling her that the Italian publisher of TFOV wanted to re-publish it and paid him an advance, he referred to the novel as 'a book I know you always deplored and were often snidely "amused at" (leaving me no defense)' ([PCJ12]). The passage, for all its ostensible casualness, is pregnant with a bitter accusation: for Rhoda to 'snide' at such a heavily autobiographical work (a passive-aggressive response that, whatever Jackson's justice in attributing it to her, would be no less understandable than Jackson's reaction to it) amounted to striking him where he felt utterly helpless.

Jackson died almost three years to the day of moving to Manhattan, being cared for during the last year of his life by his devoted new lover, Stanley Zednik, a factory worker in his early forties (Bailey, 2013: 404–405). A picture in Bailey's (2013) biography shows Zednik as fair- and wavy-haired, squared-jawed, heavy-browed, apparently quite thick-set.

Fact and fiction in TFOV

Much of the rest of this chapter proposes an interpretation of TFOV which relies heavily on extrinsic evidence both about Jackson's experience (discussed above) on and beyond Nantucket, and his experience (discussed below, across several sections) of writing and re-writing the book. One of the reasons for this approach is that, as the next section argues, authorial intent has been used to accuse TFOV of internalised homophobia; having recourse to extrinsic evidence assists me in reconstructing authorial intent and debunking this argument. The other reason for relying on this extrinsic evidence is that TFOV all but calls for such an approach. I do not know that this latter point is one that is liable to being *argued* for. Rather, I try to vindicate it by discussing, in this section, the imbrication of fact and fiction in TFOV, using three examples for their sheer power of suggestion.

Jackson maintained that his writing was both autobiographical and fictional. 'You write for yourself first', he said, about 'experiences or events which have profoundly moved [you]', and writing then 'acts like a kind of purge', even if, in writing, you 'change life to suit yourself', and thereby 'you're false to yourself' ([PCJ10]). This falsification of self is in part due to the publicity of writing: in 1964 Jackson wrote that his letters to his daughter were like a private journal, except better, because if he were writing an actual private journal, he could not help contemplating its publication, which would, in turn, result in a lack of truthfulness ([PCJ11]). In fact, as we will see later, even as small an audience as his daughters made the act of writing enough of a public performance for Jackson as to result in a falsification of the self. In any case, even in work that purports to be fully autobiographical and wholly private (as Jackson's did not), the self that experienced then can only re-appear in written form as recollected and experienced now, so that writing is both a reliving and, necessarily, a remaking of the experience.

A handwritten quote, attributed to Henry Handel Richardson, in one of Jackson's notebooks reads: 'The woof of fact and fiction is so intrinsically spun that, even for their author, the unravelling would now prove a difficult and lengthy task' ([PCJ19]). The quote illuminates the complex and dynamic relationship between experience and writing in Jackson's work. The relationship works both ways, on several planes. I will discuss three examples. In the first the act of writing synchronically shapes affective experience, which, in turn, diachronically affects writing. In the second example the experience of writing retrospectively affects (the appreciation of one's) lived experience. In the third example the written word affects lived experience prospectively.

1   Less than two months from their stay on Nantucket, Jackson sounds cheerful, worry-free, not a bit lovelorn, pensive, melancholy or whatever else one might expect him to be, having only recently laboured in the throes of an impossible desire for Vince Kramer: 'I am doing so well it's almost shameful. … THE LOST WEEKEND … is going to curl the hair of the entire country' ([PCJ13]). On the other hand, sixteen months later, when his draft of TFOV was well underway, Jackson writes in one of his letters: 'It is a very strong story, a very emotional one, and I have been punch–drunk for months because of it' ([PCJ14]). Thus, in recreating Nantucket in TFOV, Jackson conjures up *anew* (*again*, but also in a *new* way) his infatuation with the Marine Captain, and the process is so affecting that he feels dazed, 'punch–drunk'. At the time of writing this letter, as we will see, Jackson was not yet contemplating a tragic ending for TFOV; so, 'emotional' here means just that – it does not mean 'tragic'. Eerily, however, the first meaning of 'punch–drunk' is, according to the Merriam-Webster dictionary online, 'suffering from brain injury from repeated blows to the head', prefiguring – well before Jackson had *consciously* decided to make the story end tragically – Cliff's striking Grandin with the fire tongs.

2   At the end of April 1945, when Jackson is redrafting TFOV, he writes in a letter that the Marine is 'the kind of attractive-destructive personality that has never … been written about. The kind of simple-minded nice guy with a fatal charm' ([PCJ15]). This description fits neither Cliff as originally conceived in TFOV's outline from 1944 ([PCJ1]), nor Vince Kramer as

Jackson had known him in 1943, and on whom the Cliff of the outline was apparently based. Yet, by the time Jackson has reconceived Cliff as 'attractive-destructive' and 'fatal' (deadly), he comes to speak of him not just as a literary type but a real life one – even alluding at his having met just *that* version of the Marine Captain, suffering the consequences: '[I]f you meet him in life, give him a wide berth, as no good will come of it – and he will be untouched whatever happens' ([PCJ15]).

3   Jackson's preoccupation with getting every least detail true to life in TFOV – a preoccupation noted by Ray, and one that embraced train and ferry times, stations, military insignia, injured servicemen's pay, air corps' uniforms, and more ([PCJ16]; [PCJ17]; [PCJ18]) – is serviceable to remaking experience authentically, and hence successfully. One item in Jackson's archive illustrates this preoccupation particularly eloquently. It is an unidentified newspaper clipping depicting a Marine.[4] In Chapter VIII of TFOV (2016: 41), just such a photograph – 'two or three columns wide, neatly cut out with a pair of scissors which had eliminated the unnecessary caption' – is described in meticulous detail, down to 'the packed kit of some kind resting on his chest', the 'thick bare thighs and knees, slightly hairy and probably dirty', the 'couple of days' growth of beard', the 'raised' eyebrows, the 'almost pug' nose, etc. The description, running for more than half a page, is part of a scene in which Ethel discovers the photograph concealed under Grandin's blotter, while dusting his desk. The photograph that Jackson, just like Grandin, made a point of carefully cutting out of a newspaper and keeping safe, is preserved without a note explaining what it is, among a bundle of other papers and items in one of the boxes of Jackson's archive, ready for the student of Jackson to chance upon it in the kind of semi-accidental way in which Ethel stumbles upon it in TFOV. In other words, the scene in TFOV in which the woman who loves Grandin discovers the clipping under Grandin's blotter loosely scripts the experience of the lover of Jackson's work who rummages through his archive. 'The woof of fact and fiction' ([PCJ19]), it turns out, is 'intrinsically spun' not just for the author of TFOV, but for the student of it, too.

A homophobic author writing a homophobic novel?

Crowley's *Sewanee Review* essay on TFOV remains the most fully worked out academic assessment of the novel. Crowley (2006: 277) critiques what he sees as a tendency to 'misrepresent *The Fall of Valor,* in the interests of twenty-first-century identity politics', arguing that 'it is more honest to acknowledge Jackson's own homophobia'. According to Crowley (2006: 265–266, 275–276), Grandin is

4   I have a copy of the picture on file, but I cannot reproduce it because, despite having secured Dartmouth College's authorisation, there is a chance that the photograph is still under copyright, and the copyright owner is impossible to identify.

homophobic because he values heterosexual marriage more than homosexuality, and Jackson shares precisely the same view as Grandin's: this is what enables the novel's protagonist to experience, and the author to convey to the reader, the epilogue to Grandin's involvement with Cliff as a fall of valor, or loss of value. Indeed, Crowley (2006: 261, 274, 276) argues that TFOV is not a gay novel at all, but a novel about heterosexual marriage, and about the tragedy of giving up the ennobling trait of heterosexual masculinity, which participation in marriage symbolises: this explains why the book does not end with Grandin's beating, but with his realisation that now he will not be able to restore his marriage. On this view, if TFOV is to be read as a 'gay novel' at all, in the sense of a work that reveals the oppressive nature of compulsory heterosexuality, it must be in spite, rather than because, of Jackson's intentions (Crowley, 2006: 277).

The hypothetical 'queer theorist' that Crowley (2006: 264–265) imagines engaged in a project of gay-affirmative 'critical recuperation' of TFOV would not necessarily disagree with the last point – queer theorists, influenced as they are by post-structuralism are more interested in how texts are liable to exceed, and even undo, their authors' intentions than in establishing those intentions. Be that as it may, it is unclear to me that, on the basis of purely internal textual evidence, the author's intention is such that Grandin's attitude – his experiencing a loss of value – is best read as disvaluing homosexuality vis-à-vis the superiority of heterosexual marital masculinity. For all that their sexual life is wanting, Grandin genuinely loves Ethel, and she him. Grandin is also rightly proud of his professional achievements, for which he has worked hard. At the end of the book, Grandin is poised to lose all this – the love of someone he has shared the best part of his adult life with, a relationships with his children, the rewards of professional commitment. And he is due to lose it because a homophobic society has both made Grandin's homosexuality opaque to him until recently, and ill-equipped him to handle in a satisfactory way this belated discovery – indeed, making it virtually impossible for him now to accommodate homosexuality in his life without losing everything else. All of this *is* tragic, unless one is inclined to view human relationships as fungible and careers as disposable. To claim that Grandin's loss is only tragic if the desirability of the 'marital heterosexual norm' is assumed (Crowley, 2006: 275) flattens all the moral complexity of the novel as Jackson himself seems to have intended it.

A consideration of extrinsic evidence relating to the novel's genesis and evolution confirms this, and suggests that it is reductive to portray TFOV as a case of a homophobic protagonist and homophobic authorship. Crowley (2006) did not have the full benefit of this evidence at the time of the publication of his essay: although all the boxes constituting Jackson's archive were delivered to Dartmouth College by 2002, all but one remained forgotten and uncatalogued in the library's basement until they were rediscovered thanks to Bailey's (2013: 432) inquiries while he was carrying out research for his biography of Jackson. An academic consideration of this extrinsic evidence, so as to illuminate Jackson's intention in respect of TFOV is opportune, and this is what I attempt in the next several sections.

The first incarnation of TFOV: 'a sensual but warm and even kindly story of the kind of masculine affinity out of which (possibly) good can come' ([PCJ20])

When Jackson, less than one year after the Nantucket trip, first came up with the idea of writing a novel about homosexuality based on his holiday, his agent Bernice Baumgarten and his then editor Philip Wylie were 'guardedly discouraging' (Bailey, 2013: 169). Wylie told him that the book would require 'a deal of "guts and heart and sweat", the more so because it demands "exquisite writing"' ([PCJ1]). Indeed according to Jackson, his publisher Farrar & Rinehart 'were reluctant to consider this book or even read it, at first' ([PCJ14]).

Jackson responded by writing them a very lengthy letter, dated 24 May 1944, setting out a detailed outline of the novel ([PCJ1])), to show he was serious about it and already had it all in his head. As the novel was originally conceived, neither a marital rift nor a tragic ending was contemplated. This lack of drama is reflected in the title Jackson had in mind for the novel: *My Two Troubles*, from a poem by Housman. Jackson declared the poem 'says exactly what I wish to say in my story: that the thinking and feeling man is the vulnerable one, while the insensitive unimaginative perfectly average happy normal guy is the one who, while never experiencing anything very deeply, also is never troubled and thrown off base like my hero' ([PCJ1]). The 'troubled, sensitive hero' was to be Grandin, at this stage called David Williams, while Cliff was the one who is less feeling, but also 'completely right with the world, completely adjusted, and he belongs' ([PCJ1]). That the novel, at bottom, was to be a study, however understated, of a man's pining over another is made obvious from the alternative title Jackson was considering – *Who Can Wonder* – the sound of which Jackson actually preferred to *My Two Troubles*, save the disclaimer that the poem (again by Housman) from which it was extracted smacked 'a bit too much of the precious or lavender' ([PCJ1]). In the letter, ([PCJ1]) Jackson went to the trouble of typing out the poem for the benefit of his publisher:

> He would not stay for me; and who can wonder?
> He would not stay for me to stand and gaze.
> I shook his hand and tore my heart in sunder
> And went with half my life about my ways.

Read in light of what we have already learnt about the novel's autobiographical basis, and about Jackson treating his writing as a cathartic exercise, it seems plausible that at this stage the novel was closely tailored to Jackson's unrequited feelings for the young Captain with whom nothing had happened, or could happen, and whom he might well never see again. The novel was to be about 'a rather melancholy but completely normal experience in these confused times'; the wartime atmosphere provided Jackson with an affective vocabulary to express (his and) his hero's desire in duly sublimated terms, emphasising 'his prescience of death; his consciousness of youth all about him leaving – to what;

his anxiety and concern because the ideal of today is brutality and destruction' ([PCJ1]). In Jackson's words, the novel would be 'a kind of poetry in fiction about the troubled heart of man today', and 'the value and beauty of the story will be in the telling, never really in the events' ([PCJ1]). Williams (Grandin) would be aware of a feeling of 'disturbance' (as well as its drawing power) in the presence of the Marine; Ethel would sense her husband's trouble, and its nature; but this would precipitate neither arguments, nor a separation, nor indeed anything over-blown: 'There is no heavy drama or great understanding or noble sacrifice or anything crappy like that, here: it is all simple and natural and normal. ... my aim is to keep the story from ever being neurotic or "rarified"' [(PCJ1)].

The novel was to end with a strained meeting between the two men in Williams' apartment, shortly after the Nantucket holiday (Cliff is in town to have his new uniforms tailored; Ethel is at her parents' with the children). Williams becomes aware of the erotic basis of his attraction to Cliff, but manages to resist the temptation to express his fondness physically or even verbally ('Men don't say those things, least of all to a man like Cliff') ([PCJ1]). The two eventually leave the flat, both experiencing a sense of release, only now feeling authorised to make bodily contact, Cliff wrapping his arm around Williams' shoulders as they walk. 'As they part they both know that they are fonder of each other than ever before and no longer have any need of each other' ([PCJ1]). A few months later, a nephew who is in the Navy is dining at the Williamses. Cliff happens to be his Captain. The nephew reports a somewhat sleazy episode involving Cliff, a married man, randomly picking up a girl for the night. Williams is saddened that 'a chance girl in a bar' got so easily what he yearned for so intensely, but 'he can't help feel all of it is right, it all fits, all belongs: it's so like Cliff' ([PCJ1]). Earlier Jackson described Cliff's joking with another soldier about a gay man on Nantucket, comments that brought home to Williams the Marine's 'callousness and complete lack of understanding' ([PCJ1]). Taken together, Cliff's homophobia and his phi-landering are indicative of a certain ruthlessness, the very thing that makes him successful and, in Jackson's earlier words, 'completely right with the world' ([PCJ1]) – a world that values and, as Williams' own experience suggests, even eroticises the power of conventional heteronormative masculinity.

Interestingly, earlier in the letter Jackson speaks of a 'difficult and inevitable conclusion' to the novel ([PCJ1]). In light of this, Williams' feeling, with which the novel as originally conceived was meant to conclude, that 'all of it is right' ([PCJ1]) is not the same as a feeling that what has transpired *is all right*. This is in an important point to keep in mind because, I think, it helps illuminate the finale in the novel as eventually published in a way that challenges the facile reading of both Jackson and his hero as a clear-cut case of internalised homo-phobia. I will return to this later, but in this connection it is also significant that the gay character that elicits the Marines' joking comments was, in the novel as outlined by Jackson at this early stage, a homosexual 'of the most orchidaceous variety', and yet a 'rounded character and an individual, not a too-recognizable and easy type, not something laughable and ludicrous, certainly not just a stock pansy' ([PCJ1]).

Jackson concluded his outline of the novel saying that, having thus set it out in full, he felt 'uncertain about its final effect' – in fact, felt 'definitely depressed' ([PCJ1]). In response, Stanley Rinehart and Jackson's agent, Bernince Baumgarten, sent telegrams which read, respectively: 'Go ahead my friend' and 'Don't let anything or anybody stop you if you really want to write this book' ([PCJ20]). His editor, Philip Wylie, wrote a letter to the effect that his ultimate belief (as an author himself) was that good writing is about 'how you do it', not the subject matter. He added: 'So, if you want to write it that much, for God's sake, write it', and he threatened Jackson that if he did not, Wylie would chase him 'down Fifth Avenue on skis with a baseball bat' ([PCJ21]).[5] Jackson happily seized on the phallic symbolism, retorting that if he did not deliver the novel in six months he was 'going to depend on [Wylie] chasing [him] down Fifth Avenue on skis with a baseball bat (let Freud work on that one!)', adding that the symbol was Wylie's, not Jackson's own ([PCJ23]).

Despite these encouragements, the depressed feeling that Jackson was left with after fully outlining the novel in late May 1944 stuck with him. Only a week later he was writing: 'I've got to come up with practically a whole new story; certainly a whole new ending, one with "uplift", one with some meaning and point' ([PCJ20]). He felt what was missing was a proper resolution to the hero's inner conflict. Williams' 'frustration is just as bad at the finish as it was half-way through, because nothing is done about it' ([PCJ20]). The 'tense scene in the apartment' troubled Jackson most; if nothing in it happens 'in outward action' (remember that at this stage the professor makes no pass at Cliff and hence does not suffer the consequences), neither does anything really happen 'interiorly' ([PCJ20]). This leaves the two men without any 'reason whatever for the feeling of release' they feel upon leaving Williams' apartment ([PCJ20]).

Jackson lamented that he failed to understand his 'own story' (a feeling that would periodically re-emerge during the gestation of TFOV), and did not know what he 'was driving at', else 'there would be no vagueness or evasion at the climax' ([PCJ20]). It is tempting to hypothesise that in re-living the Nantucket experience, as a result of setting it out in detail in his letter to his publisher ([PCJ1]), Jackson had brought to the surface his own unresolved frustrations over Vince Kramer. Initially, he might have told himself that he could rationalise away his infatuation by ascribing it (as in the case of his hero) to oversensitivity; by not falling into the trap of idealising the Marine (hence Cliff's moral ambiguity as portrayed in the novel's outline); and by repeating to himself the impossibility of his love (which explains the ending outlined in the letter, with the two men parting without tragedy or drama). All of this now seems to have struck a false note with Jackson.

Jackson saw himself as facing a stark choice: either he had to write 'an out-&-out neurotic disturbing story of abnormal homosexuality' à la *Death in Venice*

---

5   Wylie reinforced the point at the end of the summer: 'Go ahead and write out some of your heart' ([PCJ22]).

('but what's the good?'), or 'a natural human melancholy but not unpleasant story of normal homosexuality, the kind that is a part of all men: sublimated, understood, a natural affinity of man with man, needing no physical expression', one 'we can believe in in terms of the human' ([PCJ20]). Jackson was adamant that the story should 'not fall in between' ([PCJ20]). This suggests that he could not contemplate a normal, non-disturbing story of same-sex desire that finds a physical outlet. As I will argue later, this has less to do with the genre requirements of mid-century queer fiction than with Jackson's own imaginative resistance. At the same time, Jackson was at pains not to sanitise the story too much, and not to disavow the ultimately erotic nature of that 'natural affinity of man for man' ([PCJ20]). He wanted a 'story of the kind of masculine affinity out of which (possibly) good can come', but it was to be a 'sensual' story; and, in any case, 'if you sublimate it too much, it becomes a kind of invidious pleading', a 'suspect' attempt at concealing 'earthy, fleshy, and "ulterior"' motives ([PCJ20]).

It might be argued that, given the choice Jackson set himself between a story of physically-expressed 'abnormal homosexuality' and one of physically-restrained, sublimated (but not *too* sublimated) 'normal' homosexuality, in eventually choosing to make Grandin seek physical contact with Cliff, the tragic ending of the final, published version of the story was more or less inevitable. To have had Grandin make a pass at Cliff without Cliff's responding violently would have been to envisage the *tertium* which Jackson seemed to think *non datur:* a normal, rather than deviant, story of non-sublimated same-sex desire. Such a reading, however, is premised on the assumption that, as the writing and rewriting progressed, Jackson held on to the stark alternative between physical abnormal homosexuality and platonic normal homosexuality. It is unclear, however, whether he did. As we will see, it is Jackson's final decision to make the novel a study of marriage – rather than Jackson's holding on to the view that physically expressed homosexuality is an aberration – that best accounts for the novel's tragic ending.

The second incarnation: 'the study ... of a war-neurosis' ([PCJ24])

Over that summer of 1944, Jackson's concept for the novel evolved in response to a conversation with a Hollywood physician, Dr Sam Hirshfeld, who persuaded him to bring to the fore the theme of a war neurosis. Jackson appeared very grateful for being told 'what the story was about and what it was not' (Bailey 2013: 172).

Jackson adapted his explanation of the war neurosis conceit to the audience he was writing to. In a bid not to alienate a literary critic who had liked his previous work, for example, he used language that distanced him from same-sex desire, explaining to the critic that his hero 'becomes almost a case of shell-shock, and finds release and a cure for his neurosis in only the most anti-social way' ([PCJ25]). Even more guarded and vaguer was the account he provided to Charles Brackett and Billy Wilder, who at the time were producing the motion picture of *The Lost Weekend*: 'the story is how the uniform today dominates our lives and upsets or deranges our emotional thinking' ([PCJ26]).

On the other hand, with his liberal-minded Marine friend Buck Lielenthal, Jackson could let down his guard, and drop the vocabulary of antisocial behaviour and derangement: 'Are you familiar with A. E. Housman's poems? Though they lament the death of youth by war, they are really love-poems. And Walt Whitman's becoming a nurse during the Civil War. In peacetime he wouldn't have done it, nor would Housman have written those poems. Well, my prof is something like that' ([PCJ4]).

Jackson explained the war neurosis conceit most clearly to Fred W Dupee, a politically radical literary critic, himself gay or bisexual (Reed, 2014: 10): '[A] college professor ... develops a kind of war-neurosis as a result of his obsessive preoccupation ... with the deaths of so many young men nowadays.... This neurosis takes the form of an infatuation with a young Marine ... What I am trying to say ... is that all men, whether they realize it or not, feel a homo-sexual urge toward the soldier, and this urge increases when the power of the uniform dominates our lives, as it does these days' ([PCJ14]). This account may explain why Jackson, for a long time during the novel's gestation and his pre-paration of its first and second drafts, became so sold on the idea of a war neurosis. Presumably he felt that the conceit, in implying that same-sex desire is – at least in a latent form – universally shared, offered him the formula he needed to make the story one 'we can "recognise" as being ourselves or part of ourselves' ([PCJ20]). Analogous motivations prompted Jackson to change the protagonist's designation from David Williams to 'Professor' and 'John Grandin', and eventually simply to 'Grandin', which he thought gave 'a stronger and even a kind of more "masculine" effect throughout ... so that we will care' ([PCJ16]).

Whether or not stated in homophobic terms, the idea of a war neurosis, once introduced into the novel, inevitably lent to Grandin's desire for Cliff a patho-logical quality that had been absent from the story as initially conceived. The new titles Jackson tossed about as candidates for the reconceived novel reflect this. By late September 1944 he was considering *The Middle Mist* ([PCJ27]) (which one year later ended up becoming the American title for Mary Renault's lesbian novel *Friendly Young Ladies*). This was no doubt from a sonnet by Rupert Brooke (1910), which in relevant part reads: 'There are wanderers in the middle mist, who cry for shadows, clutch, and cannot tell whether they love at all, or, loving, whom'. The passage is suggestive of the emotional/sexual derangement Jackson imputes to the domination of the uniform in wartime.

Two months later, the title had already changed to *The Fall of Valor* ([PCJ16]), from a passage in Moby Dick: 'it is a thing most sorrowful; nay shocking, to expose the fall of valor in a soul' (Melville, 1922: 112). Since by this time Jackson was still far from contemplating a tragic ending (and since the new conceit, by making the wartime atmosphere the reason for Grandin's homosexuality, relieves the hero of any responsibility for his 'neurosis') it is not entirely clear why this title was considered at this stage. Later, when Jackson dropped the war neurosis idea and made TFOV a novel of marriage with a tragic ending, he would concede that the title 'suits the new big story better than it ever did the other one' ([PCJ28]).[6]

Perhaps because of this lack of congruence between the new title and the war neurosis theme, Jackson soon came to prefer the title *So Many Captains*. As he explained in a letter to his brother 'Boom' and mother Sal, the title comes from a passage in Henry II, which 'goes like this "...Is all our travail turned to this effect, after the slaughter of so many peers, so many captains, gentlemen, and soldiers?"'([PCJ30]). The title clearly brings to the fore the idea of homosexuality as a side-effect of war. As Jackson put it: 'The quote about SO MANY CAPTAINS is especially good because the theme of the story is how the uniform today dominates our lives and upsets or deranges our emotional thinking' ([PCJ26]).

Less than three weeks before sending the full first draft of the novel to his publisher, we get the first indirect intimations that Jackson was having new doubts about the book's ending – not only because, as before, he still felt Grandin's conflict required a proper resolution, but also because, now, he was less sure about the kind of resolution he had been after. Unlike Aschenbach in *Death in Venice* who simply dies when he should do something about the discovery of his desire for Tadzio,

> Grandin has to work out his dilemma, to our satisfaction and his, and he's got to be either the better or the worse for the experience. I choose to make him better for it, but I can't help wondering whether the reader will not simply be impatient with him for his infatuation instead of sympathetic.
>
> ([PCJ31])

While a full-blown tragic ending is not yet manifestly on the cards, it seems significant that one month later Jackson briefly considered changing Cliff's rank to Sergeant, so that he would be able to title the book *Sergeant Death*. As he explained, the expression came from Hamlet: 'This fell sergeant, death, is strict in his arrest' ([PCJ2]). If this was intended, as it seems, to convey the idea that, in awakening same-sex desire in Grandin, Cliff brought a kind of metaphorical death to the professor,[7] we can see that at this stage the novel was evolving in a direction that was a far cry from the original concept of 'a kind of poetry in fiction about the troubled heart of man today' ([PCJ1]), which was much closer to the way in which Jackson had experienced his attraction for Vince Kramer on Nantucket.

Jackson completed the full first draft on 1 February 1945, but withdrew it from the publisher because he decided 'it was much too emotional, with too

---

6 Another title Jackson was considering (and preferring to TFOV) by the end of 1944 was *So Long!* ([PCJ29]).

7 Since, however, at one point Jackson was planning to have Cliff himself die ([PCJ16]), the case for this interpretation is not entirely clear-cut.

many rhapsodies about the Marine', and he wanted it to re-emerge 'more soundly and objectively' ([PCJ32]). He felt that his 'many too many qualifying clauses' made 'it look as though [he] were trying to steer a neutral course and not commit [himself] on anything' ([PCJ33]) – a concern that seems to echo his earlier desire that the story should not fall between one of 'abnormal' (physically expressed) homosexuality and one of 'normal' (sublimated) homosexuality. He was especially dissatisfied with the last portion of the work: 'The motive that resolves the story, I now discover, is all wrong and I am now casting about for a better dramatic device to present the "working out" of the story' ([PCJ33]). Yet at this stage nothing *too* dramatic was yet envisaged. In fact, it appears that Jackson in his second draft planned to retain the final scene of the first draft, which ended with Grandin and Cliff parting ways after the tense scene in the apartment ([PCJ34]) – and hence was even less climatic than the ending originally conceived in the outline: the epilogue in which the Gradins learn of Cliff's infidelity to Billie had now disappeared.

Jackson completed the second draft of the novel in June 1945 but refused to send his publisher the full thing. He held on to the last part (which he decided to entirely rewrite in a third and final draft), giving his editor, Ted Amussen, and other staff at Farrar & Rinehart, only the benefit of a summary of how the ending currently stood ([PCJ28]). According to the ending of the second draft, during the final scene between Grandin and Cliff in the former's apartment, the Marine begins to titillate the professor with dirty talk. The rationale for this turn of events is that Cliff feels an urge to cling to Grandin's (a cultured, older man) admiration, as he is now insecure both about the future of his marriage and his career in the Navy (his war injuries might prevent him from re-joining the war effort). 'But', as Jackson explained in his letter, 'this is pretty silly thinking – spurious, arbitrary, and somehow (no amount of fine writing will mask this fact) a little nasty' ([PCJ28]). Even before the final scene, while the two were still on Nantucket, Cliff had already started to become, in Jackson's words, 'a cock-teaser' ([PCJ28]). The problem was that Jackson now felt he had no compelling reason to make Cliff act in this way: '[I]t just made for good scenes – which would be all right if I were writing radio, but not all right in a novel that I hope will be honest and valuable' ([PCJ28]). After Cliff's dirty talk in Grandin's apartment, Grandin briefly leaves the room and, in his absence, Cliff tries on Grandin's coat, which he admires. When Grandin sees the Marine so attired, he feels that out of his uniform Cliff has lost his attractiveness. The two men then leave the apartment and Grandin accompanies Cliff to his tailor. In the tailor's shop, Grandin appreciates the drawing power of the uniform 'objectively', from the outside, rather than experiencing it first-hand as in the apartment. The men say farewell to each other, and 'Cliff goes off in the crowd' ([PCJ28]).

The ending of the second draft, thus, remains true to the war neurosis theme that had shaped the first draft – indeed, it makes that conceit completely explicit through the imagery of the very last scene, where the idea of 'the domination of the uniform' is literalised in the tailor's shop. That Jackson continued to hold on to the war neurosis conceit in the second draft is also apparent from the fact that one of the ways in which the second draft revised the first was by making Grandin develop an attraction for Cliff only after he had heard of the Marine's experiences in war, thus making the conceit more credible ([PCJ35]).

The third incarnation: 'a study of marriage' ([PCJ36])

Phil Rahv (literary critic and founder of the *Partisan Review*), with whom Jackson discussed the novel extensively, had suggested that Jackson should move away from the war-neurosis idea, though he appears to have done so by indirection. Jackson, invested as he had been in the idea since the summer of 1944, seemed to struggle to comprehend what Rahv was getting at, let alone take it on board:

> I will appreciate it if you could explain again just what you meant by saying that I shouldn't 'use' the war so much. I vaguely know what you mean; but because I feel I must continually have the war in the background and even an integral part of the story, I don't quite know when I am 'using' it and when it really belongs.
>
> ([PCJ37])

As Jackson was approaching completion of the second draft, however, he 'suddenly began really to grasp all [Rahv] had been talking about', hence his decision to call publication off and produce a third and final draft ([PCJ5]). Jackson wrote to Rahv to say he was being guided, in the redraft, by Rahv's last letter like 'the veritable chart I must follow' ([PCJ5]). Sending the critic a new outline of how he would rewrite the novel, he wrote:

> Over and over in the outline you will see points that you gave me.... I know you will prick up your ears when you see that bit about 'To answer such questions, he must be aware not only of the immediate problem ... but of his life as a whole'. Thank you, dear Phil, a thousand times for that: it is truly the gist of the whole novel.
>
> ([PCJ5])

What Jackson means here is that he has recognised the contrived nature of the war neurosis conceit: Grandin, to properly understand himself, needs to abstract from the way in which his same-sex desire contingently manifests in wartime (as an infatuation with the uniform), and look at the substance of what is going on (the desire itself, as something more permanent).

As Jackson explained in a letter to Amussen and others at Farrar & Rinehart, 'I was pinning it all on war', but 'my story really has nothing to do with the war whatever, or at the most very little' ([PCJ28]). 'Grandin's upset', he went on to write, 'could take place just as easily in 1935 as it could in 1955': that is,

Grandin is not 'deranged into homosexuality merely as a result of his strong feeling about war and the death of so much youth' (a notion that, Jackson now worried, would also call into question 'the integrity and honest emotion of millions') ([PCJ28]). In a suggestive, albeit throwaway, line, Jackson seemed to indicate that his own infatuation with Vince Kramer clouded his self-understanding as a man desiring other males, and that the mistake was carried through in Jackson's flawed portrayal of Grandin's troubles in the first and second draft of the novel: 'The fault of the novel is that I have allowed the Marine to carry the author away' ([PCJ28]).

Thus, a consideration of extrinsic material reveals that what Crowley (2006: 270) takes at face value as Grandin's self-understanding and the author's intention ('As Grandin himself comes to understand, the emergence of his homosexuality *can* be blamed on the eroticized wartime atmosphere') is actually best read as Grandin's self-deception; and that the author himself intended us to so read it. The author, in other words, really does know (at least about the point that homosexuality is not due to the war) better than his hero – a notion Crowley (2006: 265–266), in his critique of TFOV, seems unwilling to entertain.

Having discarded the war neurosis conceit as 'strictly topical and timely and even rather spurious' ([PCJ38]), Jackson now wanted the novel to be about marriage, crediting 'Don Stewart' (presumably the author Donald Ogden Stewart) for helping him see the flaws in the second draft ([PCJ28]). The primary flaw was that if Grandin, having realised 'his infatuation for the Marine … goes back to his marriage as if nothing had happened, that's a pretty poor excuse for an ending, and a still poorer excuse for a marriage' ([PCJ28]). Making TFOV a novel of marriage meant telling it from two viewpoints, Grandin's as well as, now, Ethel's, whose perspective 'will give a greater objectivity to the book as a whole' ([PCJ39]). Some of Jackson's letters self-consciously play up the idea that the novel was about marriage: '[I]t's far more the study of a marriage – any man's marriage (yes, dammit, yours too) – than it is merely a libidinous or teasing or sensational episode about homosexuality'([PCJ36]). Apparently, Jackson was anxious not to have the book dismissed as pulp (though TFOV eventually was reprinted as a pulp paperback, the cover design of this edition going on to become iconic). Nonetheless, note the specific words used by Jackson: to say that the novel is not 'merely a libidinous or teasing or sensational episode about homosexuality', clearly, is not the same as saying it is not about homosexuality. Since same–sex desire takes centre-stage as the force that drives the Grandins' marital troubles, it would be disingenuous to take Jackson's characterisation ('a study of marriage') too literally, when it seems ultimately designed to legitimise same–sex desire as a serious subject matter for fictional treatment.

A tragic or happy ending?

When Jackson decided to call off publication of the novel's second draft and sought more time from Farrar & Rinehart to produce a third draft, he knew the ending had to be entirely rewritten, but not how he would rewrite it. In the letter he sent to the publisher in late June 1945 ([PCJ28]), in which he set out his plan for the third draft, the novel as was finally published is largely recognisable in embryonic form, despite the fact that at this stage he was going to include incidents and characters (some surviving from earlier versions of the novel) that eventually got dropped. The crucial issue, however, was how to end the novel. In the second draft, Grandin gets over his infatuation with the Marine. But given that he has now become aware of his homosexuality, Jackson was concerned that the reader would rightly wonder about the future of Grandin and Ethel's marriage: a satisfactory ending would have to address precisely this question ([PCJ28]).

As Jackson saw it now, the question of the fate of the Grandins' marriage entailed a choice between a happy and a tragic ending. Some of the new titles Jackson was considering at this time reveal how difficult he found it to settle on either one or the other ending. *The Fall of Valor* remained a contender. Although Jackson now thought it 'pretentious', 'hard to remember', and a 'little lush all Ls', he conceded that it suited 'the new big story better than it ever did the other one' ([PCJ28]). This seems to suggest Jackson was inclined towards a tragic ending. The same seems true of the alternative title *In Will and Error*, from *Love's Labour Lost*: 'Now, to our perjury to add more terror, We are again foresworn, in will and error' ([PCJ40]). This title was dismissed by one of Jackson's agents, who tartly remarked that it 'might sound as if we were publishing Jonathan Edwards [an 18th century American preacher] instead of Charles Jackson, and we wouldn't want that idea to get around the trade' ([PCJ41]).

On the other hand, another title Jackson was considering at the time suggests he was far from ruling out a happy ending: *Courage Enough*. This was from *Pericles*: 'Courage enough; I do not fear the flaw; it has done to me the worst' [PCJ40]. Yet another candidate was *The Error of the Moon*, from *Othello*: 'It is the very error of the moon; She comes more near the earth than she was wont, And makes men mad' ([PCJ40]). With the moon symbolising, presumably, Cliff's irresistible charm, this title would have suited either a tragic or a happy ending.

In the happy ending, as Jackson envisaged it, the Grandins 'will get together and there will be complete understanding and acceptance, in the best possible way, with, for the first time, a sound hope for their future together' ([PCJ28]). This, apparently, would have required working out the basis for that sound hope, in a way which the novel's second draft had failed properly to account for, despite a portrayal of Ethel as consistently sympathetic to her husband's 'predicament' ([PCJ28]). Alternatively, Jackson considered, the novel could end in tragedy, though the tragedy was not inherent in the fact of Grandin's homosexuality, nor in his desire 'to accept it' and 'adjust his life to it' ([PCJ42]). As he elaborated:

> [T]he husband feels purged and better for the experience, glad at last to discover the truth about himself ... for whatever is so, is so. The tragedy comes when the Marine exploits the older man's interest in him, and thus brings disaster to all.
>
> ([PCJ42])

It took Jackson considerable time to make up his mind about how to end the novel as reconceived in the third draft. Between the end of June and the first third of July 1945 he seemed resolved to make the novel end tragically ([PCJ43]; [PCJ44]), but the end was rewritten several times ([PCJ45]), and in October he still declared himself undecided on 'how it's going to come out – whether tragedy or not' ([PCJ46]).

Jackson was eager to know his agent's and editors' preference with regard to a happy or tragic ending ([PCJ28]; [PCJ47]; [PCJ48]). Amussen declined to say:

> I have no right or even the ability to say whether it should be one or the other.... Whatever happens will be right, because by that point the book, if it's to be done the way you are doing it now, will resolve of itself and you won't have much say about it. The characters are acting out their lives as human beings the way they should and you wont [sic] be able to tell them what to do
>
> ([PCJ49]).

Wylie favoured a happy ending: either Grandin is only incidentally homosexual, in which case the most satisfactory ending would be for him to digest the news and go happily back to Ethel; or Grandin is basically homosexual, in which case the experience with Cliff would enlighten him about the root-cause of his marital troubles as well as about his own nature, leaving him happy in self-knowledge ([PCJ50]). According to Wylie,

> the problem is not one susceptible of tragic conclusions. Here is not a man doomed essentially from the beginning who remorselessly fights that doom in awareness of inevitable defeat. A marriage is not a doom in that sense and homosexuality is not – in that it is no sin, no matter for any but morbid atonement, and no intrinsic crime – such as, say self-murder.... So, in John's story, tragedy would be an artifice, allegorical only
>
> ([PCJ50]).

Wylie would go on to deal with homosexuality in his own books. It is clear that he did not rate homosexuality as highly as heterosexuality (in *The Disappearance* (1951), for example, he treats it as a form of relational immaturity), but neither, as his letter to Jackson here reveals, did he think homosexuality sinful or criminal. Indeed, he even castigates Jackson for 'dealing with homosexuality almost wholly through ... bodies and garments, shower baths and sun tan oil', alienating 'all those readers who will through fear (suppressed) or through prissiness (even in intellectuals) be made thereby to feel that homosexuality is merely vulgar in essence' ([PCJ50]). It is unclear whether Wylie means that Jackson's un-sanitised portrayal of homosexuality will alienate excessively defensive gay readers or, rather, sexually conservative heterosexual readers; but, clearly, he believed that those who could be made to feel that homosexuality was merely vulgar had unresolved hang-ups.

Wylie's and Amussen's responses confirm a point made by Donald Webster Cory as far back as the early fifties: that no 'gentleman's agreement' existed in the publishing industry that gay novels should end tragically (Connelly, 2001: 93). Their responses also give the lie to Jackson's claim, writing to his daughter Kate in the mid-sixties, that his publisher forced the tragic ending on him ([PCJ51]). Indeed, it will be remembered that when Jackson first outlined in full the novel – when it was still due to be a summer idyll without any 'heavy drama' ([PCJ1]) or tragic ending – his publisher, editor and agent all wrote to him very encouraging letters telling him to go ahead. Jackson's claim that Farrar & Rinehart required a tragic ending is contained in a letter which, ironically, Jackson asked Kate to save so that in future he could check whether he gave an honest account of himself ([PCJ51]). The letter is actually a very long PS to another letter that Jackson had already sealed, and went to the trouble of unsealing, in order to add this lengthy self-reflective account of his work. Jackson explains that although his novels 'were muffled through lack of discipline & illness, sickness, alcoholism, call it what you will, they were worthy efforts' ([PCJ51]). He goes on to say:

> THE FALL OF VALOR was ahead of its time ... and had a great, an important premise – then about two-thirds through turned lugubrious, too long-suffering, a miserable marriage & a "punishing" for the aberrant hero – because Farrar & Rinehart wouldn't accept my more intelligent, much more honest version – and to get it published at all, I had to accept the compromise, against my deepest wishes, for I, as an honest man honest about himself, and anybody else who thinks today, knows that in the middle of this-the-20th Century, the problem of homosexuality does not require a lugubrious treatment ... It needs only forthright statement of the fact that may be true or dormant in anybody's life, an intelligent meeting of the minds involved, and an acceptance of the facts & then a fitting of those facts into one's social life as best & intelligently as one can. It could have been a novel of discovery to a great many people, and a novel of let's-not-despair to many many others.... As it was, that novel has always been a great disappointment to me ... for having missed a great opportunity, of failing to bring it off on the high intelligent & totally absorbing level on which it starts out
>
> ([PCJ51]).

It is possible that, nearly two decades after the publication of TFOV, and considering his intervening history of addiction, Jackson's memory was not serving him well. As we will see there is evidence that Jackson, at the time of writing and publishing the book, was somewhat apprehensive about its reception; it is not incredible that, two decades later, the memory of those feelings led him astray in recalling how sympathetic his publisher had been to a non-'lugubrious' treatment of homosexuality in TFOV.

It is also possible that just as Jackson remade the Nantucket experience in writing TFOV, so now he was remaking, in epistolary form, his experience of writing TFOV. This may have been due to excusable pride: a desire to project, for the benefit of his daughter, a persona that was wiser, stronger, and more at peace with himself than he really was, or had been in 1946. But it might also be that Jackson was reinventing his past in a way that fitted the new self he was subconsciously preparing to inhabit: it will be recalled that the following year, 1965, Jackson would leave Rhoda and New Brunswick, to relocate and come out in Manhattan. Although his letter to Kate indicates that at this time Jackson was still very much hoping his marriage to Rhoda would have a future ([PCJ51]), another letter Jackson had sent her about a month before suggests that he was well underway in the process of maturing the kind of self-awareness that would enable the radical steps he took in 1965 ([PCJ52]). In this letter he explains how Plato had been recommended to him many years ago, both by Winthrop (a rich New Yorker of whom the young Jackson had been a pro-tégé) and by Ralph Monroe Eaton – a Harvard philosophy professor with whom Jackson had travelled in Italy: 'He was very good for me; ten years older, rugged, athletic … was married but got a divorce that year, we read Mann together' ([PCJ53]). But, as he goes on to explain, it was only recently, when he turned to *The Symposium,* that he had finally been able to get Plato ([PCJ53]). Jackson did not tell Kate that this specific Platonic dialogue deba-ted the merits of same-sex love, but he wrote: 'I seem to have entered a new world, one in which, though I can't explain it (and feel ridiculous using such inappropriate words), I feel better, and freer, and questions & answers seem, well, not easier, but different, on a plane where emotion & intelligence seem so perfectly match that one cannot tell one from the other and indeed in which they are the same' ([PCJ53]). Similarly, in a letter he wrote to his other daughter, Sarah, the day after telling Kate about TFOV in the long PS, Jackson declared:

> these past few year, HADRIAN'S MEMOIRS has come to be my most necessary book, to be re-read and re-read; I absolutely identify with Hadrian as with no other "character" I know of, and need him (his book and his wisdom) in my life.
>
> ([PCJ11])

Not only do these deliberate references to queer canonical texts indicate Jackson's re-orientation towards a less closeted self – one more congruent with the false story of Farrar & Rinehart requiring a 'lugubrious treatment' of homosexuality. They also suggest that it is partly through the study of these queer-affirmative, philosophical texts that Jackson was finally able (two decades too late) to make-believe a happy ending which – unlike the happy endings he had considered in the forties – would not necessarily involve the recuperation of Grandin into heterosexual marriage. Now a happy ending could mean something more open-ended and bold – 'acceptance of the facts [of one's homosexuality] & then a fitting of those facts into one's social life as best & intelligently as one can' ([PCJ51]).

The tragic ending in the published novel

The ending in the novel as published differs from the tragic ending Jackson envisaged for the third draft in his June 1945 letter to Amussen et al. ([PCJ28]). There is evidence that once Jackson decided on the tragic ending, this went through a series of different permutations. In one, Ethel committed suicide, and there was a scene in which Cliff's re-absorption into heteronormative marital domesticity was literalised through his returning to Billie ([PCJ53]). Neither of these made it to the final version of the manuscript.

According to the tragic ending as initially envisaged for the third draft, 'Grandin has pulled out, has made his adjustment with Ethel to the complete satisfaction of both – yet the error demands payment' ([PCJ28]). Payment would occur, Jackson imagined, through something Cliff does: 'It could end in Gradin's literal destruction; and even while it was happening, he could almost feel no resistance to it at all, no protest, his last and only thought being: "Ethel will ... understand"' ([PCJ28]).

In the published novel, on the other hand, the Grandins have *not* worked out things to their satisfaction – rather, they have left Nantucket separately after a succession of strained scenes. The future of their marriage is very uncertain. Then, at her parents' house, unbeknownst to Grandin, Ethel has a change of heart: she loves Grandin precisely because he is the type of sensitive man who could fall in love with another man, and she decides that she can trust him to remain faithful to her, just as he told her on Nantucket that he would be. Her understanding and her resolve to go back to him, however, are conditional on Grandin being true to her. But Grandin is not. True, it is Cliff's continually being a 'cock-teaser' ([PCJ28]) that finally prompts Grandin to make a pass, and he does so in circumstances in which he feels provoked at what he thinks is Ethel's inflexibility and lack of trust in him. But ultimately Grandin bears responsibility for initiating the physical contact with the Marine that make him untrue to Ethel and to his word to her. As a result, his final thought is not 'Ethel will understand', as in the tragic ending Jackson had outlined to Amussen at al. in June 1945, when he was about to rewrite the novel a third time; rather, Grandin's final thought in the published novel is that he has wrecked beyond repair his relationship with the woman he loves – and this as Ethel's telegram, whose conciliatory content Grandin guesses, is slipped under his door.

There is no doubt that, from the point of view of how it is constructed, this is a much more powerful ending than the possible tragic conclusion Jackson outlined in June 1945. Whereas then he imagined the Grandins entirely reconciled in mutual love and understanding, only to have that happiness wrecked by Cliff, the ending in the published version restores to Grandin a modicum of agency – so that while readers may be horrified at Cliff's homophobic violence, they can also intuit a karmic quality to what befalls Grandin, given his betrayal of Ethel. The effect – that is, reading Cliff's attack less like the homophobic violence that it is, than karma for Grandin's betrayal of Ethel – is in part enabled by the wholly impersonal quality of that violence, which makes Cliff (indeed, Cliff's *body*, the very object that prompts Grandin to betray Ethel) an instrument of karmic retribution: 'For an instant the tense body froze; then it reacted, violent and automatic, as if by reflex' (Jackson, 2016: 221). Contrast this with Grandin's movements, which triggered Cliff's reaction: while, once his hands are on Cliff's waist, they move 'involuntarily', the act of placing them on the waist in the first place was wholly voluntary, as it follows right on the heels of Grandin's telling Cliff that he is fond him, which gives the professor 'a *purpose* and a *deliberation* he had not experienced in years' (Jackson, 2016: 221, emphasis added).

Jackson must have realised the lunacy of the tragic ending he had initially envisaged, which involved accountability without responsibility, or, as he had put it, 'the hero as well as the wife having to pay to the very utmost for the flaw or stain that was beyond their control' – something that, at the time, he had thought would produce in the reader 'a kind of lofty satisfaction' ([PCJ28]). The final version of the novel turns this concept on its head. It is no longer Cliff who 'brings disaster to all' by 'exploit[ing] the older man's interest in him' ([PCJ42]). It may still be Cliff who sets in motion the tragedy that is to follow, when he proposes meeting Grandin in his apartment, and half-heartedly becomes a cock-teaser once again, impelled to excite and cling to Grandin's admiration at a time when his possible disqualification, due to his injuries, from re-joining active duty precipitates in him a crisis of self-confidence. But Cliff's agency stops there: it his *body*, rather than Cliff himself, that *automatically* reacts after Grandin, in full control, places his hands on the Marine's waist – the performative that enacts his betrayal of Ethel. In the published version of the novel then, 'the error [that] demands payment' ([PCJ28]) is no longer homosexuality itself, but Grandin's betrayal of Ethel's trust. Ironically, therefore, it is Jackson's very insistence that in its final incarnation the novel is a novel of *marriage* that enables a queer critical recuperation of TFOV as a gay novel. TFOV's being a novel of marriage invites the reading that Cliff's violence is not justifiable retribution for Grandin's same-sex desire, but (admittedly, disproportionate) karmic payment for the loss of integrity (the fall of valor) entailed in Gradin's final (albeit, possibly, only momentary) cavalier treatment of his relationship with Ethel.

After finishing the novel once and for all, Jackson declared: 'I had to abandon the story as originally outlined [in 1944] because there was no conflict in it between husband and wife, and thus Grandin's involvement with the Marine amounted to little more than a kind of summer idyll; in other words, it had little drama and hence no meaning' ([PCJ54]). This statement ties very clearly the novel's drama (the protagonist's fall of valor) to the failure of their marriage. Homosexuality, unaccompanied by this failure of Grandin's relationship with Ethel, would have made simply for a 'summer idyll' ([PCJ54]). These are neither the words nor the thinking of a homophobic, self-loathing author.

Nor is a queer recuperation of TFOV precluded by the fact that the book implies that Ethel and Grandin's marriage is something valuable, whose loss Grandin has reasons to mourn. Of course Grandin's marriage was valuable: he and Ethel had lived together for years, still loved each other, and had once had a satisfying sexual life. Recognising that the events that follow Nantucket result in a loss of value in Grandin's life need not presuppose either investing het-erosexual marriage with any kind of metaphysical value, or uncritically ratifying dominant societal norms that value marriage above other kinds of relationships. All that it requires is an understanding of human well-being's dependence on the successful pursuit of one's autonomously chosen comprehensive goals, including the cultivation of one's key interpersonal relationships (Raz, 1989). Because of how Grandin's life has gone so far, his attachment to Ethel must be counted as one such relationship, regardless of his sexual orientation.

Clearly, Grandin's same-sex desire, even before he has become consciously aware of it, has been interfering with, without necessarily negating, the success of his relationship with Ethel. Having woken up to it, the sensible option *might*, in the end, be to discontinue their relationship *as husband and wife*; but that is not how Grandin sees it by the time the book ends. Because Grandin is still invested in a marital relationship with Ethel, and because he does not consider himself released from the bonds of trust this creates between them, it is entirely congruent for him to feel that, in making a pass at Cliff, he has compromised his integrity, and even, perversely, that he has deserved Cliff's beating.

Jackson himself, for better or for worse, would choose to go on living with Rhoda for nearly two decades after writing TFOV, despite their many difficulties ([PCJ11]). In 1964, the year before they separated, he wrote to his daughters about a planned vacation with Rhoda in Strathmere, their 'first time away, alone together, in many years' ([PCJ11]), which would be 'a kind of test for us both, a good test' ([PCJ51]). As he explained to Sarah:

> Strange things happen in marriage ... and because the passage of years and all the ups-&-downs, we are no longer the same people. ... Now my sole aim is to slide down these last ten years or so of our lives together as gracefully as possible, as happily or contentedly as possible, and I think it is possible if we make the effort.... [I] am looking forward most keenly – oh, not to a happy week at Strathmere necessarily (because what is that?) but a week of knowing one another closely again, seeing one another as interesting or, if you will, not interesting, people, but at least seeing.... If we find a real communion together ... much will have been accomplished, to augur well for the fast diminishing future. If we don't, well, then we'll have to face that too. But I am hopeful, even optimistic. It's like when we came to New Brunswick, which I didn't want to do – and not wanting to, I determined to myself that I was going to like it if it killed me.
>
> ([PCJ11])

I quoted from the letter at length because Jackson's words, despite being penned twenty years after TFOV was conceived, are revealing of Jackson's intentions about the book once he had decided to make it a study of marriage. Around that time, Rahv had suggested that Jackson 'should put more of [himself] in the character of Grandin', though 'not in any autobiographical sense, necessarily', but in terms of what Jackson felt and thought ([PCJ55]). Grandin's fall of valor, then, can be understood, from Jackson's own perspective (reconstructed on the basis of this later reflection about marriage that he sent to his daughters), as a failure to act in accordance with the conviction that a meaningful relationship between him and Ethel could be restored.

Intriguingly, after receiving Rahv's recommendation to put more of what he thought and felt in Grandin, Jackson wrote to him that, in the novel's second draft, the driver behind Grandin's desire to visit Nantucket – namely, his conviction that it would make him more uxorious towards Ethel, and repair the rift that had come between them – will be 'played up now, with greater truth (I might even add "greater fidelity to fact")' ([PCJ56]). The words in brackets seem to suggest that Jackson himself may have hoped that Nantucket would make him more sexually interested in his wife, although, as we will see, at this time his marriage with Rhoda did not seem to have experienced serious troubles yet. It was two decades later that, in his sixties, Jackson would take the steps he had made the Grandins follow in TFOV – namely, to arrange a holiday (albeit in the more pedestrian location of Strathmere, rather than Nantucket) in a bid to mend their marriage, on the basis of the principle that '[a]ll (or mostly all) that any of us needs is an open-mind – a "well, let's see" attitude' ([PCJ11]).

A 'tortuous birth' ([PCJ7])

Even making allowances for artistic self-doubt, Jackson's penchant for histrionics, his addictions, and the mood swings that these addictions either engendered or were intended to assist in managing, Jackson experienced the writing of TFOV not only as laborious, but an emotionally draining experience that made him virtually neurotic.

In May 1944, when he was trying to sell his publisher the idea of TFOV, he anticipated that it would be a 'short book' (40,000 words, 'a continuous action and continuous mood'), 'completely thought out … and ready to be written', whose drafting 'would take a great deal less out of me both in heart and sweat, not to say time' than the sequel to *The Lost Weekend,* on which Farrar & Rinehart was keen ([PCJ1]). While towards the beginning of his lengthy letter he confidently stated that TFOV would 'come to be established as an American classic', the American counterpart of *Death in Venice,* by the time he had outlined it in full in the same letter he had already managed to lose some of his self-assurance. He declared himself 'depressed', and stated: 'It either is a great story or else it is a completely embarrassing one, and crap. I am simply in no position at this moment to judge it myself. Please relieve me … I want to know the truth' ([PCJ1]). The letter itself gives a very definite clue as to why Jackson would express himself in such impassioned terms: 'I don't give a damn whether the book is ever published or not; it is something I must do for myself' ([PCJ1]).

Jackson continued to describe himself as feeling 'depressed' or 'worried' about the book well into November, by which time the drafting was well underway ([PCJ20]; [PCJ27]; [PCJ57]). After ruthlessly revising the manuscript he felt sanguine enough as to write to his editor 'that this book will find a real place in current lit' ([PCJ16]), though on the same day he was writing, to people who had no stakes in the project: 'It's a most ambitious undertaking, full of pitfalls; the least false note and all is lost; I'v [sic] become all but a nervous-wreck trying to steer a safe and sane course through its dangers' ([PCJ24]).

By the time the end of the first draft was in sight, and he was anticipating sending the manuscript to the publisher as 1944 was drawing to a close, Jackson's optimism knew no bounds: 'I have nothing to fear: it is good, it is big, it is beautiful' ([PCJ29]); 'it's the best damn book you ever read in your life' ([PCJ58]); 'It's wonderful – all of it good' ([PCJ59]). But in January 1945 he was still working on the first draft and self-doubt had crept back in with a vengeance:

> I'm having terrible trouble with it.... I've never gone through anything like this in my life: it is torture, trying to handle all the points of this story in the way you know they must be handled. Just "good enough" isn't, in this case, good enough ... when the story begins to be "dramatized," it doesn't measure up.... The story kills me to write it: I've never attempted or done anything that takes so much out of me; and during the past month it's gotten me down so that I've become neurotic as hell, nervous, depressed, and even at times have thought that the only solution is suicide. You give so much to a thing and then, because you simply don't have the equipment needed, it doesn't come off, or, if it does come off, what of it? It's just another story. I keep wondering is it worth it, the hell you go through.... You get to the point when you simply do not know when an image or symbol is arbitrary & when it's an integral part of the whole. The sexual symbols are so many & so constantly insisted upon that I begin to wonder if the story is simply nothing more than prurience – a kind of prolonged "tease."... Another thing that disgusts me with myself is my inability as a writer to stand on my legs.... I shouldn't have to submit in aguish to someone else & then have them tell me what the story is or is not.
>
> ([PCJ31])

Eventually, after having 'worked literally night and day, at a pitch of fever', 'worked harder' on it than 'on anything in [his] life', he submitted the manuscript towards the end of January, only to reread it and find it 'sloppy, overdone, over-written, overemotional, overlong' ([PCJ60]) – the last four parts, particularly, 'very mediocre' ([PCJ61]). So, he called the whole thing off, despite the fact that 'it raised hell with F&R's publishing schedule' ([PCJ62]). He pronounced himself 'tired out and awfully let down' ([PCJ61]), but the book had to be 'completely right' ([PCJ63]), 'a masterpiece or not at all' ([PCJ64]): 'I have chosen a theme that is difficult and dangerous in the extreme ... I am trying to put into THE FALL OF VALOR absolutely everything I have' ([PCJ60]).

Jackson felt that the last few parts of the book must 'take a new line altogether', and (much to his agent's frustration) ([PCJ39]), discussed the book with several people to help him find it: 'God, don't I feel foolish writing a story I am so interested in – and yet calling on everybody else to help me out' ([PCJ34]). Eventually, following a discussion in New York with literary critic Rahv ([PCJ65]), he declared: 'I have at last achieved an understanding of the kind of story I want to write' ([PCJ2]), though in fact, as will be remembered, Rahv's suggestions (and particularly his recommendation to abandon the war neurosis conceit) did not sink in until much later.

By the last week of March 1945 his excessive anxiety 'to make it a good and lasting book' was hampering progress ([PCJ66]), and he wrote to his agent that he was 'tempted to chuck' it, but would finish it 'if only to solve the insoluble problem' it posed, though he anticipated giving up if the second draft fell short like the first ([PCJ67]). As, the 'intense requirements' ([PCJ30]) of writing the book, as well as his Seconal addiction (Bailey, 2013: 189), resulted in Jackson's hospitalisation, the deadline to submit the second draft kept slipping ([PCJ68]; [PCJ69]). Jackson said he had been living with the manuscript so long that he could 'scarcely make sense out of it any more' ([PCJ69]): 'One moment I think it's the greatest thing I ever read, the next that it's rubbish' ([PCJ15]).

Although by the end of May he felt that the book was 'so good now, and so right' ([PCJ70]), one month later he had 'a terrific upheaval and facing-up with himself' [PCJ71] and withdrew the finished draft again to rewrite it a third time. Promising Farrar & Rinehart that the final version would vindicate all the tarrying and redrafting, he told them, exhausted, that he was 'ashamed', because the story 'leaves us with nothing to care about, teaches us nothing', and pleaded: 'I've got to satisfy myself with this book, else why write at all?' ([PCJ28]).

The redrafting took several more months, during which Jackson got far too little sleep ([PCJ5]; [PCJ36]; [PCJ46]; [PCJ72]; [PCJ73]), and started sounding more than a little manic: 'this book grows bigger and bigger; it will be purely dramatic' ([PCJ74]); 'it grows and grows, bigger and finer, all the time' ([PCJ43]); 'my eyes filled with tears.... I have in my hands such a wonderful story to tell' ([PCJ44]); 'it will be the best novel published in American in many years' ([PCJ72]); 'I am simply astonished at how interesting and alive it is' ([PCJ46]); 'I am going like a house afire' ([PCJ73]). Again and again he insisted that TFOV would be far superior to *The Lost Weekend* ([PCJ44]; [PCJ75]; [PCJ54]; [PCJ76]). These statements – immodest though they are – should be read in light of the sheer degree of Jackson's investment not just in writing, but in this particular project: 'I honestly ... don't care whether it sells or not; all I want to do is to dominate that story and make it my own and be satisfied with it myself' ([PCJ39]); 'I have given it everything that's in me ... I have never worked harder on anything in my life' ([PCJ72]); 'I worked much too hard on it for too long, and it almost killed me to do it' ([PCJ77]). There is some evidence that after submitting the manuscript in the spring of 1946, he started doubting the book again ([PCJ78]), and indeed he rewrote some scenes even after the book was in galleys, and then again when it was in page-proof ([PCJ45]; [PCJ79]).

Despite Jackson's generally sanguine attitude while redrafting the book a third time, it had not been smooth sailing. Towards the end of March, after submitting the third draft, Jackson was hospitalised a second time after collapsing in New York (Bailey, 2013: 213). Rhoda wrote to Jackson's brother, a former co-worker with whom she maintained a life-long friendship (Bailey, 2013: 62):

> But the dreadful thing is that I have no feeling of missing Charlie at all, nor have the kids. He has been such an irritant and problem for so long it seems much more like home with him away.... I can't face the same Charlie we've had for the last year or so, even without any pill problem. I can't live with such egocentricity, such unreasonableness, such perverted sense of value. The insatiate lust for fame, for recognition
>
> ([PCJ80]).

Not only had writing TFOV 'almost killed' Jackson ([PCJ77]), but also wrecked his marriage. Even setting aside Jackson's addictions, his wife could not bring herself to see Jackson's investment in the project as anything other than self-centred and unreasonable. One year later, even with the book now published, the situation had not improved. In July Rhoda wrote to her brother-in-law again: Jackson had decided to leave her, and she wanted him to go, for they could not go on like this ([PCJ81]). But Jackson had a change of heart at the last moment ([PCJ82]). They would go on to live together for another two decades, for all that Rhoda appears to have found him over-bearing ([PCJ82]; Bailey, 2013: 383), and that Jackson may not have lived up to the high marital standards he made his fictional alter ego set himself (and ultimately betray) in TFOV.

Indeed, judging by a letter sent by Jackson to one 'Patrick' ([PCJ83]), as early as 1953 Jackson had become quite the consummate flirt. The letter concerns the plan that Patrick should come over in August to assist Jackson with his writing,[8] light-heartedly discussing pay and accommodation. It starts 'Angel Patrick ...', but refers to Patrick as 'Pat' and a 'girl' throughout, and mentions Pat's 'husband', whom Jackson calls 'the handsome Mr William Edgar' ([PCJ83]). The letter ends as follows: 'I do think we'll have fun. There is one story in particular that I am eager to try, called SOLITAIRE – and I don't know why exactly, but I have a hunch that you are the very girl to try it out on. Or with' (the last two words handwritten on the typescript) ([PCJ83]). The Jackson who wrote of Grandin's fall of valor for his betrayal of Ethel might have felt let down by the Jackson who sent that letter to Pat in 1953.

Rhoda placed the beginning of her marital troubles to about April 1945 ([PCJ80]). Eerily, towards the end of March 1945 Jackson was writing to his editor that now that he had resolved to make the book 'as much ... a story about the "fatigue" of marriage ... as the story of a war-neurosis' he might do 'a better job of it – more objective, *less personal*, etc'. ([PCJ68], emphasis added). That, so soon after these words were typed, marriage fatigue would set in in

---

8   Bailey (2013: 188) mentions one 'Pat Hammond, a secretary who helped with Jackson's prolific story output in the early 1950s'.

earnest for the Jacksons themselves adds another element of complexity to the curious pattern of imbrication of fact and fiction in Jackson's life.

Critical reception of TFOV

The scrapbook Jackson made for TFOV suggests that his emotional investment in the project did not end with the book's publication. It contains many clippings of reviews from newspapers and magazines. Reviewers who attacked the book on account of its homosexual content tended to describe the ending as inevitable; many other reviews were, for different reasons, critical of the ending itself.

The inevitable ending

Charles Denecke, who taught at the Jesuit institution Woodstock College (Carey, 2010: 104), wrote a scathing review of the book, describing it as 'offensive and indecent' ([PCJ84]). The book's being about homosexuality is enough to condemn it to failure: the reader will only feel 'an indifferent contempt' for Grandin, who exhibits 'a less mentionable deviation from the normal' than alcoholism, the subject of Jackson's previous book ([PCJ84]). Denecke resents that Grandin accepts his homosexuality as a fact, and even 'experiences a sense of relief' at his discovery, for 'no man … submits to a degrading humiliation without at least a show of resistance' ([PCJ84]). Denecke even projects onto Grandin sadistic desires purportedly induced by his homosexuality, crudely oversimplifying Jackson's account of how the protagonist's preoccupation with war and war heroes was inflected with same-sex pulsions. Having conceptualised yielding to same-sex desire in terms of degradation, humiliation, and moral failure, it is a foregone conclusion that Denecke regards the book's 'violent climax' as 'inevitable' ([PCJ84]).

These sentiments are echoed in another review, published in the *Meridien (Conn.) Record* ([PCJ85]). In line with the contemporary social treatment of homosexuality as a psychological aberration and same-sex sexual activity as a crime, this review oscillates between treating Grandin as a clinical case and a case of deliberate immorality. The reviewer attacks what it views as the book's portrayal of homosexuality as an unwilled plight deserving of sympathy; yet, with its reference to 'a rotten spot at the core to cause so sudden a moral collapse' in Grandin, the reviewer equivocates on whether Grandin's actions are ultimately willed or determined by his inner constitution ([PCJ85]). Similarly baffling is the reviewer's point that the book 'traces the disintegration of a homosexual who, in all justice, must pay the price for his flaw' – which exacts retribution not for a guilty act, but for an unwilled defect ('flaw'), a point reinforced by the claim that Grandin belongs not in a prison, but in an 'asylum' ([PCJ85]). It will be remembered that when Jackson had initially envisaged a tragic ending, he himself had subscribed to similarly incongruous notions of accountability without responsibility. Clearly, the oppressive interlocking of legal and medical discourses on homosexuality around the middle of the twentieth century was not bound by respect for the rules of logic. Finally in claiming that Grandin does not belong 'between the covers of a book', and that homosexuality should not be afforded fictional treatment ([PCJ85]), the review hearkens back to the century-old *topos* of homosexuality as the unmentionable vice.

Another reviewer similarly maintained both that homosexuality should be handled by medicine and not literature, and that 'it was undoubtedly necessary to bring about the main character's revulsion at his own degradation' in the final scene ([PCJ86]).[9] All these reviews expressly claim that the book's tragic ending is the inevitable and even befitting consequence of Grandin's giving in to same-sex desire. Their moralistic condemnation of homosexuality, ironically, misses the actual moral significance of Grandin's making a pass at Cliff – namely, his betrayal of Ethel.

The underdetermined ending

Another group of reviewers took issue with TFOV because they saw the ending as *not* inevitable ([PCJ88]; [PCJ89]). Harriet Zines, for instance, states that Jackson has not 'fully embodied the cowardice of John Grandin's perverse despair', and that the book leaves the reader 'entirely unprepared for the end' which, as a result, becomes 'mere sensation, a cheap device' ([PCJ90]). Grandin, in other words, is depicted too sympathetically for a homosexual; as a result we are left in shock at his beating – when really, if only Jackson had correctly insisted on Grandin's cowardice and perversity, we would have no reason to be.

The most fully worked out version of the position that the ending of TFOV is underdetermined is by journalist and literary critic John Chamberlain, who argues that in great works of literature the ending is compelled by circumstances and characterisation ([PCJ91]). The problem with TFOV is that the ending is 'reversible' ([PCJ91]): a different outcome would have been equally credible. This could have been remedied, for example, if the book had shown how the drudgery and sedentary nature of academic work perverted Grandin's youthful love of heroes, preventing him from 'taking his love of masculine action out in harmless forms of combat', instead leaving him prey to 'a momentary surge of feeling that leaves John Grandin shaking and ready for a loathsome adventure' ([PCJ91]).

In constructing an account of why the not 'basically homosexual' ([PCJ91]) Grandin is nonetheless impelled to make a pass at Cliff, Chamberlain imagines what outlet, other than homosexuality, Grandin could have had for his

9   The reviewer for the *Hartford Times*, who, unlike the other reviewers discussed, is inclined to speak of homosexuality as 'the complexity of sex in its relation to the distribution of hormones', states more equivocally that the tragic ending 'is inherent in character and is foreshadowed from the first page' ([PCJ87]). The inevitability of the tragic ending here is possibly seen as tied to the specific way in which TFOV is constructed, rather than to its homosexual subject matter.

penchant for hero-worship. With the book being set during WWII, Chamberlain inevitably lights on the idea of 'combat' ([PCJ91]). Yet, here a serious difficulty arises: with the bombing of Hiroshima having taken place the year before the book was published (1946), any kind of romanticisation of warfare and combat, as a counterpoint to the supposed harmfulness of same-sex sexual activity, is likely to have struck a false note. Jackson himself, in a 1945 letter to Thomas Mann, had stated that the 'small moral problem' addressed in TFOV, 'seems very unimportant indeed' in the aftermath of the atomic bombing ([PCJ92]). Chamberlain resolves the paradox of his line of argument, by speaking not of combat *simpliciter*, but '*harmless* forms of combat' ([PCJ91], emphasis added), whatever those might be. Conversely, he plays up the harmfulness of homosexuality by resorting to the over-the-top vocabulary ('loathsome' ([PCJ91])) traditionally associated with sodomy, recourse to which had always been a way of rhetorically establishing what resists rational argumentation – namely, the moral badness of same-sex sexual activity.[10] Elsewhere, Chamberlain manufactures the badness of homosexuality by drawing up a contrast between 'the seaminess of [Jackson's] theme' and 'the clean, sea-washed backdrop of Nantucket'([PCJ91]), crediting this contrast to Jackson himself, when in fact the choice of Nantucket as a setting for TFOV was dictated by autobiographical considerations.

The indeterminate ending

Some reviewers rated the book in a positive light because, apparently, they read the ending as foreclosing any prospect, however remote, of future happiness for Grandin. This is the case with Alice Dixon Bond, who refers with finality to 'the tragic disintegration and destruction of a marriage through the weakness and helpless perversion of the husband', and whose praise for the book is made subject to the disclaimer that 'it is for adults only and not, I think, for too many of them' ([PCJ93]).

Conversely, other reviews took issue with Jackson's book because they felt the ending is indeterminate. Thus, Edmund Wilson critiqued the inconclusive ending for failing to provide a satisfactory resolution: Cliff's beating of Grandin deludes the reader into thinking Grandin's problem has gone away, but it has not (Connelly, 2001: 105). A more egregious example is the review penned by Harold C Gardiner – the Jesuit literary editor of *America*. In his day, Gardiner was known for 'his broad reading habits', for defending 'novels many readers considered to be morally repugnant', and for arguing that novels are not inevitably immoral merely by virtue of portraying immorality (McDonald, n.d.). Apparently, however, these high-minded principles did not hold in respect of TFOV. Gardiner writes of

---

10   Other reviewers avoid the use of such vocabulary, but make obvious their distance from same-sex desire through an elaborate show of affected naïveté, eg: 'It may have been our own lack of sophistication, but we didn't have any idea where this story was leading'; and: 'Perhaps if we had been tremendously concerned with the subject …' ([PCJ92]).

TFOV that '[t]he danger is inevitably lurking on almost every page' because 'the theme is, of its very nature, flushed with a sickly cast', so that the 'book is unhealthy; it cannot but be' ([PCJ94]). The risk, presumably, is that the book will corrupt its readers' moral standards, and weaken their defences against 'homosexualism' – a 'moral malady' which 'may be spreading' ([PCJ94]).[11]

More significantly for our purposes, Gardiner also laments that the story lacks closure: 'the book does not end' ([PCJ94]).[12] What troubled him, presumably, was Jackson's refusal conclusively to either redeem Grandin into heterosexual domesticity, or kill him off as a result of Cliff's assault. When the book ends, Ethel is about to return to her husband, determined to forgive him. Will she keep her resolve once she has found Grandin hurt and learnt that it is as a result of acting out his same-sex desire? And what will Grandin himself do? Will he seek to make amend, resume making love to his wife, fight against his tendencies – and will he be successful or reduced to a guilt-ridden wreck, perhaps tyrannised by a resentful wife? Or will the Grandins go their separate ways, which could lead either to his ultimate undoing, or to a new life, possibly a fulfilled one, as a self-accepting homosexual? The latter possibility seems remote, but Jackson ultimately gives us no absolute reassurances that it is not on the cards. Gardiner's complaint that 'all is suspended in confusion' ([PCJ94]), thus, draws attention to the actual extent of finality of TFOV's tragic ending. Strictly speaking TFOV's final tragedy turns out to be an *interim* tragedy; while it may be more likely than not that further loss and sorrow will await Grandin, a less gloomy resolution cannot be ruled out.

The gratuitous ending

Those who saw the ending as gratuitous range from readers who appear free from homophobia and those who adopted the view that homosexuality is not immoral, but an unfortunate and curable psychological condition.

To the former group belongs an undated review, signed 'RR', which blames the failings of TFOV on the 'encroachments' of 'literary suppressionists' and Hollywood clichés ([PCJ96]). The review describes the ending as implausible, inconsistent with Cliff's characterisation as same-sex attracted, and employing a 'facile key' of 'perversion-doesn't-pay' ([PCJ96]). It also criticises no less Cliff's volte-face than Grandin's being 'without earlier intimations of his sexual tendencies' ([PC96]).[13] The effect is that we are not 'moved by', but rather

---

11 Like its unmentionable nature, the exceptional potential for communicability of same-sex desire is a century-old *topos*: indeed, the main reason why sodomy was the unnameable vice had always been that mere mention of it might put ideas in folks' heads (Zanghellini, 2015).

12 This criticism was echoed by Dorothy Quick, who would have liked a more 'definite conclusion' (PCJ95]), and the *Miami Herald* review ([PCJ88]).

13 Another review also takes issue with Grandin's belated 'tragic discovery' of his same-sex desire, though for different reasons ([PCJ97]). This reviewer professes to be 'shocked' and 'doumbfunded', for homosexuality is 'a fault or flaw in the human character' whose fictional treatment, if it is not to be 'altogether harmful', requires

'moved to wonder at [Grandin's] plight' ([PCJ96]). Another review, along similar lines, describes the ending as 'obscene, violent and pathetic', Grandin's belated realisation of his homosexuality contrived, and the conclusions 'false' ([PCJ98]). Behind the observations of both these reviewers one senses queer readers protesting against TFOV's missed opportunity to avoid both a tragic ending, and a portrayal of gay men as inescapably stuck in denial, resulting either in self-opacity (Grandin) or inner conflicts exploding in raging violence (Cliff).

Psychiatrist and celebrity analyst Lawrence S Kubie, who later would become Jackson's own therapist (Bailey, 2013: 240), also considered the book's conclusion gratuitous. In a 1946 letter to Laura Hobson[14] he declares himself 'troubled' by the ending, on the basis that it misses the opportunity to enlarge the readers' imagination and insight ([PCJ99]). Kubie would have favoured a slower realisation on Grandin's part of his own attraction to Cliff, one that did not necessarily lead him to make a pass at him, and that would have enabled him to reconcile himself with his homosexual tendencies, thus paving the ground for a mending of his relationship with his wife. As a psychiatrist, Kubie regards homosexuality as 'the heritage of all men and women, one of those universal problems which like the common cold cannot be brushed aside as normal merely because it is ubiquitous' ([PCJ99]). Kubie remonstrates not only against Grandin's attempting to consummate his relationship with Cliff, but also against the violent way in which Cliff repels him: 'I do not see that it was necessary to have Grandin conked on the head. I suspect that something in Jackson made him punish Grandin in this fashion' ([PCJ99]). The clear implication is that this 'superfluous' ending was due to Jackson's own failure to reconcile himself to his own same-sex desire, a point also made in the early fifties by Cory in respect of all mid-century gay novels having tragic endings (Connelly, 2001: 104–105).

Conclusions

Taken together, the reviews of TFOV reinforce the points made in chapter two about the social and cultural climate that shaped many mid-century lesbians' and gay men's ambivalent relationship to their sexuality – including Jackson's own, as well as his concerns about the book's reception. Apart from (and often in combination with) plainly homophobic attitudes, the reviews betray anxieties characteristic of much mid-century discourse on same-sex desire – a discourse working with an array of contested minoritising and

---

strict conformity with scientific knowledge ([PCJ97]). What the reviewer seems to find intolerable is the thought that (in contrast to what his psychological knowledge indicates) homosexuality might suddenly creep up on one without warning, leading one to act like Grandin – forgetting his 'sense of dignity' and accepting 'a revolting proposal and its disastrous consequences' ([PCJ97]).

14 Hobson was a novelist who knew Jackson, and Kubie's former lover (Bailey, 2013: 240).

universalising taxonomical typologies of homosexuality (inversion vs situational and/or opportunistic homosexuality), as well as deterministic (post-Freudian) and non-deterministic conceptions of agency (including sexual and criminal agency). What is one to make, for example, of Chamberlain's urge to write 'basic' ([PCJ91]) homosexuality out of John Grandin? Is it an attempt at reassuring himself, and his male readership, that if they experience and even (like Grandin) act on same-sex desires, they need not draw the conclusion that they are *really* queer?

Jackson was all too aware of the homophobia surrounding him, frequently having recourse to humour and irony in order to exorcise his anxieties. Commenting on why a representative of his literary agency never delivered a copy of the book to their London branch Jackson stated: 'Perhaps he was so shocked (or maybe even frightened) that he threw it overboard' ([PCJ100]). Elsewhere he quipped 'If the book isn't banned in Boston on publication day, what's the use of writing?' ([PCJ101]). He was also fully aware of how hard it would be to sell TFOV for a Hollywood adaptation ([PCJ102]). Finally, Jackson had no illusions about his (or at least Grandin's) romanticisation of the uniform: if the Marine Corps Headquarters had 'known the nature of THE FALL OF VALOR', he wrote when informing Rahv of his being invited by them to join them on a Pacific Ocean trip as war correspondent, 'they'd [have] beaten me up instead' ([PCJ5]).

The mainstream understandings of homosexuality that transpire from most of the reviews also go a long way towards illuminating why, despite his protestations to his daughter Kate in 1964,[15] TFOV ultimately reveals Jackson's despair, in 1946, of the odds of same-sex relationships faring well in the face of social hostility to same-sex desire. A different ending – one in which, say, Cliff is receptive to Grandin's advances, and they are left with the task of navigating the dilemmas of doing good by their wives as well as each other – remained abstractly conceivable, presumably even for Jackson. But make-believing, as opposed to merely conceiving of, such a denouement would have committed Jackson to assenting to a different kind of story – one that challenged, if only on the aesthetic plane, the heteronormative constraints that shaped Jackson's own life. This, in the early forties, Jackson could not bring himself to do. Indeed, as I intimated above, it was only in the 1960s that Jackson seemed able to overcome his imaginative resistance to a happy ending that did not involve Grandin's recuperation into heterosexual marital domesticity.

If, as we have seen, some rare reviews betoken a lack of patience, on the part of some (presumably queer) readers, with the mid-century gay novel's tragic ending script, a personal letter to Jackson from Thomas Mann illustrates queer writers' own difficulties with breaking free from that script ([PCJ103]).[16]

---

15 '[I]n the middle of this-the-20th Century, the problem of homosexuality does not require a lugubrious treatment' ([PCJ51]).

16 A portion of Mann's complimentary letter was later used by Jackson's publisher, Rinehart, to advertise the book in the print media, as shown by a clipping from an unidentified magazine or newspaper preserved in Jackson's scrapbook for TFOV.

Among other things, Mann specifically addresses the book's ending – the only part of the review where his positive assessment becomes more tentative. After mentioning that initially he had some psychological doubts about 'Cliff's brutal reaction to the revelation of feelings which he has unwittingly nurtured', Mann concedes that it 'must be accepted as congruous, after all', adding that, in any case, 'it is possible, and I could not say how to do it differently' ([PCJ103]). These remarks point to queer writers' imaginative resistance to committing happier endings to paper, even as they are not fully convinced by the tragic ones: 'I could not say how to do it differently' ([PCJ103]) implies that though an alternative must be possible, bringing it off eludes no less Mann's than Jackson's imaginative powers. Indeed, Mann goes on to tell Jackson about his own new novel, involving the seduction of 'a lonely artist, a figure somewhat like Nietzsche' by a 'young man of impish traits', who, however, unlike Cliff in TFOV, 'does not then grab the poker' ([PCJ103]). This is not, however, because Mann felt that a hopeful ending was called for; rather, as he immediately clarifies, it is the seduced artist 'who takes deadly revenge for his defeat' ([PCJ103]).

Like twenty-first century critics, virtually all the reviews that discussed the book's ending (and virtually all did) read the book's tragic ending as commentary on Grandin's homosexuality. Of course, Cliff reacts violently out of internalised homophobia, that is, because of the homosexual nature of Grandin's pass at him. But it is a mistake to let the concern with the same-sex nature of Grandin's advance make us lose sight of the broader point that TFOV wants to make in respect of the implications of Grandin's pass for his relationship with Ethel. As I have argued through a detailed examination of the imbrication of fact and fiction in Jackson's life, according to Jackson's own intentions the book (in its final, published incarnation) is a study of marriage. Grandin's beating at Cliff's hands, to the extent that Grandin knows that he has 'brought it on himself, asked for it' (Jackson, 2016: 221), is less punishment for Grandin's homosexuality than karma for his betrayal of Ethel's trust (underscored by Ethel's telegram being slipped under the door when Grandin comes round) – for all that Grandin's homosexuality and Cliff's homophobia are the vehicles through which the karmic punishment hits him.

Francis Downing's 1946 review of the book perhaps came closest to appreciating this point, despite being clouded by his heteronormativity and homophobia. According to Downing, the novel is about 'the central social problem of our times – the failure of our marriages' ([PCJ104]). Grandin and his wife Ethel epitomise 'our defect of will'; their failure to make their marriage work is symptomatic of our lack of 'the internal strength to carry the burden of living' ([PCJ104]). It is this failure that spells the awakening of Grandin's latent homosexuality, which becomes symbolic of our being 'drawn terribly, yet fascinated, toward what we know to be evil' ([PCJ104]). Downing's heteronormative and homophobic rhetoric turns TFOV into a novel about the institution of marriage, rather than (as I think was Jackson's intention) a novel about the marriage of John and Ethel Grandin, and people similarly situated. But buried under this rhetoric is a point that eludes both other moralistic reviewers from the forties and the modern critics who accuse TFOV and Jackson of homophobia: that Grandin's letting his relationship with Ethel flounder for the sake of a fairly meaningless (and doomed) infatuation is in itself a tragic outcome.

This reading of TFOV as a non-homophobic text – according to which Grandin falls from valor less because of his homosexuality than because of his betrayal of Ethel – is viable under the premise that Grandin and Ethel, despite their difficulties in recent years (and despite the difficulties' origin in Grandin's own suppressed same-sex desire), still love each other. The novel is particularly insistent on Ethel's undiminished love for Grandin, on the unmitigated success of the early years of the relationship, and on its continuing to offer a source of meaning and value for both Grandin and Ethel – which is precisely why the difficulties they are now facing loom quite so large.

These were not, necessarily, the conditions of the Jacksons' own marriage from about the time Jackson started writing TFOV, and until their separation in 1965. Although Rhoda, toward the end of her life, would say that Jackson was the best thing that happened to her (Bailey, 2013: 427), from as early as the mid-forties she expressed a wish that he would leave her ([PCJ82]). After their decision to separate, she wrote to her daughter Sarah: 'You worry that I'll withdraw from life as a result of the separation. I've withdrawn for years – and now I feel free. I won't have this censure weighing down on me, burying me' (Bailey, 2013: 383). Jackson's own experience of the last two decades of his marriage may or may not have been similarly benighted, but, in any case, it seems unlikely that he could have been oblivious to Rhoda's unhappiness. Under these conditions, the fall from valor that Jackson himself may have been guilty of was quite the opposite of Grandin's: it was his imaginative resistance to striking out on his own as a queer man. It might have been kinder to Rhoda, and to himself, if Jackson had left her sooner.

Jackson settled on a tragic ending for TFOV only after the process of writing, re-writing, and counter-writing his Nantucket holiday collapsed the space between fact and fiction, forced a degree of self-reckoning, and intensified his awareness of the tensions and constraints characterising his own life as a heterosexually-married, homosexually-attracted man. His protesting that the novel's first incarnation – where Grandin and Cliff separate amicably, each going contentedly his own way – provided no resolution to the hero's inner conflict seems a confession that he himself could no longer cathect with a Grandin that so easily – without pain, angst, or regret – freed himself of the need for a male beloved. The original happy ending was, in other words, spurious: Jackson's mind could still represent it, but he could no longer assent to it. He could, that is, no longer genuinely make-believe it. At the same time, neither could he assent – whether or not he could represent it – to a happy ending that involved a future together for the intellectual and the Marine. Heteronormative constraints made such a same-sex happy denouement as unimaginable in the novel as in his own life in the mid-forties.

Currie and Ravenscroft (2002: 8–9) point out that 'imagination' has many meanings, including the faculty of 'seeing, thinking about, and responding to the world as the other sees, thinks about, and responds to it', where the other can be another, but also 'our own future, past, or counterfactual self'. They call this 'recreative imagination'. This contrast with the 'creative imagination', displayed when 'someone puts together ideas in a way that defies expectation or convention … [leading] to the creation of something valuable in art, science, or practical life' (Currie and Ravenscroft, 2002: 9). Currie and Ravenscroft (2002: 9) go on to say that while creative imagination does not necessarily require the use of re-creative imagination, 'if we can place ourselves, in imagination, in situations other than our own, current situation, our capacity to engage with what is merely possible – and hence to make the possible actual – is greatly enhanced'. Using these concepts, we might say that throughout the 1940s and 1950s, heteronormative constraints affected Jackson's recreative imagination, engendering a resistance to seeing and responding to the world from the perspective of his future (1960s) self. This, in turn, affected his creative imagination in the context of his project of self-authorship: it made it difficult, in his practical life, for him to engage with the possible in a way that challenged heteronormative expectations and conventions. When finally, shortly before the end of his life, Jackson overcame his imaginative resistance to same-sex happy endings, and embarked on a relationship with Stanley Zednick, he seems to have been 'happy most of the time' (Bailey, 2013: 405).

References

Bailey, B (2013) *Farther & Wilder: The Lost Weekends and Literary Dreams of Charles Jackson* (New York: Alfred A Knopf).

Bronski, M (2016) 'Introduction' in Jackson, C, *The Fall of Valor* (Richmond, VA: Valancourt Books) v–ix.

Brooke, R (1910) *Sonnet: I said I Splendidly Loved You; It's Not True*, available at www.rupertbrooke.com/poems/1908-911/sonnet_i_said_i_splendidly_loved_you_its_not_true/

Carey, PW (2010) *Avery Cardinal Dulles, SJ: A Model Theologian, 1918–2008* (Mahwah, NJ: Paulist Press).

Caserio, RL (1997) 'Queer Passions, Queer Citizenship: Some Novels about the State of the American Nation 1946–1954', *Modern Fiction Studies*, vol 43(1) 170–203.

Connelly, M (2001) *Deadly Closets: The Fiction of Charles Jackson* (Lanham, MD: University Press of America).

Crowley, JW (2006) 'Charles Jackson's Fall of Valor Revaluated', *The Sewanee Review*, vol 114(2), 259–277.

Currie, G and Ravenscroft, I (2002) *Recreative Minds* (Oxford: Oxford University Press).

Jackson, C (2016) *The Fall of Valor* (Richmond, VA: Valancourt Books).

Melville, H (1922) *Moby Dick: Or the White Whale* (Boston: St Botolph Society).

McDonald, J (n.d.) 'Gardiner Against Catholic Philistines', *Dappled Things: A Quarterly of Ideas, Art, & Faith*, https://dappledthings.org/7390/gardiner-against-the-catholic-philistines/ (accessed 14 May 2019).

[PCJ1] Letter from Charles Jackson to Philip Wylie, 24 May 1944, *Papers of Charles Jackson*, Dartmouth College Library, MS-1070, box 1, folder 141.

[PCJ2] Letter from Charles Jackson to Bernice Baumgarten, 12 February 1945, *Papers of Charles Jackson*, Dartmouth College Library, MS-1070, box 1, folder 5.

[PCJ3] Letter from Max to Charles Jackson, 19 July 1943, *Papers of Charles Jackson*, Dartmouth College Library, MS-1070, box 2, folder 6.

[PCJ4] Letter from Charles Jackson to Buck Lielenthal, 28 February 1945, *Papers of Charles Jackson*, Dartmouth College Library, MS-1070, box 1, folder 66.

[PCJ5] Letter from Charles Jackson to Phil Rahv, 29 June 1945, *Papers of Charles Jackson*, Dartmouth College Library, MS-1070, box 1, folder 97.

[PCJ6] Charles Jackson's address book, Papers of Charles Jackson, Dartmouth College Library, MS-1070, box 3, folder 45.

[PCJ7] letter from Charles Jackson to Cue-ball 7 August 1946, *Papers of Charles Jackson*, Dartmouth College Library, MS-1070, box 2, folder 4.

[PCJ8] Letter from Charles Jackson to his mother Sal, 26 June 1951, *Papers of Charles Jackson*, Dartmouth College Library, MS-1070, box 2, folder 6.

[PCJ9] Letter from Charles Jackson to Rhoda Jackson, 18 August 1948, *Papers of Charles Jackson*, Dartmouth College Library, MS-1070, box 4, folder 24.

[PCJ10] Brown DE, 'Rutgers unveils Noted "Lost" Writer', article published in unidentified newspaper in New Brunswick, NJ, 4 October 1964, *Papers of Charles Jackson*, Dartmouth College Library, MS-1070, box 3, folder 50.

[PCJ11] Letter from Charles Jackson to his daughter Sarah, 2 August 1964, *Papers of Charles Jackson*, Dartmouth College Library, MS-1070, box 4, folder 26.

[PCJ12] Letter from Charles Jackson to Rhoda Jackson, 6 June 1968, *Papers of Charles Jackson*, Dartmouth College Library, MS-1070, box 4, folder 25.

[PCJ13] Letter from Charles Jackson to Thorberg, 17 September 1943, *Papers of Charles Jackson*, Dartmouth College Library, MS-1070, box 2, folder 6.

[PCJ14] Letter from Charles Jackson to Fred W Dupee, 8 January 1945, *Papers of Charles Jackson*, Dartmouth College Library, MS-1070, box 1, folder 31.

[PCJ15] Letter from Charles Jackson to Tom Powers, 26 April 1945, *Papers of Charles Jackson*, Dartmouth College Library, MS-1070, box 1, folder 87.

[PCJ16] Letter from Charles Jackson to Ted Amussen, 21 November 1944, *Papers of Charles Jackson*, Dartmouth College Library, MS-1070, box 1, folder 3.

[PCJ17] Note from Charles Jackson to Captain Anderson, undated, *Papers of Charles Jackson*, Dartmouth College Library, MS-1070, box 1, folder 1.

[PCJ18] Letter from Charles Jackson to Moss Hart, 10 April 1945, *Papers of Charles Jackson*, Dartmouth College Library, MS-1070, box 1, folder 47.

[PCJ19] Charles Jackson's notebook, *Papers of Charles Jackson*, Dartmouth College Library, MS-1070, box 7, folder 48.

[PCJ20] Letter from Charles Jackson to Stan (Stanley Rinehart), 2 June 1944, *Papers of Charles Jackson*, Dartmouth College Library, MS-1070, box 4, folder 21.

[PCJ21] Letter from Philip Wylie to Charles Jackson, 7 June 1944, *Papers of Charles Jackson*, Dartmouth College Library, MS-1070, box 1, folder 141.

[PCJ22] Letter from Philip Wylie to Charles Jackson, 13 September 1944, *Papers of Charles Jackson*, Dartmouth College Library, MS-1070, box 1, folder 141.

[PCJ23] Letter from Charles Jackson to Philip Wylie to, 12 June 1944, *Papers of Charles Jackson*, Dartmouth College Library, MS-1070, box 1, folder 141.

[PCJ24] Letter from Charles Jackson to Jim and Liz Hart, 21 November 1944, *Papers of Charles Jackson*, Dartmouth College Library, MS-1070, box 1, folder 48.

[PCJ25] Letter from Charles Jackson to Mr Jackson, 5 December 1944, *Papers of Charles Jackson*, Dartmouth College Library, MS-1070, box 1, folder 57.

[PCJ26] Letter from Charles Jackson to Charles Brackett and Billy Wilder, 12 February 1945, *Papers of Charles Jackson*, Dartmouth College Library, MS-1070, box 1, folder 12.

[PCJ27] Letter from Charles Jackson to Philip Wylie, 23 September 1944, *Papers of Charles Jackson*, Dartmouth College Library, MS-1070, box 1, folder 141.

[PCJ28] Letter from Charles Jackson to Ted Amussen et al., 25 June 1945, *Papers of Charles Jackson*, Dartmouth College Library, MS-1070, box 1, folder 3.

[PCJ29] Note from Charles Jackson to Elling Aannestad, stamped 5 December 1944, *Papers of Charles Jackson*, Dartmouth College Library, MS-1070, box 1, folder 2

[PCJ30] Letter from Charles Jackson to his brother Boom and mother Sal, 27 March 1945, *Papers of Charles Jackson*, Dartmouth College Library, MS-1070, box 4, folder 7.

[PCJ31] Letter from Charles Jackson to Phil Rahv, 12 January 1945 (misdated 1944), Papers of Charles Jackson, Dartmouth College Library, MS-1070, box 1, folder 97.

[PCJ32] Letter from Charles Jackson to Phil Cook, 9 March 1945, *Papers of Charles Jackson*, Dartmouth College Library, MS-1070, box 1, folder 26.

[PCJ33] Letter from Charles Jackson to Philip Rahv, 29 January 1945, *Papers of Charles Jackson*, Dartmouth College Library, MS-1070, box 1, folder 97.

[PCJ34] Letter from Charles Jackson to Bernice Baumgarten, 30 January 1945, *Papers of Charles Jackson*, Dartmouth College Library, MS-1070, box 1, folder 5.

[PCJ35] Letter from Charles Jackson to Jesse Lielenthal, 15 February 1945, *Papers of Charles Jackson*, Dartmouth College Library, MS-1070, box 1, folder 66.

[PCJ36] Letter from Charles Jackson to Leland Hayward, 1 July 1945, *Papers of Charles Jackson*, Dartmouth College Library, MS-1070, box ox 1 folder 50.

[PCJ37] Letter from Charles Jackson to Philip Rahv, 14 February 1945, *Papers of Charles Jackson*, Dartmouth College Library, MS-1070, box 1, folder 97.

[PCJ38] Letter from Charles Jackson to Phyllis Haydon, 28 June 1945, *Papers of Charles Jackson*, Dartmouth College Library, MS-1070, box 1, folder 49.

[PCJ39] Letter from Charles Jackson to Philip Rahv, 12 July 1945, *Papers of Charles Jackson*, Dartmouth College Library, MS-1070, box 1, folder 97.

[PCJ40] Letter from Charles Jackson to Bernice Baumgarten, 1 July 1945, *Papers of Charles Jackson*, Dartmouth College Library, MS-1070, box 1, folder 5.

[PCJ41] Letter from Jean to Charles Jackson, 25 July 1945, *Papers of Charles Jackson*, Dartmouth College Library, MS-1070, box 1, folder 38.

[PCJ42] Letter from Charles Jackson to Ludwig, 3 October 1945, *Papers of Charles Jackson*, Dartmouth College Library, MS-1070, box 1, folder 21.

[PCJ43] Letter from Charles Jackson to Bernice Baumgarten, 30 June 1945, *Papers of Charles Jackson*, Dartmouth College Library, MS-1070, box 1, folder 5.

[PCJ44] Letter from Charles Jackson to Ted Amussen, 11 July 1945, *Papers of Charles Jackson*, Dartmouth College Library, MS-1070, box 1, folder 3.

[PCJ45] Letter from Charles Jackson to Carl, 16 July 1946, *Papers of Charles Jackson*, Dartmouth College Library, MS-1070, box 1, folder 19.

[PCJ46] Letter from Charles Jackson to Bernice Baumgarten, 20 October 1945, *Papers of Charles Jackson*, Dartmouth College Library, MS-1070, box 1, folder 5.

[PCJ47] Letter from Charles Jackson to Philip Wylie, 28 June 1945, *Papers of Charles Jackson*, Dartmouth College Library, MS-1070, box 1, folder 141.

[PCJ48] Letter from Charles Jackson to Bernice Baumgarten, 25 June 1945, *Papers of Charles Jackson*, Dartmouth College Library, MS-1070, box 1, folder 5.

[PCJ49] Letter from Ted Amussen to Charles Jackson, 8 July 1945, *Papers of Charles Jackson*, Dartmouth College Library, MS-1070, box 1 folder 3

[PCJ50] Letter from Philip Wylie to Charles Jackson, 16 July 1945, *Papers of Charles Jackson*, Dartmouth College Library, MS-1070, box 1, folder 141.

[PCJ51] Letter from Charles Jackson to his daughter Kate, 1 August 1964, *Papers of Charles Jackson*, Dartmouth College Library, MS-1070, box 4, folder 26.

[PCJ52] Letter from Charles Jackson to his daughter Kate, 30 June 1964, *Papers of Charles Jackson*, Dartmouth College Library, MS-1070, box 4, folder 26.

[PCJ53] Letter from Charles Jackson to Kay, 9 May 1946, *Papers of Charles Jackson*, Dartmouth College Library, MS-1070, box 2, folder 5.

[PCJ54] Letter from Charles Jackson to Charles Brackett, 16 August 1946, *Papers of Charles Jackson*, Dartmouth College Library, MS-1070, box 1, folder 12.

[PCJ55] Letter from Charles Jackson to Elling Aannestad, 13 February 1945, *Papers of Charles Jackson*, Dartmouth College Library, MS-1070, box 1, folder 2.

[PCJ56] Letter from Charles Jackson to Phil Rahv, 1 March 1945, *Papers of Charles Jackson*, Dartmouth College Library, MS-1070, box 1, folder 97.

[PCJ57] Letter from Charles Jackson to his brother Boom, 11 November 1944, *Papers of Charles Jackson*, Dartmouth College Library, MS-1070, box 4, folder 6.

[PCJ58] Letter from Charles Jackson to Norma Chambers, 4 December 1944, *Papers of Charles Jackson*, Dartmouth College Library, MS-1070, box 1, folder 20.

[PCJ59] Letter from Charles Jackson to Ted Amussen, 7 December 1944, *Papers of Charles Jackson*, Dartmouth College Library, MS-1070, box 1, folder 3.

[PCJ60] Letter from Charles Jackson to Arthur Rober, 12 February 1945, *Papers of Charles Jackson*, Dartmouth College Library, MS-1070, box 1, folder 60.

[PCJ61] Letter from Charles Jackson to his brother Boom, 29 January 1945, *Papers of Charles Jackson*, Dartmouth College Library, MS-1070, box 4, folder 7.

[PCJ62] Letter from Charles Jackson to Jim and Liz Hart, 9 March 1944, *Papers of Charles Jackson*, Dartmouth College Library, MS-1070, box 1, folder 48.

[PCJ63] Letter from Charles Jackson to Charles Brackett, 29 January 1945, *Papers of Charles Jackson*, Dartmouth College Library, MS-1070, box 1, folder 12.

[PCJ64] Letter from Charles Jackson to John Retzer, 14 February 1945, *Papers of Charles Jackson*, Dartmouth College Library, MS-1070, box 1, folder 96.

[PCJ65] Letter from Charles Jackson to Philip Rahv, 12 February 1945, *Papers of Charles Jackson*, Dartmouth College Library, MS-1070, box, folder 97.

[PCJ66] Letter from Charles Jackson to LB Fischer, 21 March 1945, *Papers of Charles Jackson*, Dartmouth College Library, MS-1070, box 1, folder 71.

[PCJ67] Letter from Charles Jackson to Bernice Baumgarten, 23 March 1945, *Papers of Charles Jackson*, Dartmouth College Library, MS-1070, box 1, folder 5.

[PCJ68] Letter from Charles Jackson to Ted Amussen, 27 March 1945, *Papers of Charles Jackson*, Dartmouth College Library, MS-1070, box 1, folder 3.

[PCJ69] Letter from Charles Jackson to Helen (editor), 5 April 1945, *Papers of Charles Jackson*, Dartmouth College Library, MS-1070, box 1, folder 81.

[PCJ70] Letter from Charles Jackson to his brother Boom, 22 May 1945, *Papers of Charles Jackson*, Dartmouth College Library, MS-1070, box 4, folder 7.

[PCJ71] Letter from Charles Jackson to Elling Aannestad, 25 June 1945, *Papers of Charles Jackson*, Dartmouth College Library, MS-1070, box 1, folder 2.

[PCJ72] Letter from Charles Jackson to his brother Boom, 8 October 1945, *Papers of Charles Jackson*, Dartmouth College Library, MS-1070, box 4, folder 7.

[PCJ73] Letter from Charles Jackson to Leland and Paul, 24 October 1945, *Papers of Charles Jackson*, Dartmouth College Library, MS-1070, box 1, folder 50.

[PCJ74] Letter from Charles Jackson to Bernice Baumgarten, 28 June 1945, *Papers of Charles Jackson*, Dartmouth College Library, MS-1070, box 1, folder 5.

[PCJ75] Letter from Charles Jackson to Bernice Baumgarten, 11 July 1945, *Papers of Charles Jackson*, Dartmouth College Library, MS-1070, box 1, folder 5.

[PCJ76] Loose leaf from a letter from Charles Jackson to (apparently) an unidentified art dealer (somewhat rambling, probably written under the influence), undated, *Papers of Charles Jackson*, Dartmouth College Library, MS-1070, box 2, folder 8.

[PCJ77] Letter from Charles Jackson to his mother Sal, 10 March 1946, *Papers of Charles Jackson*, Dartmouth College Library, MS-1070, box 4, folder 8.

[PCJ78] Letter from Charles Jackson to Ted Amussen, 13 May 1946, *Papers of Charles Jackson*, Dartmouth College Library, MS-1070, box 1, folder 3.

[PCJ79] Letter from Charles Jackson to Jesse Lielenthal, 7 August 1946, *Papers of Charles Jackson*, Dartmouth College Library, MS-1070, box 1, folder 66.

[PCJ80] Letter from Rhoda Jackson to her brother-in-law Boom, 10 April 1946, *Papers of Charles Jackson*, Dartmouth College Library, MS-1070, box 4, folder 8.

[PCJ81] Letter from Rhoda Jackson to her brother-in-law Boom, Tuesday [1] July 1947, *Papers of Charles Jackson*, Dartmouth College Library, MS-1070, box 4, folder 8.

[PCJ82] Letter from Rhoda Jackson to her brother-in-law Boom, 3 July 1947, *Papers of Charles Jackson*, Dartmouth College Library, MS-1070, box 4, folder 8.

[PCJ83] Letter from Charles Jackson to Patrick, 21 July 1953, *Papers of Charles Jackson*, Dartmouth College Library, MS-1070, box 2, folder 6.

[PCJ84] Review of TFOV (Denecke, C, *Best Sellers*, 3 October 1946), The Fall of Valor Scrapbook, *Papers of Charles Jackson*, Dartmouth College Library, MS-1070, box 13, folder 1.

[PCJ85] Review of TFOV (Meridien (Conn.) Record, 9 November 1946) The Fall of Valor Scrapbook, *Papers of Charles Jackson*, Dartmouth College Library, MS-1070, box 13, folder 1.

[PCJ86] Review of TFOV (Hunter, AC, Savannah Morning News, undated) The Fall of Valor Scrapbook, *Papers of Charles Jackson*, Dartmouth College Library, MS-1070, box 13, folder 1.

[PCJ87] Review of TFOV (Hartford Times, undated) The Fall of Valor Scrapbook, *Papers of Charles Jackson*, Dartmouth College Library, MS-1070, box 13, folder 1.

[PCJ88] Review of TFOV (Miami Herald, 6 October 1946) The Fall of Valor Scrapbook, *Papers of Charles Jackson*, Dartmouth College Library, MS-1070, box 13, folder 1.

[PCJ89] Review of TFOV (Dallas Times Herald, undated) The Fall of Valor Scrapbook, *Papers of Charles Jackson*, Dartmouth College Library, MS-1070, box 13, folder 1.

[PCJ90] Review of TFOV (Zines, H, *St Louis Post Dispatch*, 7 October 1946) The Fall of Valor Scrapbook, *Papers of Charles Jackson*, Dartmouth College Library, MS-1070, box 13, folder 1.

[PCJ91] Review of TFOV (Chamberlain, J, *The New*, undated) The Fall of Valor Scrapbook, *Papers of Charles Jackson*, Dartmouth College Library, MS-1070, box 13, folder 1.

[PCJ91] Review of TFOV (Worcester Mass. *Sunday* Telegram, 6 October 1946) The Fall of Valor Scrapbook, *Papers of Charles Jackson*, Dartmouth College Library, MS-1070, box 13, folder 1.

[PCJ92] Letter from Charles Jackson to Thomas Mann, 10 August 1945, *Papers of Charles Jackson*, Dartmouth College Library, MS-1070, box 1, folder 71.

[PCJ93] Review of TFOV (Bond, AD, *The Boston Herald*, 30 October 1946) The Fall of Valor Scrapbook, *Papers of Charles Jackson*, Dartmouth College Library, MS-1070, box 13, folder 1.

[PCJ94] Review of TFOV (Gardiner, HC, 19 October 1946) The Fall of Valor Scrapbook, *Papers of Charles Jackson*, Dartmouth College Library, MS-1070, box 13, folder 1.

[PCJ95] Review of TFOV (Quick, D, *East Hampton Star*, 17 October 1946) The Fall of Valor Scrapbook, *Papers of Charles Jackson*, Dartmouth College Library, MS-1070, box 13, folder 1.

[PCJ96] Review of TFOV (RR, undated) The Fall of Valor Scrapbook, *Papers of Charles Jackson*, Dartmouth College Library, MS-1070, box 13, folder 1.

[PCJ97] Review of TFOV (Cleveland Press, 15 October 1946) The Fall of Valor Scrapbook, *Papers of Charles Jackson*, Dartmouth College Library, MS-1070, box 13, folder 1.

[PCJ98] Review of TFOV (Providence Journal, 6 October 1946) The Fall of Valor Scrapbook, *Papers of Charles Jackson*, Dartmouth College Library, MS-1070, box 13, folder 1.

[PCJ99] Letter from Stanley L Kubie to Laura Z Hobson, 17 September 1946, *Papers of Charles Jackson*, Dartmouth College Library, MS-1070, box 13, folder 1.

[PCJ100] Letter from Charles Jackson to Bernice Baumgarten, 16 May 1946, *Papers of Charles Jackson*, Dartmouth College Library, MS-1070, box 1, folder 5.

[PCJ101] Letter from Charles Jackson to Fredric, 21 March 1944, *Papers of Charles Jackson*, Dartmouth College Library, MS-1070, box 1, folder 71.

[PCJ102] Letter from Charles Jackson to Carl (agent), 15 July 1946, *Papers of Charles Jackson*, Dartmouth College Library, MS-1070, box 1, folder 19.

[PCJ103] Letter from Thomas Mann to Charles Jackson, 5 October 1946, *Papers of Charles Jackson*, Dartmouth College Library, MS-1070, box 1, folder 71.

[PCJ104] Review of TFOV (Downing, F, *The Commonweal*, 1 November 1946) The Fall of Valor Scrapbook, Papers of Charles Jackson, Dartmouth College Library, MS-1070, box 13, folder 1.

Raz, J (1986) *The Morality of Freedom* (Oxford: Oxford University Press).

Raz, J (1999) *Engaging Reason: On the Theory of Value and Action* (Oxford: Oxford University Press).

Reed, TV (2014) *Robert Cantwell and the Literary Left: A Northwest Writer Reworks American Fiction* (Seattle: University of Washington Press).

Schwartz, M (2017) 'Love's Longing Lost', *The Gay & Lesbian Review Worldwide*, vol 24 (3), 39.

Sedgwick, EK (1985) *Between Men: English Literature and Male Homosocial Desire* (New York: Columbia University Press)

Wylie, P (1951) *The Disappearance* (New York: Reinhart).

Zanghellini, A (2015) *The Sexual Constitution of Political Authority: The Trials of Same-Sex Desire* (Abingdon, UK: Routledge).

4 Gillian Freeman's *The Leather Boys* (1961)

Introduction

Gillian Freeman first published her story of male same-sex desire, *The Leather Boys* (TLB), under the name of Eliot George. By conjuring up, through an inversion of her *nom de plume*, Mary Ann Evans' ghost, Freeman's choice of pseudonym seemed calculated less to allow her to pass as a male author, than to leave her identity and gender playfully shifting and undefined[1] – save for her publisher Anthony Blond then spoiling the effect by disclosing on the jacket that 'Eliot George … conceals the identity of a well-known woman novelist' ([PGF1]). Freeman's husband, Edward Thorpe, whom I interviewed in his London home in 2019, about six months after his wife's death from 'complications of dementia' (Genslinger, 2019), is keen to clarify that Freeman's use of a pseudonym for the novel's first edition was not due to concerns about its subject matter. She was simply precluded from using her real name while under contract with her previous publisher.

A film, directed by Sidney Furie, was adapted from Gillian's 1961 novel and completed as early as March 1963, though its showing in theatres was subject to a 'notoriously long delay' of almost one year (TK, 1964). In respect of both the novel and the film, it has been claimed that they contributed to the change in social attitudes that led to homosexual law reform in England and Wales (Jordan, 2019), through the belated implementation of the *Wolfenden Report* (1957) via the Sexual Offences Act 1967. Yet, when I ask Thorpe if Freeman had a political motivation in writing TLB, if she saw herself as working towards the kind of shift in attitudes that would be ripe for homosexual law reform, he tells me that that was not 'in the forefront of her mind'. She did not think 'she was doing something specific towards that end', though she was certainly hoping people might become more 'empathetic' towards homosexuals as a result of reading her work. Her main concern, Thorpe says, was to write a book, hoping that it would be good and successful as a novel.

---

1   In this, Freeman's literary alias is in fact more akin to the Brontës' 'ambiguous choice' of pen names (Brontë, 1997: 135) than Evans' more straightforwardly masculine one.

DOI: 10.4324/9781003188797-5

Freeman got her wish: the book quickly became a best-seller, with re-printings into the seventies and eighties.

In this chapter I will discuss not only the differences between the novel and the film, but also between both of these and the original screenplay for the film, preserved among the papers of Gillian Freeman in the special collections of the University of Reading, of which Freeman was an alumna. I will argue that these three texts show different degrees of openness to same-sex happy endings: as the spirit of the story transmigrated from novel to screenplay to film, the degree of openness decreased, and the work became less politically savvy. I will also use my interview of Freeman's husband to throw light on some of the authorial choices transpiring from the novel.

What's in a title, and in a book cover

At face value, 'The Leather Boys', as a title, may be taken simply to point to the background against which the tale develops – a community of leather-clad bikers. The cover blurb of the 1961 Anthony Blond edition made much of this setting, pandering to societal anxieties about the changes brought about by post-war reconstruction and the economic boom, which threatened to unsettle class and age-based social hierarchies (Robinson, 2007: 14). The blurb describes its protagonists – Reggie and Dick – and their mates as 'working class boys with a big wage packet and nothing to do', who 'for their expensive machines … need expensive leather jackets and are generally aimless, lawless, cowardly and vain' ([PGF1]).

This preoccupation with the erosion of class distinctions is overshadowed, in the blurb of the New English Library 1975 edition, by a concern with young women's sexual morality. However, the new blurb also confirms the longevity of the trope of the leather-clad biker as an outlaw par excellence: 'They're Britain's "Wild Ones", the motorcycle cowboys who live for fast machines and faster girls … terrorising drivers and defying the law … who experience sex too young, marry unthinkingly and live only for the next kick' (Freeman, 1975). The blurb goes on to say that TLB is a novel 'of these aimless young men and women', (Freeman, 1975) and, true to this, the cover photo displays a heterosexual (male/female) pair of bikers.

In this picture, a slight, narrow-shouldered, not particularly tough-looking young man is dwarfed by a blonde woman in the foreground, wearing a leather overall. Her legs are planted wide apart in the unmistakable attitude of someone who means business. Her expression is equally threatening: despite the partially opened zip, provocatively revealing a glimpse of breast, this is no playboy bunny winking at the camera. She is, rather, a woman in charge of her sexuality – and, probably, her male partner's. Not only is the focus of the cover of the New English Library 1975 edition on a dominant female biker who, incongruously, does not feature in the narrative; but the cover blurb, oddly, presents the central same-sex romance as merely incidental. TLB, we are told, 'is *also* the story of Dick and Reggie' (Freeman, 1975, emphasis added).

In contrast, the 1961 Anthony Blond edition's blurb had made it very clear that the problem of lawless bikers was '*in the background* of THE LEATHER BOYS which is the story of two of them', Dick and Reggie, whose 'friendship develops into love' ([PGF1], emphasis added). The original book cover design bore this out, showing beautiful woodcut-like artwork by Oliver Carson, depicting two James Dean lookalikes, as broad-shouldered and narrow-hipped as any Tom of Finland's creation.

The blurb of the 1975 New English Library edition, in an ill-conceived attempt to turn TLB into the pulp that it so clearly is not, characterises the boys' desire for each other – evidently against any authorial intention – as 'curious and twisted' (Freeman, 1975). Conversely, the 1961 book blurb expressly states, with much greater truth, that the novel 'does not treat homosexuality as a personal or social problem' and that Dick and Reggie's love 'could exist between two human beings at any time at any place' ([PGF1]).

One can only speculate about the reason why New English Library found it necessary to mislead TLB's readers about the book's content in the 1970s.[2] The ludicrously incongruous choice of cover photograph, with its dominant female, suggests perhaps a desire to clock up sales by exploiting the heterosexual British public's fascination with BDSM. Freeman (1969: 79) herself, in her intelligent study of pornography, *The Undergrowth of Literature*, noted that already in the late sixties 'almost all of the pornography available in England must be centred around sadism'. She went on to say that '[i]t isn't merely the violence that keeps the sales steady, but those attendant accessories; the boots, the gloves, leather … and of course, the dominating, calculating, omnipresent women with the whips' (Freeman, 1975: 103). The blonde on the cover of the 1975 edition of TLB may lack gloves and whips, but she certainly has the leather suit, boots, and, all-importantly, the attitude.

Jordan (2019) notes that the novel's title, with its reference to leather, acquired a special erotic resonance for gay men in more recent years (Jordan, 2019). However, there is actually good evidence that Freeman's choice of title and setting was not serendipitous, but deliberate. Freeman was aware of both the erotic appeal of leather for many gay men at the time she was writing, and of that appeal being grounded in bikers' culture. Specifically, in her chapter on homosexual pornography in *The Undergrowth of Literature*, Freeman explains, quoting from the annual magazine *Male Classics*: 'Of the motor-cycle we learn that "it replaced the horse in physique fiction as an alternative prop – it was also more hygienic in a small studio." With the introduction of the motorcycle came "the leather jacket, the jeans, the boots." Later "the motorcycle faded away somewhat, but the leather remained"' (Freeman, 1969: 65). Freeman (1969: 66) goes on to note that 'the leather cult is indissolubly ravelled with sado-masochism', and that by the mid-sixties sadomasochism itself had become

2   It is possible the publisher started doing so before 1975: between new editions and reprints, New English Library issued no fewer than five printings between 1969 and 1975.

central to gay erotic fantasies, in a way in which it did not appear to be in the early fifties (69). This chapter of *The Undergrowth of Literature* was originally published as an essay in the *London Magazine* in 1965, a mere four years after TLB first appeared in print. Thus, about the time when she wrote her novel, Freeman was aware of gay leather/biker fetishes, strongly suggesting that the title and setting were a nod to her gay male readership.[3]

Edward Thorpe, Freeman's beautifully-spoken husband, confirmed this to me. During our interview, Thorpe told me that the idea of setting the novel amongst motorcycle buffs was actually his own suggestion. This suggestion followed a visit to Hollywood, where Freeman and he had learnt about gay leather culture through a friend of a friend. He had taken them to watch so-called 'lavender movies'; one of them, Thorpe reminisces, featured exclusively 'leather-men'. One reason why Thorpe's suggestion of setting the novel in a bikers' community seemed a good idea, apart from resonating with gay leather fetishes, was also that it provided a device to let the characters move, as it were, beyond a traditional working-class background, giving Reggie and Dick something of 'the freedom of having a horse in cow-boy times'.

The novel

In the novel, Dick and Reggie, the two main characters, are in their late teens. Reggie is a labourer. Despite his youth, he is already married to Dot – early marriage and earlier sex being quite the done thing amongst their peers. Dot is rather immature and slovenly; she and Reggie do not have much in common, and he prefers hanging out on his motorbike or with his mates at a bikers' café,[4] without his young wife. Unlike Reggie, Dick is still a virgin and unemployed. He moves in with his grandmother after his grandfather's death, which brings him into the same part of town as Reggie's, and into his circle of friends. They become mates, and partake in acts of petty criminality masterminded by Les, gang leader, who frequents the same bikers' café where Reggie hangs out. Meanwhile, Reggie apparently having lost interest in sex with Dot, she starts sleeping around. The two young spouses have a row and, after spending a day at the seaside with Dick, Reggie, instead of going back home to Dot, is a guest of Dick's, in the room he occupies in his grandmother's house. They share Dick's bed and, '[q]uite without deliberation, without intention, without thought' (Freeman, 1975: 63) they make out. Dick and Reggie realise they are in love with each other. Their living and sleeping arrangement continues through Dick's grandmother's hospitalisation, as well through further criminal activities under Les's leadership. Dick, however, realises the precariousness of the arrangement and proposes that he and Reggie should sail with the

3   This is despite the fact that the story itself does not deliberately eroticise either leather or BDSM: they happened to be not Freeman's (1969: 36) cup of tea.
4   On the significance of cafés and milk bars to youth culture in Britain from the 1920s and into the 1960s see Bradley (2015).

Merchant Navy. It is a prospect to give their relationship a future, away from Dot and from the gang. Reggie announces to Dot that he will join the Merchant Navy, but before he does so he intends to give her the money she will need for an abortion – Dot having falsely claimed to be pregnant in a bid to get Reggie to return to her. To procure the money needed for their plans, the boys plan a burglary at a cinema; it is to be their last, and, this time, without the gang. But Les learns of Dick and Reggie's plan. Before the burglary, Dick goes to Southampton Port to organise their sailing. There he meets some very camp sailors and is none too impressed with their looks and lewdness, but he trusts his relationship with Reggie will be different. The burglary yields no goods, shattering the boys' dream of breaking free from their hopeless present. Outside the cinema, Les and his gang are awaiting Reggie and Dick, and brutally attack them. Reggie dies; Dick is hospitalised. Dick is called as a witness against Les and his gang in their trial for murder. After his examination, he leaves the court and mounts Reggie's bike, unable to shake off the 'tightness in his chest', 'an ache compounded by loneliness and guilt', and the fact that there is 'no one, no one, no one he could tell' that Reggie and he 'loved each other' (Freeman, 1975: 125). He still feels he needs to get away from it all and plans to board the ship alone; but as another motorcycle draws near him, he accepts 'the unspoken challenge' and they start racing away.

Before writing TLB, Freeman was already a published novelist. It was her agent Anthony Blond, who by then had set up his own publishing business, issuing a number of novels dealing with homosexuality, who commissioned Freeman to write TLB. What Blond wanted was an intense love story between working-class men – something for which, at the time, there was virtually no precedent in fiction. As Thorpe told me:

> Most of the books which touched on gay subjects up until that time dealt with what was then, as I described, the gay scene as being amongst intellectuals, intellectuals who'd look for simple lovers, transient lovers and so forth … cultured people, artists, writers, actors, dancers, whatever – which was the sort of … upper section of the gay scene.

This state of affairs in respect of fictional treatments of male same-sex desire reflected a cultural association in the British collective imaginary between homosexuality and the upper classes. This association was a legacy of high profile same-sex scandals dating from the late Victorian era, including the Cleveland Street scandal, which cast homosexuality as a vice of a degenerate aristocracy preying on innocent males of lower station (Zanghellini, 2015: 141–150), as well as Oscar Wilde's trial, one of whose effects was to establish an identity between the homosexual and the dandified 'leisure class man' (Sinfield, 1994: 122). Freeman's agent was keen on a story that would effect a departure from what Salmon (2018: 118) calls 'the stereotypical class dynamics of homosexual representation'. As Thorpe goes on to elaborate:

What Anthony [Blond] wanted was two ordinary working-class boys having this relationship, not perhaps knowing how to deal with it, psychologically, how to express their sexuality, which was… worrying to them, but nevertheless having a sexual relationship, or a loving relationship even.

Freeman's novel, in this respect, participated in ushering in 'a new figure within [the] typologies of queer urban life' to be found in 'sociological and literary texts' from the fifties and sixties (Houlbrook, 2005: 193). As Houlbrook (2005: 193) explains, men 'who wore work clothes, who were "rough" … had participated in London's sexual landscape for decades'; but only now, 'rather than being understood as "normal" or trade, such men were increasingly thought of – and considered themselves – as "homosexual"'. Houlbrook (2005: 193) takes the (secondary) character of Terry, in Rodney Garland's (1953) *The Heart in Exile,* as the prototype for this new figure, of which he considers Dick and Reggie in TLB 'the mirror image'. Yet TLB went beyond *The Heart in Exile* in centring a relationship between two such men, rather than following the more familiar script of a relationship between a wealthier, more cultured man and a working-class one.

Reportedly, Blond asked Freeman to write the same-sex working-class equivalent of Romeo and Juliet (Gunn, 2014: 120; Kremer, 2015: 55; Smith, 2019). The reference to Shakespeare's tragedy might make it sound as if Blond specifically required a tragic story of same-sex love. But Thorpe is very clear, during his interview with me, that this was not the case: the story's conclusion was entirely Freeman's choice – not Blond's, and not Thorpe's own, with whom Freeman 'very rarely conferred' on matters of her creative writing. Thorpe's explanation of why his wife chose to end the novel in tragedy aligns with my hypothesis about mid-century authors' imaginative resistance to same-sex happy endings. As we will see below, he even independently brings up the central role that the criminalisation of homosexuality must have played in engendering such resistance.

Ninety-three at the time of our interview, Thorpe would have been in his mid-thirties in the early sixties, when Freeman wrote and published the book. Though not homosexual himself, Thorpe's perspective of what it was like to speak and write about same-sex desire at the time was moulded by his experience of living as an adult through the post-war years. His insight was made keener by his unusually close familiarity – for a heterosexual man – with homosexuality. Both as a 'boy actor at the age of fifteen', and as an army recruit for three and a half years before meeting Freeman, Thorpe had come into contact with queer men early on in his life. In fact, his boyish good looks (he tells me he was probably the 'most feminine-looking' man in the army) made him prized as an object of same-sex desire in both the world of theatre and the army, and forced him to 'endlessly' fend off the attentions of both actors and soldiers. Many of the latter were working-class men and dockers from the East End of London; their advances, Thorpe recalls, were rather less gentle than those of the former

Further opportunities to mingle with queer people came from Thorpe's renting an attic room in the London home of Louis Golding (then a famous novelist), while Thorpe was studying at the Royal Academic of Dramatic Art, after his stint in the army. Every weekend, Golding invited to his house half a dozen sailors, for whom Golding had 'a penchant'. Golding's friends would also 'be coming in, and they would be having parties, and drinking, and pairing off and going up to sleep together'. Many sailors at the time, Thorpe explains, were not averse to light same-sex sexual activity if given a roof to sleep under and a lift to their ship the following day. Thorpe and Freeman (whom Golding had appointed as his literary secretary, resulting in her meeting Thorpe) witnessed all this, and quickly learnt to regard it as a normal, benign facet of human experience.

As someone who was closely familiar with the queer scene and yet not of it, Thorpe's observations seem to me especially valuable in illuminating his wife's choices in writing of same-sex desire. Like him, Freeman was both sympathetic to same-sex attracted people, and yet not a sexual outsider herself. When discussing TLB's tragic ending, Thorpe tells me:

> They shouldn't live happily ever after ... because it was still illegal, because it was a taboo subject ... in order to deal with the subject at all, you would have to make it unhappy at the end ... or there was something that conspired to make it unhappy.

Thorpe does speculate that publishers might also not have accepted something that could be read as 'promoting homosexuality as an enjoyable lifestyle', so that you 'couldn't make it look as if by being gay you're automatically set for a happy life'. This may have been true during the fifties, though we have seen in chapter two that by the time Freeman published her book, obscenity legislation had changed, and publishers could afford being more daring. In any case, Thorpe's point about publishers being possibly unwilling to publish same-sex happy endings is added almost as an afterthought to his earlier, more fundamental point that 'there was something that conspired to make it unhappy', and his insistence that Blond did not specifically require TLB to end in tragedy.

Thorpe also draws out the self-same connection I drew in chapter one between writers' imaginative resistance to same-sex happy endings and same-sex attracted practical agents' imaginative resistance to happy outcomes in their own lives. He does so, furthermore, by making law central to his account:

> I think that intrinsically one felt that, because of the law – not because of any physical feeling between people, between human beings ... but because of the law, it was enforcing an unhappy situation: the law *made* it unhappy, the law drove people to depression ... or [to feel] that they would find some extreme where they would go against the law, which would end unhappily.... I mean the law was *there,* the law was the evil thing that drove people to unhappy endings, in one way or another – emotionally or

physically or criminally, or whatever. They were forced to break the law if they wanted to live as their sex determined.... You're really being forced to be an outlaw – literally.

Nonetheless, Thorpe immediately, if indirectly, qualifies this assessment about the centrality of legal prohibition to queer lives. He does so by showing his awareness of the role that societal homophobia and heteronormativity play in constraining same-sex attracted people's ability to script their own happy life-stories even when legal prohibitions have been repealed. He recounts to me an episode where, in recent years, after a dinner party at a friend's, where the gay subject-matter of Freeman's books had come up, another guest, a young workman, approached him to tell him he thought he had feelings for other men, but could do nothing about it. The lad was in a double-bind: he felt that he could neither leave his mates (to seek, as Thorpe had suggested to him, sexual and romantic fulfilment in London), nor come out to them.

The screenplay

The text of the screen adaptation of TLB, which Freeman herself authored, is preserved in her literary archive at the University of Reading ([PGF2]). This adaptation differs significantly from the book, and in minor but important ways from the film itself.

The two main characters in the screenplay are named Reggie and Pete. As in the book, Reggie is employed and married to Dot, and owns a motor-cycle, but here it is he and not Pete who has a grandmother and a dying grandfather. In the screenplay, the differences between Reggie and Dot start becoming apparent during their honeymoon, when Dot prefers social activities and Reggie one-to-one intimacy. Their marital woes grow more serious during the subsequent six months, what with Dot's slovenliness and appalling house-keeping, Reggie's neglect (including sexual neglect) of her, her refusal to accede to his request that they move in with his grandmother after her hus-band's death, and Reggie's spending too much time at the bikers' café. At the café Reggie meets Pete, who also owns a motor-cycle, and has a past in the Merchant Navy. Pete is being evicted by his landlady, and Reggie arranges for him to move in with his own grandmother. Soon, Reggie's difficulties with Dot having reached breaking point, he moves into his grandmother's house himself, sharing a double-bed with Pete, with whom he grows more and more intimate (but without any fondling or sex) after a day at the seaside. Dot, having visited the boys' room during their absence, confronts Reggie at the café and publicly accuses them of being queer. Back in their bedroom at Reggie's grandmother's, Pete suggests they should sail off somewhere to get Reggie away from Dot. There are some tense moments where Reggie makes clear that if it were true that Pete is queer, their friendship would be over; but it all ends in a pillow-fight. The boys take part in a motor-cycle race to Scot-land organised by the gang's leader, Les, a much more benevolent figure in the screenplay than in the novel; so does Dot, riding on the backseat of the motor-cycle of a new boyfriend. On the way back from Scotland, in a café, there is reconciliation between Reggie and Dot, much to Pete's dismay; and it is on her husband's motor-cycle, not her boyfriend's, that Dot makes the rest of the return trip to London. Reggie wins the race and is carried away by Les and the other bikers to celebrate. Dot, tired of waiting for him, returns home with her boyfriend after all. Reggie, having realised this, spends the night at his grandmother's, in the room he shares with Pete. In the morning, however, he is determined to move back with Dot, explaining to Pete that his marriage to her gives some meaning to his otherwise aimless life. Pete tries to persuade him to stay, culminating in his claim: 'You're better off with me than 'er. You been happier with me'. Reggie replies, 'Do I have to put it in plain English, mate? I need a bird. And don't ask me for what'. Pete retorts, 'We could 'ave that together too', ([PGF2]: 99) but Reggie leaves. A scene between Dot and Reggie ensues in their flat, where her boyfriend has spent the night. The boyfriend taunts Reggie for his presumed queerness, but Reggie takes little notice and asks Dot if she wants to get back together. Upon her failure to say yes or otherwise unequivocally indicate that she does, Reggie returns to Pete, telling him, 'I decided to go to sea with you mate, if that's what you still want' ([PGF2]: 104). The boys head for Southampton and manage to secure their place (as workers) on a ship heading for Buenos Aires. Before embarking, they go to a dockside pub, where they run into sailors formerly known to Pete. The sailors start engaging in camp and lewd, if vague, banter about what awaits Reggie on his voyage. As they leave the pub, the sailors' 'mincing gait is more apparent' ([PGF2]: 109). In response to their continued banter to the effect that he'd better watch Reggie on the ship, Pete says, 'Don't worry. 'E's my mate…. 'E left his wife for me' ([PGF2]: 109). At this point Reggie states, disgusted, that he will not sail after all, that he does not want to become like Pete's friends, and that he, Pete, should go back to them. Pete replies, 'We couldn't never be like them', and adds, 'I don't want them, Reggie, I want you. I love you. I'll come back with you'. But Reggie is unmoved: 'I don't want you' ([PGF2]: 110). He leaves Pete behind, who is left with no choice but to make for the ship with the other sailors. Back in Dot's flat, Reggie is exhausted. They have a genuine reconciliation; she makes him a cup of tea.

A handwritten note on the cover of the typescript preserved in Reading University's special collections indicates that this is the 'first draft', not the 'final screenplay' ([PGF2]). Yet, it is clearly not the very first draft, for whole segments running for several pages have been crossed out and rewritten. It is also unclear what Freeman's brief was – that is, how much artistic freedom was afforded her by the director or producers in adapting the story for the screen. It seems that certain conditions were imposed that were non-negotiable. Specifically, when I point out to Edward Thorpe that, unlike the book, the boys do not make out in the screenplay, he tells me, 'they wouldn't have any consummation in the film, no'. He added that Freeman had 'no compunction' about the characters having a 'sexual affair' on screen, and even seems to remember that she 'was rather upset that they did not go through with it' in the film.

In general the screenplay is rather a tame affair compared with the book. Not only do Reggie and Pete not have sex, but both are employed, there is no criminal activity, no burglary, no assault, and no death. Quaintly, the worst that Pete and Reggie do in the screenplay is encroach on a children's playground, scaring off its legitimate users, and being duly rebuked for it. The novel's and screenplay's endings are also quite different. Towards the end of the novel, heterosexual domesticity is poised to reassert its primacy by default (through the failure of the burglary, and of the promise it held to set Reggie free from Dot); but a violent outcome (Reggie's killing) sweeps away both it (the prospect of reconstituting the heterosexual family) and any hope of a queer alternative – namely, Reggie and Dick's romantic escape by sea. At the end of the story as reconceived for the screenplay, on the other hand, heterosexual domesticity reasserts its full power over both Reggie and Dot. Reggie chooses Dot over Pete: for with Pete comes the risk of becoming a mincing queer (Pete: 'We couldn't never be like them'; Reggie: 'I ain't running the risk' ([PGF2]: 110)). As for Dot, in the screenplay's final scene, 'for the first time [she] seems to have a vulnerable sweetness' and, at her husband's behest ('I could do wiv a cup of tea'), she dutifully puts the kettle on ([PGF2]: 112). Finally, Pete is left with the only choice really open to men like him: to be reabsorbed into camp, promiscuous, queer camaraderie.

Queer life beyond queer camp

Not unlike Jackson's (at least initial) failure to conceive a third alternative to an 'abnormal' story of consummated homosexuality and a 'normal' story of sublimated homosexuality,[5] TLB's screenplay foreshadows but immediately forecloses the option (a committed same-sex affair) that challenges the binary choice between heterosexual domesticity and submission to the rules of queer society. In the novel, too, the kind of same-sex affair embodied by Dick and Reggie is one that – had Reggie' death not put a premature end to it – was positioned precisely in the same no man's land of neither fish (heterosexual domesticity) nor flesh (queer promiscuity). Interestingly, the possibility of this same-sex bond between the boys seems to articulate with their attempt at performing gay identity in novel ways on the aesthetic plane, too. Specifically, Salmon (2018: 121) argues that the boys' 'hesitancy and inarticulation' points to 'a desire to move away from the overt performativity of camp', a desire to subvert 'the representational language of what was emerging as more of a queered, subcultural appropriation of the masculine biker figure'.

While in the novel Reggie's death means he does not have a chance to confront queer camp on the docks, Dick (Pete in the screenplay) does come up against it when, as we have seen, he goes down alone to Southampton port to arrange their passage by sea, prior to the burglary. Here, coming across a group of queer sailors and their camp banter, Dick reflects:

5   See Chapter 1.

He had never thought of his relationship with Reggie as being homosexual, he hadn't labelled it or questioned it. It wasn't like this. They would never be like these men. He thought he didn't really want to be at sea with people like that. Would he be able to keep out of their way, would they leave him and Reggie alone?... But he and Reggie would be able to stick it.... They would have each other. After Friday they wouldn't have to bother about anyone else.

(Freeman, 1975: 100–101)

Salmon (2018: 122) argues that this passage in the novel could be criticised for the caricatured representation of queers and for Dick's homophobic reaction to them. In fact, the description of the sailors that Dick (in the novel), or Pete and Reggie (in the screenplay) meet on the docks seems both realistic and believable. Studies of mid-century queer communities onboard ships (Baker and Stanley, 2014), and accounts provided in works of fiction from the same period, authored by gay men who had experienced life at sea (Lauder, 1962), document a world of over-the-top, in-your-face, camp performativity.

Indeed, even without my raising this point with him at all, Thorpe tells me that the scene of the camp sailors on the docks was based on real-life experience – albeit his own rather than Freeman's. He recounts that when he was young, an Australian friend of his had convinced him that there was a theatrical scene in Australia that it would be worth Thorpe's while to become acquainted with, for his professional development (at the time, Thorpe was an actor). So, Thorpe had worked his way to Australia on board an immigrant ship, where it turned out that the restaurant staff and 'cabin stewards were nearly all gay', most of them being 'very effeminate, tremendously effeminate', with regular drag shows in the evenings at the crew's bar. It is this that provided the inspiration for the scene which, in the novel, reinforces Dick's commitment to Peter ('he and Reggie would be able to stick it', Freeman, 1975: 101), and conversely, in the screenplay, sets the test for Reggie's commitment to Pete – a test Reggie fails.

Salmon (2018: 122) also argues that this dockside scene is problematic because of Dick's apparently homophobic reaction. Yet, this reaction is perfectly congruent with Dick's background. Dick's resistance to the idea of his and Reggie's being 'homosexual' and 'like these men' aligns with subsequent studies that have shown working-class men who have sex with men being less likely to self-describe as 'gay' and to participate in the gay community (Barrett and Pollack, 2005; Connell, Davis and Dowsett, 1993) than gay men with higher income and education. Dick's investment in a dyadic relationship vis-à-vis the more ribald life he imagines the sailors to lead at sea – 'he and Reggie would be able to stick it.... They would have each other' (Freeman, 1975: 101) – similarly accords with studies that have shown working-class men who have sex with men to value sex within long-term relationships (elusive though that ideal may remain) more highly than sex outside them (Connell, Davis and Dowsett, 1993).

Salmon (2018: 122) herself goes on to qualify her critique of the dockside scene in the novel by arguing that Dick's apparently homophobic reaction could be read as a valuing of the kind of 'sincerity' that Dick and Reggie's intimacy instantiates, compared to the artificiality of 'overt performance'. Be that as it may, the key point for my purposes is that what is denied Reggie and Dick/Pete in both the book and the screenplay, is the fruition of a relationship – even a shared life – on their own terms, not those scripted for them by either heterosexual society or queer subculture. But it is to radically different effect that this form of life remains elusive for the boys in the book as compared to the novel.

In the novel, it is an accident of fate (Reggie's death following the failed burglary) that sweeps away the option of a committed same-sex relationship *alongside* the option of Reggie's re-absorption into heterosexuality (which in the novel, he had ruled out anyway at the time he committed to Dick). This outcome symbolically creates a kind of value parity between those two options. Conversely, in the screenplay Reggie makes a very deliberate choice not to take the risk (namely, absorption into queer society) involved in pursing the option of sailing off as Pete's lover; nor is Reggie's heterosexual return to Dot marred by anything more serious than some tiredness resulting from the facing-up with himself he has just experienced. Indeed, in the screenplay Reggie's reabsorption into heterosexual domesticity is ratified by the marital harmony rediscovered around the domestic rite of tea-making. Thus, although both texts fail to bring to fruition the promise of a shared life for the boys, it is only the screenplay that does so in a way that ultimately re-establishes the superiority of the heterosexual option.

The film

The film itself, directed by Sidney Furie, was released in 1964, a mere three years after the book's publication. Furie's film follows the general trajectory of the plot as described in the screenplay preserved at Reading, with some slight differences, but also, as we will see, a key one.

Occasionally, the changes made in the film are improvements on the original screenplay. For example, the scene in the boys' bedroom, after Dot has accused them of being queer, is handled more subtly in the film than in the screenplay. In the screenplay, when Reggie confronts Pete, none too amicably, with the possibility of his homosexuality, Pete responds with 'You're as screwy as what [Dot] is' and 'Cut it out' ([PGF2], 82). In the film, on the other hand, Pete does not deny the charge, but makes as if to leave the room. This gesture allows him to maintain his integrity as a queer man, but can be conveniently mistaken by (the heterosexual and homophobic) Reggie as Pete taking offence at the accusation, leading smoothly to their reconciliation via a pillow fight. Another improvement is the disappearance from the film of the very final scene in the screenplay (after Reggie has abandoned Pete in Southampton), with its heteronormative literalism of Dot making Reggie his cup of tea.

Conversely, the return to London after the bike race to Scotland, which provides the context for the rapprochement between Reggie and Dot, is more heavy-handed in the film than in the original screenplay. In the film, Reggie and Dot end up dancing to a romantic tune from a juke box in a service station's café along the way, and later scramble up to a bench on a hilltop, with a countryside vista. Here they realise Reggie is now bound to lose the race (which in fact, in the film, he does), but he declares that he does not 'give a damn', now that he and Dot have made their peace. It is only good acting that saves this moment from starry-eyed sentimentality.

The most significant difference between screenplay and film – one that changes the overall valence of the two texts, to the film's detriment – comes at the point when, after the race in Scotland, Reggie announces to Pete his intention to go back to Dot. In the film, Reggie eventually drowns out Pete's muttered objections by snapping: 'For crying out loud Pete, I need a woman, don't I?' Pete's half-hearted response comes after a moment's silence, in which he turns to stare at Reggie, who is giving him his back. But Pete does not say, as in the screenplay, 'We could have that, too'. Rather, in the film Pete simply assents, 'Yeah'. Thus in the film, unlike the screenplay, Pete fails to unequivocally come out to Reggie. As a result, in the film, when Reggie – after finding out that Dot has spent the night with her boyfriend – decides to sail off with Pete after all, he does not do so in the knowledge of Pete's sexuality. Contemporary reviews of the film make this amply clear, describing Reggie as 'naively blind, as the audience won't be, to Pete's repressed homosexual proclivities' (TK, 1964) – a blindness that Jordan (2019) argues 'is emblematic of the difficulty of accommodating homosexuality with masculinity'.

It follows, too, that the final scene on the docks of Southampton, where Reggie abandons Pete, has a subtly but crucially different meaning in the film compared to the screenplay. Because Reggie sets out to embark on an adventure with Pete when he still believes him heterosexual, the reason why he gives him up in the film is his belated realisation, upon meeting the queer sailors in the dockside pub, of, as contemporary reviewers put it, 'the homosexual implications of his friendship with Pete' (Harcourt, 1964), or Pete's 'homosexual past' (TK, 1964). On the contrary, recall that in the screenplay Reggie was prepared to start a new life with Pete on the understanding that he and Pete 'could have that [namely, sex] together too' ([PGF2]: 99); and Reggie only pulls back when he becomes convinced that by having 'that together too', they run the risk of turning into the mincing queers he despises.

Reggie's response upon meeting Pete's former queer associates is, on its face, less homophobic in the film than in the screenplay. In the film there is no discussion between Pete and Reggie. There is no attempt on Pete's part to convince Reggie to stay with him, to draw a distinction between the kind of queerness Pete believes he and Reggie can embody, and the kind of queerness they are confronted with on the docks. For his part, Reggie, unlike his counterpart in the screenplay, says nothing as crude as 'You want us to be like them', or 'They make me sick', or 'I don't want you' ([PGF2]: 110); in the film he just quietly walks away, with what contemporary reviews described as 'no more than a disguised grimace' (Harcourt, 1964) and 'revulsion' (TK, 1964) – though it looked more like pain to me, with, as Jordan (2019) puts it, 'little sign of homophobic panic'. Pete, after following Reggie for a while, eventually lets him go.

While this lower-key finale in the film may be aesthetically more pleasing than the more open confrontation between Reggie and Pete in the screenplay (let alone the screenplay's further scene between Dot and Reggie with their cup of tea), Freeman's screenplay was politically more interesting than Furie's film in two ways. First, in the screenplay Reggie was not a straightforward case of heterosexuality. If only for a short time, he considered a sexually involved relationship with Pete, having heard him say 'we could have that together too' ([PGF2]: 99), and nonetheless deciding to sail off with him, 'if that's what [Pete] still want[ed]' ([PGF2]: 104). Secondly, the screenplay presented the audience with the possibility, if not the actual fulfilment, of a variety of differ-ent forms of queerness. By insisting that he wants and loves Reggie, that he'll leave the docks and go back with him, that they could never be like the camp sailors they have just met, Pete asserted his faith in an alternative queer way of being, one that need not take the ready-made (ribald, oversexed, camp) forms pre-packaged by queer communitarian norms.

It would be reductive to dismiss this aspiration on Pete's part, together with his rejection of 'homosexual' as a self-descriptor, as simply a case of internalised homophobia – at least if we are to take seriously an insight of which the screenplay, here, seems to show a certain pre-science: that to attach oneself to one's 'identity by a conscience or self-knowledge' – particularly the kind of self-knowledge that is facilitated by modern pseudo-scientific categories, such as 'homosexuality' – is to play in the hands of disciplinary power (Foucault, 1982: 212). From this perspective, in affirming his relationship with Reggie as something other than 'homosexuality', Pete's thinking, however rudimentary it might be, gestures towards a kind of queer self-fashioning beyond the limits of identity politics – for all that Reggie's lack of cooperation ultimately signals the apparently utopian quality of Pete's vision.

On the other hand, the film makes Reggie a fully heterosexual lad who just happens to be taken in by his own naiveté, and who turns his back on same-sex desire as soon as it becomes apparent to him that this is what he is confronting in Dick. In doing so, Furie's film elides the more complex and sophisticated treat-ment of straightness and queerness that is apparent in Freeman's original screen-play. All that survives of that kind of treatment in the film itself is a line delivered by Pete, still in his biker's outfit, a few sequences before the end, when the boys are back in their bedroom after the race to Scotland. 'If we had stuck together', Pete says shortly before passing out on the bed, 'we could have won'.

'They hadn't got the nerve of facing the government['s Board of Censors]': this is why, Thorpe maintains, in the film Pete does not suggest to Reggie 'We could 'ave that together too' ([PGF2]: 99), and Reggie, accordingly, never questions his heterosexuality at all. The film's rating suggests Thorpe may be right: even with a fully straight protagonist who very clearly rejects homo-sexuality, TLB was rated suitable only for people over 16.

Furie has been praised for not allowing 'even the most discrete allusions to pervasive and often insidious homosexual stereotypes' (Kremer, 2015: 65) and for supporting actor Dudley Sutton's determination to play 'Pete beyond any posturing or caricaturing' (Kremer, 2015: 58). Be that as it may, the way in which, as I argued, the cinematographic text very deliberately flattens some of the screenplay's complexity makes it hard to agree with Kremer (2015: 65) that the film 'probes how intense and elastic … a relationship [such as Reggie and Pete's] can be and mines the gray area between platonic and erotic'.

Despite some reviews betraying homophobic prejudice, the film's critical reception was on the whole positive on both sides of the Atlantic, but parti-cularly in the US (Kremer, 2015: 63; Jordan, 2019). This may be largely due to Sutton's non-threatening rendition of Pete as a harmless (at times even clownish) ordinary bloke, an effect magnified by his rather unprepossessing physical appearance. Moon-faced, thin armed, a little barrel-chested, Sutton was, even in full biking gear, no James Dean: he must have saved many a straight male viewer the inconvenience of sexual self-questioning that might have attended casting in Pete's role an actor with more obvious erotic allure. But if mainstream critics largely approved of the film it may also be due pre-cisely to the way in which, as I have argued, the motion picture ultimately reduces Reggie's choice to a simple binary between heterosexuality and queerness, obscuring the – potentially more unsettling – third way envisaged, at least as a theoretical possibility, in Freeman's original screenplay.

Conclusions

Gillian Freeman died in March 2019, only a few months before I decided to embark on this book project and interviewed her husband. In addition to TLB, Freeman (1970) wrote another novel partially centred on same-desire, *The Alabaster Egg*; and her essay on male same-sex smut (Freeman, 1965) preceded publication of her book-length study of pornography – in which the essay was re-published in modified form – by two years, having originally appeared in the *The London Magazine*. When I told Thorpe that it was interesting that his wife should care about male homosexuality, he told me that what makes it more interesting is that she was a

> nice, middle-class Jewish girl who wanted to write novels … and I don't suppose she had actually come up against [the subject of homosexuality] until we met in the house of Louis Golding.… She came from a very liberal Jewish, well-read family; she was open-minded about things, she had no inhibitions about other people; throughout her life she was a very giving and forgiving, nonjudgmental person; she was interested in what motivated people, or their lifestyle … because she was instinctively a writer … She wasn't in the least sentimental, but she was … understanding.

In centring the mutual feelings of two working-class queer lads, TLB not only covered unfamiliar ground in British queer literature, but also offered some visibility and, despite its tragic ending, even some validation to the reality of queer working-class folks. As we know from Chapter 2, opportunities for same-sex attracted people to express and experience their sexuality had flourished in possibly unprecedented ways during the war years, but traditional sexual morality powerfully bounced back when the war ceased. The postwar years are also a time when class distinctions were in some respects being blurred, with the working classes enjoying new affluence permitting them to participate in consumer culture (Robinson, 2007: 14). The phenomenon is well illustrated in TLB, with its motor-cycle owning working-class youth. Yet, class consciousness persisted in Britain; and left-wing parties throughout much of the fifties continued to marginalise the experiences and aspirations of working-class queers, holding on to the doctrine that male homosexuality was a symptom of bourgeois decadence, far removed from the heterosexual masculinity of working-class men (Robinson, 2007: 16–30). In this context – despite the fact that, after the publication of the *Wolfenden Report* (1957), some changes were afoot – the political significance of TLB is apparent.

Indeed, TLB's representation of working-class queerness remained ground-breaking well beyond the decade the novel was published. Content author Christopher Brocklebank (2010), speaking about his coming of age in the late nineties, asserts that even at the turn of the twenty-first century TLB resonated with him in a way that far outdid any of

> the gay novels I'd come across ... [which] either featured languid toffs in white flannels lying on river banks and making allusions to their 'prodivities' and dreaming of the stable boy back at the parents' estate, or two solicitors from Richmond meeting at the gents in Paddington and one finding the other dead by his own hand after six tentative months of clandestine meetings.

Brocklebank (2010) – who goes on to lament the continuing dearth of representations of working-class queerness in British novels and films – also states that TLB spoke to him at a time when he did not feel his reality represented by the then wildly popular TV series *Queer as Folk,* with its unapologetic portrayal of a partying, oversexed, drug-using gay culture, then 'lauded as a realistic a representation of gay life as we'd ever seen'. Brocklebank's reflections are consistent with my argument that the boys' affair – as either realised and then cut short in the novel, or envisioned by Pete and briefly considered by Reggie in the screenplay – gestures towards a queer ontology and mode of relationality that eschews the disciplinary constraints and trappings of either compulsory heterosexuality or gay subculture.

Jordan (2019) has made a claim to the effect that TLB film compares favourably with the novel's focus on two 'vainglorious petty thieves' whose love is 'mutual' and 'consummated': 'By removing the criminal context and by not privileging one sexual orientation over another, Furie could focus ... impartially' on what he himself described as 'the reality of human relationships'. Kremer (2015: 65) also praises the film's treatment of 'homosexuality', which 'is never thematically overdrawn; it is a single point in a larger story, rather than an unbearably heavy focal point around which the film single-mindedly revolves'.

One could as well say, however, that in sanitising both the surrounding context (by removing the boys' criminal activity) and the boys' relationship (by removing both the mutuality of the boys' desire and their same-sex sexual activity) the film is much less daring than the novel. Indeed, it is less courageous than the original screenplay, too, where, as we have seen, Reggie decides to leave England with Pete on the understanding that they 'could 'ave *that* together too' ([PGF2]: 99, emphasis added); and where the prospect of a same-sex relationship on the boys' own terms figures at least as a possibility, however fleetingly. Certainly, the novel demonstrates that it was perfectly possible for the film to focus the story more boldly on homosexuality without being either heavy-handed (Kremer's (2015) concern) or less 'impartial' in the treatment of interpersonal relationships (Jordan's (2019) concern). It seems apparent that, in terms of their sheer political significance, the novel – ironically, despite its tragic ending – outdoes the screenplay, and the screenplay fares better than the film. All three texts fail to bring off a happy same-sex outcome, but the openness to that outcome is greatest in the novel, and least in the film.

The happy outcome would be one in which the boys strike out together as lovers, without bending either to the demands of compulsory heterosexuality or those of queer communitarian norms. In the novel, the actualisation of that same-sex outcome is subordinated to one condition: procuring the money that Reggie must hand over to Dot in order to feel relieved of his responsibility towards her. Perversely, Reggie's ethic of responsibility drives Dick and him to commit a criminal act, which (like Grandin's betrayal of Ethel in Jackson's novel) is karmically bound to end in tragedy, negating the happy outcome that seemed briefly within their reach. At the same time, while both boys are alive in the novel, they do manage to steer their own course between the Scylla of heterosexuality and Charybdis of subcultural queerness, negotiating what Salmon (2018: 123) describes as 'a position of personal priority at their points of undefinition'.

Chapter 1 argued that as a regulatory regime, heteronormativity generates not only moral prescriptions, but aesthetic ones too. Freeman's work demonstrates indisputable empathy for same-sex attracted folks, and a non-phobic, supportive attitude towards same-sex desire. Thus, the most compelling way of making sense of her novel's falling in with the general pattern of mid-century's queer fiction's tragic endings is to postulate that heteronormative constraints (including, as Thorpe pointed out to me, the state of the law) triggered authorial imaginative resistance to a same-sex happy ending on aesthetic, rather than moral, grounds. This is consistent with how Thorpe accounted for his wife's choice of denouement, explaining to me that with people still being 'sent to prison' for consensual same-sex sexual activity, as a writer 'you can't make it all happy', with your heroes 'going to have a happy life in defiance of the law'.

In the screenplay, the same-sex happy outcome is chosen by Reggie with rather less deliberateness, almost like a second-best option, only after he has convinced himself that the first best option (namely, returning to Dot) is no longer available to him. Even so, it is significant that once his relationship with Dot appears to him incapable of mending, the Reggie of the screenplay does not seek consolation in other heterosexual affairs: he chooses Pete and the prospect of same-sex love – the prospect of he and Pete having 'that together too' ([PGF2]: 99). In light of this subsequent choice, Reggie's decision to go back to Dot after the motor-cycle race (before her lack of conviction makes him turn to Pete) is perhaps less the choice of heterosexuality in and of itself that it initially appears to be, than the option he perceives most conducive to his well-being. Recall that at one point in the screenplay Reggie says to Pete that in his otherwise aimless life, his marriage to Dot seemed to him to offer a chance for finding value and meaning. In the event, Reggie's commitment to Pete falters when, after coming up against the queer sailors in the dockside pub, he becomes convinced that by having 'that together too' ([PGF2]: 99), he and Pete would get more than they bargained for, despite Pete's protestations to the contrary. Reggie, that is, renounces the same-sex happy outcome and chooses the heterosexual solution only because he has lost faith in the possibility of the former.

The screenplay's ending seems overdetermined. On the one hand, as in the novel, heteronormative constraints may have triggered authorial imaginative resistance, on aesthetic grounds, to a same-sex happy ending. On the other hand, the specific choice to end the screenplay by making Reggie return to Dot – reinstating as it does the dominance of the heterosexual norm in a way that the novel does not – was probably entirely due to Freeman's beliefs about what the director, producer, Board of Film Censors, or audience required of a film dealing with same sex desire. As I explained in Chapter 1, this kind of reason for a fictional outcome is not in and of itself a case of authorial imaginative resistance.

In any case, the screenplay's ending can also be read as making quite a different point: namely, a point about Reggie's immature and even cowardly decision-making processes – thereby putting squarely on his shoulders the responsibility for making the same-sex happy outcome flounder. For the final scene of Reggie's return to Dot (when only a few hours ago he had given her up as hopeless) reveals, ultimately, Reggie's impulsiveness, which makes him treat his commitments to Pete and Dot unthinkingly, rather like a zero–sum game: one commitment contracts and the other automatically expands, and vice-versa. In this light, the screenplay's failure to bring off a same-sex happy outcome is contingent on Reggie's own imaginative resistance – a resistance grounded in a homophobic dread of being absorbed into queerness: 'I ain't running the risk' ([PGF2]: 110).

Finally, in the film, unlike the screenplay, the happy same-sex outcome (a committed same-sex relationship) has no legs at all: Reggie never even contemplates it for a moment, making Pete's faith in it delusional from the get go. In this respect, the chance meeting with the sailors at the dockside pub, which resolves Reggie to leave Pete behind, is merely a device (and an entirely fungible one) to show the happy same-sex outcome up as the non-starter it was to begin with. To this extent, the floundering of the same-sex happy outcome is predetermined in the cinematographic text in a way in which it is neither in the original screenplay, nor the novel. It might well be that heteronormativity and heterosexism generated this narrative outcome in the film by imposing non-architectural (normative) constraints on Furie's own imagination. But studies of how cautiously the British Board of Film Censors dealt with homosexual texts during the 1960s (Hargreaves, 2012) suggest that even a director who had freed himself from such imaginative constraints would have remained practically bound by the requirements of the Board. The case of *Victim* shows that these requirements could be asserted at both pre- and post-production stages, even if only with a view to awarding the film an X certificate (Hargreaves, 2012) – the same rating attracted by Furie's own film.

References

Baker, P and Stanley, J (2014) *Hello Sailor!* (Abingdon: Routledge).

Barrett, DC and Pollack, LM (2005) 'Whose Gay Community? Social Class, Sexual Self-Expression, and Gay Community Involvement', *The Sociological Quarterly*, vol 46(3), 437–456.

Bradley, K (2015) 'Rational Recreation in the Age of Affluence: The Café and Working-Class Youth in London, c1939–1965' in Rappaport, E, Trudgen Dawson, S and Crowley, MJ (eds) *Consuming Behaviours: Identity, Politicis and Pleasures in Twentieth-Century Britain* (London: Bloomsbury) 71–86.

Brocklebank, C (2010) 'The Leather Boys (1961) – Gillian Freeman', *Polari Magazine*www.polarimagazine.com/classicbooks/leather-boys-1961/.

Brontë, C (1997) 'Biographical Note of Acton and Ellis Bell' in Orel, H (ed.) *The Brontës: Interviews and Recollections* (Iowa City: University of Iowa Press) 133–140.

Connell, RW, Davis MD and Dowsett, GW (1993) 'A Bastard of a Life: Homosexual Desire and Practice among Men in Working-class Milieux', *Australian and New Zealand Journal of Sociology*, vol 29, 112–135.

George, E (1961) *The Leather Boys* (London: Anthony Blond).

Foucault, M (1982) 'The Subject and Power' in Dreyfus, HL and Rabinow, P (eds) *Michel Foucault: Beyond Structuralism and Hermeneutics* (Brighton: Harvester) 212–221.

Freeman, G (1965) 'Under the Counter Magazines II: Amigo USW', *The London Magazine*, vol 5(7), 59–65.

Freeman, G (1969) *The Undergrowth of Literature* (London: Panther Books).

Freeman, G (1970) *The Alabaster Egg* (London: Anthony Blond).

Freeman, G (1975) *The Leather Boys* (London: New English Library).

Genslinger (2019, 8 March) 'Gillian Freeman, Groundbreaking Novelist on a Gay Theme, Does at 89', *The New York Times*.

Garland, R (1953) *The Heart in Exile* (London: WH Allen).

Gunn, DW (2014) *Gay Novels of Britain, Ireland and the Commonwealth 1881–1981: A Reader's Guide* (Jefferson, NC: McFarland).

Harcourt, P (1964) 'The Leather Boys', *Sight and Sound*, vol 33(2).

Hargreaves, T (2012) 'The Trevelyan Years: British Censorship and 1960s Cinema' in Lamberti, E (ed.) *Behind the Scenes at the BBFC: Film Classification from the Silver Screen to the Digital Age* (London: Palgrave Macmillan).

Houlbrook, M (2005) *Queer London: Perils and Pleasures in the Sexual Metropolis 1918–1957* (Chicago: University of Chicago Press).

Jordan, PER (2019) 'Repressing the Male Gaze? Sidney J Furie's The Leather Boys and the Growing Pains of Post-War British Masculinity', *Film Criticism*, vol 43(1).

Kremer, D (2015) *Sydney J Furie: Life and Films* (Lexington, KY: University Press of Kentucky).

Lauder, S (1962) *Winger's Landfall* (London: Eyre & Spottiswoode).

[PGF1] Text for the first (Anthony Blond) edition of TLB's cover blurb, University of Reading Library, *Papers of Gillian Freeman*, MS930, box 1, folder 2.

[PGF2] The Leather Boys – A Screenplay by Gillian Freeman (Raymond Stross Productions Ltd), *Papers of Gillian Freeman*, MS930, box 1, folder 3.

Robinson, L (2007) *Gay Men and the Left in Post-War Britain: How the Personal Got Political* (Manchester: Manchester University Press).

Salmon, Y (2018), 'Certain Circles: Gay Fiction and Cultural Attitudes of the 1960s' in Tew, P, Riley, J and Seddon, M (eds) *The 1960s: A Decade of Modern British Fiction* (London: Bloomsbury) 111–136.

Sexual Offences Act 1967.

Sinfield, A (1994) *The Wilde Century: Effeminacy, Oscar Wilde and the Queer Moment* (New York: Columbia University Press).

Smith, H (2019, 12 March) '"Leather Boys" Novel Fractured Boundaries', *The Washington Post*.

TK (1964) 'Leather Boys, The, Great Britain, 1963', *Monthly Film Bulletin*, vol 31(360).

Wolfenden Report (1957) *Report of the Committee on Homosexual Offences and Prostitution* (London: HMSO).

Zanghellini, A (2015) *The Sexual Constitution of Political Authority: The Trials of Same-Sex Desire* (Abingdon: Routledge).

5 Patricia Highsmith's *The Price of Salt* (1952) and *The Talented Mr Ripley* (1955)

Introduction

Patricia Highsmith's 1952 lesbian novel *The Price of Salt* (TPOS) is widely reputed to be the first homosexual novel with a happy ending. Whether or not justified,[1] this reputation makes it of particular interest for this study. The book was originally published under a pseudonym, as was, at Highsmith's insistence, even the re-print issued more than three decades later: Highsmith worried about being pigeonholed as a writer of homosexual novels (Wilson, 2004: 171, 396–397).

TPOS is the story of an artistically-inclined, orphaned young woman, Therese, who falls in love with an older woman, Carol. Carol is based in New Jersey and is in the process of divorcing from her husband. The affair is a coming-of-age experience for Therese herself, who must learn to handle the pangs of first love, and find a way of breaking off with Richard, her heterosexual date. It is also a process of self-discovery for Carol, who has only ever had one other lesbian affair before, which she thought would be her first and last. From New York, where they met, the women organise a road trip westward. It is during the trip that they first have sex together. Unfortunately, Harge, Carol's husband, who has temporary custody of their young daughter, sends a detective after the women, to collect evidence of their relationship. This is then used against Carol to force her to give up any claims to her daughter's custody, and to blackmail her into giving up her relationship with Therese in order to retain contact with the child. The women have a period apart, and Carol breaks up with Therese. It is a blow for the younger woman, but slowly she starts recovering from her disappointment. When the women meet again some weeks later, Therese has made some strides forward in starting a career as a set designer. Carol, who has moved to Manhattan, informs Therese of her refusal to bow to Harge's conditions after all, and asks Therese to move in with her. Therese, who is still burnt by Carol's initial readiness to put their relationship behind other concerns, declines. Shortly after the women

---

1 The honour probably goes to *Imre: A Memorandum,* by Edward Prime-Stevenson, first printed in Naples in 1906.

DOI: 10.4324/9781003188797-6

have already parted, however, Therese decides to take Carol up on her offer and goes to the restaurant where she knows Carol is dining with an acquaintance. As Therese's eyes scan the restaurant's tables, Carol notices her and immediately understands her purpose. She enthusiastically waves her hand to catch her lover's attention, and Therese makes her way towards her. Hesford (2005: 227) notes that this happy ending becomes possible only once the women have left both Carol's New Jersey house and the middle-America of their road trip: only in the anonymity offered by the city can the women 'escape the glare of a heteronormative national culture'.

TPOS lends itself to critical readings foregrounding different axes of oppression. The controlling behaviour displayed by both Harge and Richard, Therese's boyfriend, and Carol's loss of relationship with her daughter for not meeting gendered expectations of good motherhood, for example, are clearly of both historical and political interest from a gender-based perspective. I will, however, pursue a 'divergentist' reading (Halley, 2006: 26) of TPOS that largely backgrounds gender, in the interest of advancing this book's arguments centred on same-sex happy endings and same-sex attracted practical agents' quality of life. A reading of TPOS that centres same-sex desire rather than gender seems to me also more attuned both with the text's intention and with authorial intention. As to the text's intention (Eco, 1990), the novel expressly assimilates male and female same-sex relationships, contrasting them with heterosexual ones (Highsmith, 2010a: 273), rather than insisting on the incommensurability of male homosexual and lesbian experience. As to the author's intention, Highsmith's lesbianism was not – as it would be for the so-called 'woman-identified woman' (Radicalesbians, 1970) – of the political variety, but desire-driven. In fact, for better or for worse, Highsmith declared to have little time for women who got entangled in heteronormative domesticity, on the ground that they should have seen 'that particular trap' coming (Wilson, 2004: 300)!

In what follows, I begin by clarifying what exactly the happy ending envisioned by Highsmith in TPOS is – namely, an enduring same-sex romance. Highsmith is entirely unapologetic in making this the *telos* of her novel, and remarkably successful in making it happen without sentimentality or melodrama – despite her apprehensions in this respect when the novel was republished by Bloomsbury in 1990 (Wilson, 2004: 442). A full-fledged same-sex attachment of the sort promised at the end of TPOS can be seen as the limit case of mid-century queer imaginative resistance, in the sense that it is this particular same-sex happy ending that is least intelligible from the point of view of mid-century heteronormativity. McDermid (2010: vii), in her introduction to the 2010 Bloomsbury paperback of the novel, aptly describes TPOS's happy ending as '*unimaginabl[e] for 1952*' (emphasis added). What, then, made it possible for Highsmith to make-believe it? I will suggest an explanation after delving into aspects of Highsmith's life, relying, specifically, on Wilson's (2004) acclaimed and detailed biography of the author. As well as interviews with Highsmith's close friends and lovers, Wilson's (2004) work draws on Highsmith's voluminous literary archive held by the Swiss National Library in Bern, comprised of Highsmith's manuscripts, diary, letters, as well as her 'cahiers', in which she annotated observations she considered directly relevant to her creative output (Wilson, 2014: 7). I will suggest that Highsmith's alignment with queerness – in its broader sense of *strangeness* – is key to understanding why in TPOS she was able to make-believe, and commit to paper, the kind of same-sex happy ending which elicited imaginative resistance in many other authors of queer fiction that were her contemporaries.

The second half of the chapter considers the perverse same-sex 'happy ending' in Highsmith's best-known fictional work, her 1955 novel *The Talented Mr Ripley* (TTMR). In TTMR the eponymous protagonist kills Dickie Greenleaf, a wealthy young man, and proceeds to impersonate him and enjoy his privileged lifestyle, while foiling all attempts at bringing him to justice. I will make a case for why any adequate reading of this novel must make same-sex desire central to it. I will then argue that the selfsame conditions of possibility of TPOS's happy ending – Highsmith's psychic alignment with queerness and marginality – also enabled her to bypass the happy/tragic ending dichotomy in TTMR.

The Price of Salt: Happy ending as the endurance of same-sex romance

The contours of the same-sex relationship that counts as a happy ending in TPOS are well-defined. Therese traces them unequivocally towards the end of the book, when she is debating with herself whether to go back to Carol: 'To live with her and share everything with her, summer and winter, to walk and read together, to travel together' (Highsmith, 2010a: 298). And, in the book's last paragraph: 'It would be Carol, in a thousand cities, a thousand houses, in foreign lands where they would go together, in heaven and in hell' (Highsmith, 2010a: 307). It is apparent that this is the familiar ideal of romantic love, not an attempt at crafting a queer alternative to it.

Highsmith does not portray lesbian love as qualitatively different from romantic love generally. When Therese reports to her female lover Richard's words to the effect that he cannot compete with Carol – unnervingly bringing home to the older woman Richard's knowledge of the nature of the two women's relationship – Carol states that these are the 'classic' lines of a spurned lover: 'it's the same play repeated with different casts', she says, asking Therese what 'they say makes a play a classic'. Therese's answer is 'a basic human situation' (Highsmith, 2010a: 169). The play that drives Richard to act in the way he does, and Carol and Therese to feel apprehensive about their love affair becoming public knowledge, is a basic human situation: one that has been acted countless times before by different casts, in which the gender of the actors becomes a mere accident or detail.

The point is reinforced later, when Carol talks of her feelings for her previous lesbian lover and says, 'I don't know, why not call it love, it had all the earmarks', which leads Therese to wonder, 'What was it to love someone, what was love exactly, and why did it end or not end?' (Highsmith, 2010a: 207–208). Elsewhere, it is Therese who re-affirms the capacity of the vocabulary of romantic love to embrace same-sex relationships, while at the same time rejecting Richard's reductively sexualised account of same-sex desire. When she asks him if he was ever in love with a boy, or at least if he has heard of it, and Richard answers, 'You mean people like that?', Therese replies: 'I don't mean people like that. I mean two people who fall in love suddenly with each other' (Highsmith, 2010a: 99).

Neither Therese nor Carol, that is, feel the need to make use of a separate set of coordinates to make sense of same-sex attachments: same-sex love is simply love, of the all-too-familiar variety. Yet, if same-sex love is a manifestation of the familiar ideal of romantic love, it is also a more complete incarnation of that ideal. Harge and his lawyers' devaluation of same-sex love prompts in Carol the thought 'that the rapport between two men or two women can be absolute and perfect … and perhaps some people want just this, as others want that more shifting and uncertain thing that happens between men and women' (Highsmith, 2010a: 273).

Confronted with Harge and his lawyers' suggestion that if she carries on like this she will sink to 'the depths of human vice and degeneration' (Highsmith, 2010a: 273), Carol turns the table on that notion. Degeneration, she argues, is 'to live against one's grain' (clearly meaning a same-sex attracted person forcing heterosexuality on herself); or to settle for a life where one 'is spied upon, attacked, never possessing one person long enough so that knowledge of a person is a superficial thing' (Highsmith, 2010a: 273–274). Carol implies that if she were to keep hers and Therese's relationship clandestine, in order to appease Harge and not lose contact with her daughter, she would indeed be settling for some kind of degenerate love. Carol here draws attention to the ways in which homophobic persecution may thwart same-sex love – forcing one either to give it up (as Carol at this stage has resolved to do with her relationship with Therese) or to trivialise it, make it something other, lesser, than it can be by stealing from it the dimension of continuity that love demands.

Indeed, it is their relationship's power to endure that is both Carol's and Therese's central preoccupation. The temporal dimension of same-sex love affairs becomes the standard against which same-sex happy endings are measured. This becomes apparent early on in the novel, on Carol and Therese's first date (not premeditated as a romantic one). After providing a perfunctory account of her background, Therese – who feels that only now, speaking to Carol, she has truly started to live – states that nothing 'could be duller than past history' (Highsmith, 2010a, 49). Carol's retort that 'futures that don't have any history' may be even duller seems to allude to a premonition (as it turns out, a false one) that hers and Therese's same-sex affair – which officially has not even started yet – might well not end happily. To the extent that same-sex relationships may feature in one's future, Carol seems to suggest at this early stage, they may be transient rather than enduring, and therefore without 'any history' (Highsmith, 2010a, 49). This reflects, as we will see, Highsmith's own concern with the transience of her relationships, and same-sex relationships more broadly.

Therese seems to seize on a similar sense of foreboding on her next rendezvous with Carol. But, through a process of transvaluation, the foreboding emerges in Therese's lovesick mind as a kind of romantic death-wish. The women are on their way to Carol's New Jersey house, which, according to Hesford (2005: 226–227), functions as 'a hollow monument to middle-class hetero-normativity', whose 'normative claims' the women will later try to escape when they set off on their road trip. As they drive through a tunnel, the younger woman feels a desire that it might collapse and kill them, while leaving no mistake about her and Carol's togetherness, enduring even beyond death: for Therese's death-wish is so that their bodies might be dragged out of the tunnel together (Highsmith, 2010a: 59). This death-wish is a way of both calling forth and thwarting heterosexual society's decree of same-sex relationships' futurelessness. Tom Ripley in TTMR, as we will see, shares with Therese a similar fantasy to outwit the same-sex tragic/happy ending binary. But, whereas for Therese the death-wish remains a flash of her overactive, romantically intoxicated, imagination, Tom will act out his fantasy by killing the object of his love.

In her youthful enthusiasm, Therese is quite uncompromising that love cannot possibly be a fixed-term affair. She is thrown at the idea that Carol could fall out of love with her previous same-sex lover after only two months, quite refusing to entertain the idea that true love could be so short-term (Highsmith, 2010a: 207). But she is reassured by Carol's insistence that when their road trip is over, nothing will change between them, even if they will not be able to cohabit on account of Carol's daughter (Highsmith, 2010a: 214). Eventually, the first panic that they might be driven apart, which had set in after they realised they were being followed, is superseded by Therese's calm knowledge that one cannot 'be afraid and in love' and that her bond with Carol is growing 'stronger every day … [a]nd every night' (Highsmith, 2010a: 222). The enduring quality of romantic relationships has, in fact, preoccupied Therese since early on in the novel. Dismayed by a colleague's apparently fairly uninvolved relationship with her husband, as well as by the popular notion that love dies after two years of marriage ('That was a cruel thing, a trick'), Therese tries – and fails – to 'imagine Carol's face, the smell of her perfume, becoming meaningless' (Highsmith, 2010a: 77).

It is, again, Carol's apprehension about their affair's ability to endure that underlies her criticism of Therese on the ground that she has 'a private conception of everything', including Carol herself (Highsmith, 2010a: 186). Carol asks Therese how she thinks she can 'create anything' when she gets all her 'experiences second-hand'. Though the rebuke can, at first blush, be seen to apply to Therese's creative capacities as a set designer, it seems clear that it is the two women's chance of creating a lasting love affair that worries Carol. She fears that Therese's interest in her will fade once the younger woman wakes up to Carol being less than the idealised picture Therese has painted in her own imagination. If Carol were contemplating anything less than a lasting bond with Therese, such a preoccupation with the younger woman's false impressions of her would not loom nearly as large in her mind.

The dramatic tension of the novel, in short, is built around the chances of endurance of the two women's romance. Carol is apprehensive about it; Therese needs reassurance about it; eventually the women get to the stage where they are sure enough of each other that they feel they can weather whatever comes. After a dramatic confrontation with the detective in Harge's pay, however, the prospects of their love succeeding shrink again, as Therese realises that 'the whole world was ready to be their enemy, and suddenly what she and Carol had together seemed no longer love ... but a monster between them, with each of them caught in a fist' (Highsmith, 2010a: 245). The passage conveys a point I made earlier in this book, namely, that experience of the good is mediated through social forms, and hence is partly contingent on inter-subjective validation – a validation that, as far as same-sex affairs were concerned, was conspicuous by its absence in mainstream US culture at the time Highsmith was writing.

Thereafter, as things take a turn for the worse, Therese oscillates between recovering her faith in the bond she shares with Carol – 'I don't see why it should mean [breaking up] for ever' (Highsmith, 2010a: 246) – and despairing that it can endure, so much so that for a brief moment she contemplates jumping off a hotel window (247). At only sixty pages from the end of the novel, this ghost of a suicide scene generates a certain intertextuality – one might even be tempted to call it an interpolation – between TPOS and other mid-century queer novels, making its actual happy ending all the more remarkable.

Towards the end of the novel, before Therese has decided to return to Carol, she briefly finds comfort in the idea that she might have an affair with an attractive English actress who is clearly drawn to her, 'and though she would never become entangled, might be loved herself' (Highsmith, 2010a: 305). But Therese considers this option only briefly, before realising – 'as if some prognostic voice were speaking' – that the thread connecting her to the actress 'did not lead anywhere' (Highsmith, 2010a: 305). An uninvolved same-sex affair – compared to the web of reciprocity in which she can become entangled with Carol – features as a non-place, underscoring the futility of a project of self-authorship that takes it as its destination.

The elusive ideal of enduring same-sex romance

Carol's rebuke of Therese to the effect that the younger woman's overly idealised image of her is a recipe for disaster (Highsmith, 2010a: 186) portends the observation that sociologist Ellen Hill, one of Highsmith's lovers, would later make about Highsmith herself. Highsmith, according to Hill, formed a stubbornly idealised image of her lovers and put an end to the relationship upon realising that the reality fell short of the ideal (Wilson, 2004: 177). At least another of Highsmith's lovers echoed the same point (Wilson, 2004: 238), as did Highsmith herself in a poem dating from 1977, when she had become infatuated with a 25-year-old exponent of the Berlin lesbian avant-garde scene,

Tabea Blumenschein. In the poem Highsmith declares that she is in love with a picture rather than a human being, one that must not be touched lest it should be destroyed (Wilson, 2004: 366). All the while, however, Highsmith still desperately nursed a hope for a shared future with the young woman (Wilson, 2004: 368–369).

In 1984 Highsmith stated that love is a 'state of madness' that has 'nothing to do with reality', something that is purely 'in the eye of the beholder' (Wilson, 2004: 55). The notion was already apparent in her poetry from the late sixties (Wilson, 2004: 291), and Wilson (2004: 110) identifies the writer's allegiance to this understanding of love as early as the mid-1940s. He traces its beginnings to Highsmith's reading Proust during her college years, resulting in her appropriation of his eidetic understanding of love, both in her fiction and her own life (Wilson, 2004: 79).

Highsmith's tendency to fall madly in love at first sight is consistent with this eidetic understanding of love. In 1948, as a twenty-seven-year-old shop assistant working in a Manhattan department store, Highsmith had a *coup de coeur* while serving an attractive, refined customer, who had come to purchase a doll as a Christmas present for her daughter. Highsmith sketched the plot for TPOS the following day: her encounter in the department store served as the initial incident bringing Therese and Carol together (Wilson, 2004: 1, 152).[2] Several months after this encounter, Highsmith would go to the extraordinary lengths of tracking down the woman she had assisted in the shop, making it as far as her house – not once but twice, though on either occasion she eventually lost nerve and did not attempt to make contact with her (Wilson, 2004: 1–3). Wilson (2004: 91) suggests that Highsmith shared Julian Green's view that art is borne of the artist's frustrations, that it works as compensation for what life has denied one. Indeed, Highsmith became immersed in writing TPOS at a time when she had suffered a significant blow in her romantic life; Carol then became a temporary substitute for a real-life romance, to the extent that Highsmith declared she was so in love with her character that she could hardly consider a real-world affair (Wilson, 2004: 166–167).

Highsmith's sexual awakening was in her late teens, when she started experimenting with numerous women (and men), detailing these affairs in her diary (Wilson, 2004: 78–79). Not long after this, Highsmith tentatively identified sex as the subject-matter of her fiction, for it featured centrally in her life in the form of, as she said, 'repressions and negatives' (Wilson, 2004: 88–89). Writers, she felt, should harness that which was least normal about them if they were to stand a chance of revealing the truth about the human condition (Wilson, 2004: 88–89).

---

2   The conceit of Carol and Therese being spied upon and recorded in hotel rooms to collect evidence to be used in the custody case of Carol's daughter also had a biographical basis, being inspired by the experience of one of Highsmith's most prized lovers and primary literary muses, Virginia Kent Catherwood (Wilson, 2004: 132).

Only one year or so into this phase of sexual experimentation, Highsmith, who was then in love with a partnered and unattainable woman, reflected on the neurotic quality of her attachments: unrequited or impossible love felt safer and easier, carrying with it none of that 'fear of perfection' that would accompany a mutual love affair (Wilson, 2004: 82). In 1944, Highsmith concluded that, as a result of drifting in and out of short, serial (and sometimes simultaneous) love affairs, she had dulled her capacity for feeling (Wilson, 2004: 116). But later in her life (in a diary entry from 1962) she imputed this incapacity (up to the age of thirty) to the need she felt, as young woman, to suppress her same-sex desire, which also resulted in suppressing her emotional life more broadly (Wilson, 2004: 53).

In 1948 Highsmith took stock of her past affairs and the reasons for their failure, concluding, in her words, that she 'lack[ed] sympathy' and was 'impatient with that which attracted' her, and 'resolv[ing] to do better' (Wilson, 2004: 138). Doing 'better', as it turned out, included a (failed) therapeutic attempt to turn heterosexual for the sake of Marc Brandel (Wilson, 2004: 147, 153), a British writer whom Highsmith later declared was attracted to her 'for homosexual reasons' (Wilson, 2004: 162). After accepting his marriage proposal she backtracked, admitting to herself that she dreaded both heteronormative domesticity and heterosexual sex (Wilson, 2004: 155).

Two decades later, in the late sixties, Highsmith concluded that there was something compulsive about her falling in love. It 'is not love', she said, 'but a necessity of attaching myself to someone' (Wilson, 2004: 283). In a letter to a friend dating from this period she coolly dissected her stormy romantic life, imputing her rejection of steady commitment, and her tendency to bond with women who would hurt her, to childhood trauma − specifically, the sense of abandonment and betrayal she experienced at the hands of her mother, which, she believed, she found herself under a compulsion to re-enact with her lovers (Wilson, 2004: 48).[3] Highsmith admitted to vaguely masochistic tendencies (130, 138, 269) and resolved (without really believing she would manage it) to avoid lovers who had sadistic inclinations (239). But, addicted to her 'normal diet of passion' (204), she would prolong affairs with volatile lovers that drove her mad (204–210).

About the time TPCS was accepted for publication, Highsmith − who felt strongly that having a lover was essential to her well-being (in fact her 'survival'), as well as her creativity as a writer − had already found herself contrasting the novel's happy ending with her own very different experience of love affairs (Wilson, 2004: 171). By 1955 she candidly acknowledged that in her fiction she could come to solutions that were 'somehow satisfying, as my personal solution

---

3   Throughout his biography, Wilson (2004: 74) makes a convincing case that the pattern of Highsmith's relationship of 'love and loathing' with her mother − Highsmith wondered about a same-sex oedipal complex (83) − tended to manifest itself in the writer's relationships with her lovers. As late as the early seventies, Highsmith made inquiries about the possibility of legally 'divorcing' her mother (336).

can never be' (200). Both her promiscuity and her proneness to falling victim to crushes and romances made Highsmith worry for her mental health and her grip on reality (Wilson, 2004: 166). Yet, her romantic sensibility made her feel that she needed love both to soothe her and find beauty in life (Wilson, 2004: 132, 134) – to give it *salt,* in Therese's figurative language (Highsmith, 2010: 278).

Imagination at the edge of normality

Given her tumultuous love affairs – a pattern that started early in her love life and was to last throughout it – it is not entirely surprising that Highsmith initially envisaged a tragic ending for TPOS. But she also wrote an alternative, happy ending, surmising – correctly – that her agent would prefer it (Wilson, 2004: 163). What made it possible for Highsmith to write the kind of same-sex happy ending that seems to have remained out of other mid-century writers' imaginative reach? I think the answer to this question is partly to be found, paradoxically, in the selfsame factors that explain why Highsmith found it difficult to experience this particular kind of happy outcome in her own life.

Highsmith loathed bourgeois domesticity. Being part of a family unit would, she thought, drive her to murder (probably a child!) (Wilson, 2004: 324). Housewives were the epitome of drab ordinariness, normalcy, law-abidingness (224, 300) – everything that her politico-aesthetic sensibility was repelled by. Negotiating the kind of lasting same-sex attachment she craved, without feeling somehow sucked into *some* version of domesticity by the unavoidable rituals of a shared life, was a tall order indeed. More importantly for my argument, however, the counterpart of Highsmith's dread of normalcy was her queer feeling of allegiance for 'nuts, kinky, kooky people' and criminals (224). Indeed, in 1969 Highsmith drew a connection between her attraction to evil in her writing and her attraction to less than 'honest' women in real life, hastening to add, however, that she could not consider herself 'the good side of this picture' either (303).

Even as a child Highsmith experienced school as a straightjacket robbing her of individuality, and she longed for a life free from external control (Wilson, 2004: 43). Later, during Highsmith's formative years as a writer, the bohemian atmosphere of Manhattan's Greenwich Village in the post-war years – where writers and artists fashioned an anti-mimetic sense of self at odds with the mainstream – nurtured Highsmith's nonconformist tendencies (117–118). The writer Ronald Blythe, who became a good friend of Highsmith's when she moved to Suffolk, England, in the early sixties, declared that she was cut-off 'from what most people see as the "real world"' (255). Wilson (2004: 316), her biographer, speaks of her 'awareness of herself as a marginal figure'. Highsmith's own diaries reveal an explicit pull towards counternormativity – expressly locating the source of creative forces in the marginal, abnormal, and perverse (97).

I think that this fact – Highsmith's inhabiting a psychic space outside the mainstream – goes some way towards explaining why her imaginative capacities were less susceptible to the (hetero)normative shackles at work on other authors of mid-century queer fiction, enabling her, but not them, to make-believe and commit to paper a denouement such as Therese and Carol's same-sex happy ending. In fact this is just what phenomenology would suggest. Sedimented structures of meaning, including action-guiding ones that articulate values and norms, give our social world a quality of pre-givenness, which may be more or less difficult to de-stabilise. The difficulty is partly a function of how integrated such structures are with others that make up our web of signification; but it is also a function of individual experience and temperament. The genius, the madwoman, the eccentric (Highsmith, perhaps, had a dash of all three) may well find it easier to depart from normative semantic structures than ordinary folks (Rubin, 1998).

The Talented Mr Ripley as a queer novel

It has been argued that Highsmith's 'immediate context', including 'her love affairs', does little to illuminate her novels (Wagers, 2013: 242). If TTMR is anything to go by, however, I think this claim may need to be revised. On the first of two occasions when she stalked Kathleen Senn − Carol's real-world counterpart − Highsmith wrote in her diary:

> For the curious thing yesterday, I felt quite close to murder too, as I went to see the woman who almost made me love her a moment in December, 1948. Murder is a kind of making love, a kind of possessing. (Is it not, too, a way of gaining complete and passionate attention, for a moment, from the object of one's attentions?).
>
> (Wilson, 2004: 2)

Highsmith, who claimed that, when writing TTMR, she felt as if she was channelling Tom Ripley (Highsmith, 1966: 76), fictionally enacted this very equation between love and murder at the point of TTMR's narrative climax − where Tom, the novel's antihero, bludgeons to death Dickie Greenleaf, the object of his (unacknowledged) same-sex desire. Or, at least, this is so on the assumption that Tom's relationship to Dickie is actually structured around same-sex attraction. Anthony Minghella's 1999 film adaptation obviously portrays Ripley as same-sex attracted. Highsmith, however, is on record as having denied, at least on one occasion, that her character was homosexual. He was merely, she suggested, 'lukewarm toward women' (Wilson, 2004: 452).

Some critical analyses of Highsmith's work have also claimed that Tom's sexuality is 'vague' (Harrison, 1997: 22). Others either ignore or bracket his sexuality (Cheng, 2019; Dill, 2014; Messent, 2013). Still others find that Tom's sexuality is merely incidental to the main thrust of the book, or of the Ripliad as a whole. For example, Abel (2007: 108) argues that Tom's descent into homicidal violence is triggered by an accusation of queerness that may or may not be true, but which works to generate in Tom the feeling of guilt necessary to unleash it. This implies that the interesting message in TTMR is about the operation and experience of guilt − something that in the book happens to relate to an accusation of homosexuality, but only contingently so. Meanwhile, Hesford (2018: 111–112) reads Ripley as enacting (and sometimes apolitically subverting) the logic of heteronormative commodification – mostly in the subsequent Ripley novels. This reading has the effect of reducing Tom's homosexuality in TTMR to a metonym for 'the burden of authenticity' from which Tom is set free by his killing of Dickie (Hesford, 2018: 109).[4] Shannon (2004) takes to an extreme this tendency on the part of various commentators to explain away Tom's homosexuality. He argues that Tom Ripley has a fetishistic desire for things rather than people, and that he really does not love Dickie at all. Yet, Shannon's (2004) argument is largely based on Tom's internal monologue, and so must assume that Tom and his motives are transparent to himself.

It is true that, starting from *Ripley Underground* (Highsmith, 1966), the second of her five Ripley novels, Highsmith presents Ripley as happily married to Heloise. The relationship between Tom and Heloise is interesting in its own right: in their bond Highsmith manages to make-believe what her imagination was probably most resistant to – a heterosexual marriage that avoids the dreariness of domesticity. Tom and Heloise have no children, nor do they appear remotely interested in producing any. Since they have a live-in maid, neither spouse need attend to any cooking and cleaning (unless it is Tom washing the blood of one of his victims out of the cellar floor). Neither has a five-to-nine job, relying as they both do on private incomes (Tom those derived from fraud and forgery or various description). Both enjoy a relatively jet-setting lifestyle (Heloise for the purpose of recreation, Tom to attend to his shadowy business), which ensures a degree of healthy independence. They have, in sum, all the advantages of companionate marriage (falling asleep in each other's arms, buying each other gifts, mutual support, etc) without any of the drawbacks.[5]

---

4   This reading is hard to reconcile with certain passages in the Ripliad where Tom explicitly rejects monetary, rather than aesthetic, modes of valuing (Highsmith, 2001: 83).

5   I think that the same attempt at envisioning conjugal domesticity without the dreariness that Highsmith instinctively felt for it explains one passage in TPOS that Harrison (1997: 100) finds 'bizarre' – namely, the point at which Carol tells Therese, on one of their first encounters, that one day Therese will see a house in Italy and fall in love with it. Harrison (1997: 100) ascribes Carol's remark to what he identifies as Highsmith's tendency to romanticise commodification, arguing: 'Surely, when thinking of the almost limitless possibilities of an attractive 19-year-old woman's future, one thinks of the men, or in this instance perhaps the women (but certainly people), that she will meet and possibly fall in love with'. But for a same-sex attracted woman in the 1950s the possibilities of successful romances were far from limitless. The house in Italy is Carol's way of wishing on Therese (at a time when their romance is yet to fully blossom) a future far removed from the routines of heterosexual domesticity in which Carol herself is trapped, one in which the romanticism and exoticism of geographic location (Italy) stands in for the romance and (hopefully) non-humdrum quality of lesbian companionship.

By the time (five or six years after the events narrated in TTMR) we find him married to Heloise, however, Tom is a mature man, almost unrecognisable: suave, outwardly self-assured, cultured, inwardly mostly at peace, and much inclined to humour. On the other hand, in TTMR we meet Thomas Ripley still in the green. And Thomas Ripley in the green is both rather angsty and decidedly same-sex attracted. The tell-tale signs of Tom's queerness are scattered throughout the novel – coded, but supremely eloquent.

When we first meet Tom he is still in Manhattan, and we learn that he spent a period at one Marc's, a beringed man with a private income, often absent in Florida, who takes into his home young men in financial difficulties, and proceeds to lord over them (Highsmith, 1985: 25–26). We are not told that Marc demands sex in return, but why else would Tom insist on Marc's ugliness, if not to underscore the resentment of having to sleep with him? Next, we learn of Cleo, Tom's female friend, who is described as unmistakably eligible girlfriend material, but with whom Tom does 'none of the ordinary things that a young man is expected to do with a girl' (Highsmith, 1985: 26), Cleo being, rather, an all-understanding confidant. Later Tom recalls that, as a twelve-year-old, the aunt that brought him up cruelly taunted him before one of her friends: 'Sissy! He's a sissy from the ground up!' (Highsmith, 1985: 34).

Early in the novel, Tom is charged with the wealthy father of Dickie Greenleaf (with whom Tom used to have a relatively casual friendship) with the task of bringing Dickie back home. When Tom reaches the Amalfi Coast, where Dickie has settled, he needs a bathing suit. Having decided that none of the shorts on sale fit him, 'or at least not adequately enough to serve as a bathing suit', he settles on 'a black-and-yellow thing hardly bigger than a G-string' (Highsmith, 1985: 38). Other items stereotypically featuring in gay sexual fantasies randomly pop up at different points of the novels. Thus, visiting Paris for the first time, Tom finds it imbued with the atmosphere he dreamed about, which includes a doubly phallic imagery of 'public *urinals* and *columns* with brightly coloured theatre notices on them' (Highsmith, 1985: 96, emphasis added). Gay meccas (Tangiers, Capri) or countries with homoerotic associations (Greece) feature prominently among the travel destinations Tom fantasises about visiting with Dickie (Highsmith, 1985: 59–60).

When Tom does meet Dickie and his girlfriend Marge for the first time, his impression of the latter is as follows: 'she wasn't bad-looking, Tom supposed, and she even had a good figure, if one liked the rather solid type. Tom didn't, himself' (Highsmith, 1985: 41). Conversely, he quickly becomes aware of Dickie's handsomeness (Highsmith, 1985: 54), as he does of other random young male characters throughout the novel (104, 170–171) – always without any of the qualifications he applies to his appreciation of Marge's looks. He is also conscious of wanting 'more than anything else in the world' to 'make Dickie like him' (54–45). A stunt he puts up to that end is to show off his talents at impersonation – choosing an English lady as the camp subject of his pantomime (48).

When Tom sees Dickie's quarters, he remarks to himself with relief that Marge does not appear to share them (Highsmith, 1985: 50). He attempts to arrange meetings with Dickie that deliberately exclude her, and is clearly worried that they might be in love, though Dickie disclaims anything of the sort (51). On a trip together to Naples, Tom and Dickie show no sexual interest in girls and Dickie's attempt to talk about them feels perfunctory, while Tommy's response, as he brings up Marge, hostile (55–56). Tom becomes increasingly jealous of Marge' closeness to Dickie, feeling an urge to barge on them while they are spending time together, both allured and repulsed by the thought of their physical intimacy (62, 63). Much later in the novel, when Dickie is already dead, the sight of Marge being pawed by a rich American makes Tom queasy (183).[6]

There is, in short, a wealth of clues that give Tom's same-sex desire away. Harrison (1997: 24–25), who picks on some further ones that I have not detailed here, nevertheless claims that what is most significant is that we are never told that Tom has sex with men, or indeed women, or that other characters (notably Dickie and Marge) do. According to Harrison (1997: 25), this lack of sex – he calls it 'asexuality', but the terminology is misleading, because the novel is rife with Tom's suppressed same-sex desire – holds the key to understanding the novel: it 'underscores the extreme isolation of these individuals'. Harrison (1997: 27) goes on to argue that the central (albeit unconscious) idea behind the story, and the driver of Tom's actions, is the fact that he has 'cathected his libido onto things' (those that his murder of Dickie and the appropriation of his money will enable him to enjoy). He also argues that this passionate investment into things liable to ownership is characteristic of many of Highsmith's novels.

This sort of analysis effectively writes off Tom's same-sex desire as purely accidental, as it could never be in the work of a same-sex attracted writer who, in her cahiers, coded her thoughts on homosexuality with the acronym NOEPS: 'notes on *ever present* subject' (Wilson, 2004: 99, emphasis added). Not only is Tom less attracted to specific things than to a lifestyle (Dickie's); but his enjoyment of that lifestyle presupposes, subconsciously, Dickie's phantasmatic presence to share in it, even after he has killed him. This is because, as I will argue, Tom's murder of Dickie achieves, perversely, the same-sex union between the two that Tom's subconscious craves.

Subverting the happy/tragic ending dichotomy

The first climax of the novel comes when Tom spies Dickie being intimate with Marge in her house. Tom rushes back to Dickie's house, where he is

---

6   Trask (2010: 601–602) also draws attention to the sexualised imagery evoked by the proper name '*Dickie Greenleaf*' (reminiscent of 'fig leaf'), and even Dickie's boat 'Pipistrello' (bat, in Italian), which Marge abbreviates to *Pipi* when discussing its *size* relative to other boats. While Trask's (2010: 602) point is that through this sexualised imagery TTMR draws attention to Dickie's 'endowments' – namely, the worldly goods Tom so passionately covets – it seems clear that the imagery's primary function is to underscore the erotic appeal that Dickie has for Tom.

staying as a guest; in Dickie's room, while wearing Dickie's clothes, he acts out a fantasy in which Dickie violently – in fact, homicidally – rejects Marge's advances. 'You were interfering between Tom and me – No, not that! But there *is* a bond between us', he says aloud while imagining to strangle her (Highsmith, 1985: 63). Dickie supervenes on the scene, only just missing the drama Tom has enacted, but surprised to find Tom in his own room, wearing his clothes. They have an argument, in which Dickie tells Tom *he* is not queer, even if Tom himself, Marge said, might be. Tom is humiliated: 'Nobody had ever said it outright to him, not in this way' (Highsmith, 1985: 64).

From this point on, Dickie starts more or less subtly to push Tom away. Tom later will blame the rupture of their rapport on this incident, telling himself that if he had not misjudged Dickie and Marge's relationship, they would eventually have drifted apart and he '*could* have lived with Dickie for the rest of his life' (Highsmith, 1985: 204). This is clearly a fantasy very much recognisable as Highsmith's ideal of same-sex happy ending. Its status as an impossible fantasy in T̄MR, however, is underscored not just by the fact of Dickie's death by the time Tom articulates the fantasy, but also by its being underpinned by Tom's wilful delusion that Dickie and Marge never had an affair after all. Later in the story Tom is 'ashamed that he *could* have believed' that they did (Highsmith, 1985: 182).

The change in the young men's rapport supervening this incident is symbolised by the acquisition of a refrigerator. Dickie and Marge – like the worst suburban married couple – invest a disproportionate amount of time viewing different models and debating their relative merits. The stolid, bulky appliance becomes a symbol of a settled life and heteronormative domesticity, one that overshadows the two young men's vague plans of travelling together, or relocating to Paris or Rome (Highsmith, 1985: 75).

Tom and Dickie have a last trip together to Cannes. An exchange ensues between the two men that, Trask (2010: 602–603) argues, reveals their class consciousness, through Tom's blundering queer self-betrayal, vis-à-vis Dickie's sophisticated, verse-quoting cultivation of sexual ambiguity. In the exchange, Dickie is left disgusted by Tom's enthusiasm for a group of queer, G-string-donning acrobats on the beach: 'Why don't you stay here and watch the acrobats? I'm going back'. Tom himself is torn between annoyance, and shame/denial: he disassociates himself from homosexuality by projecting it onto Dickie (why else would he be so fixated on it, Tom wonders) and onto the 'fairies' on the beach (Highsmith, 1985: 78). It is not simply that here, as Tuss (2004: 96) argues, the 'closeted' Tom 'fears discovery, fears being known as a pervert himself'. Rather, Tom fears knowing *himself* as queer, which makes him, technically, not even closeted, if being in the closet presupposes a *deliberate* attempt to make opaque to others one's *self-transparent* same-sex desire. This interpretation is consistent with an unpublished interview excerpted in Peters (2016: 154), in which Highsmith conceded that Tom is attracted to males but will not act on his desire, because he does not acknowledge his attraction.

The pattern of denial resurfaces at different junctures in the story, as when Tom, by now living in Rome, invites an attractive young American man to his flat, but apparently makes no pass at him, choosing instead to put on an impersonation of Wildean dandyism, by 'serving him his best brandy and strolling about this apartment discoursing of the pleasures of life in Rome' (Highsmith, 1985: 104). Tom's denial of his homosexuality is also apparent when he commits his second murder – the victim being Freddie Miles, one of Dickie's friends, who comes to snoop about Tom's place after Tom has killed and started impersonating Dickie. Tom, who kills Freddie because the latter was on the scent of something underhand, considers his death 'unnecessary' and 'unfair' to him (Highsmith, 1985: 112). But he finds comfort in the thought that Freddie was rather unlikable, with his 'stinking, filthy suspicions' of 'sexual deviation' (Highsmith, 1985: 111, 112) between Dickie and Tom himself.

It is Tom's murder of Dickie, however, that is the novel's high dramatic point, after which much of the plot is driven by Tom's subterfuges to avoid justice. Killing off Dickie is the device through which Highsmith subverts the mid-century queer novel's happy/tragic ending dichotomy. The murder happens after Tom and Dickie have left Cannes for San Remo, where they rent a small motor-boat. By this time Tom has more or less resolved to kill Dickie, who does not conceal his impatience, irritation and distaste in Tom's company. When Dickie had made him angry or disappointed before, Tom briefly experienced a desire to kill him, immediately followed by shame; but this time, as he fully feels the pain and outrage of Dickie's rejection and disdain, the desire lingers (Highsmith, 1985: 79).

While on the boat, on a hazy day, Tom realises that no one would be able to see what he might do to Dickie: 'he could have hit Dickie, sprung on him, or kissed him, or thrown him overboard' (Highsmith, 1985: 81). This sequence of fungible possibilities establishes the very equivalence between love and murder that Highsmith had toyed with in her 1950 diary entry quoted at the beginning of this section, and written the day after her first trip out of New York to the address of Kathleen Senn, Carol's real-world counterpart, whom Highsmith had served as a shop assistant in Bloomingdale in December 1948.

Haggerty (2006: 174) rightly argues that 'the desire to kill Dickie' is 'clearly connected to [Tom's] desire to make love to Dickie'. The homoeroticism of this scene – which has not gone unnoticed by other commentators (see Harrison, 1997: 24) – is heightened by the fact that, right before Tom decides to strike, both men are taking their clothes off (Tom having dared Dickie to jump into the high water and have a swim). Tom is also holding an oar between his legs, 'as casually as if he were playing with it' (Highsmith, 1985: 81) – this phallic implement being then used to inflict death on his semi-naked companion. Indeed, Baldwin (2020: 143–144) argues that 'the description of the violence' of the killing itself 'includes sexualised imagery of penetration', though this is less obvious to me.

Thereafter, Tom proceeds to impersonate Dickie, which enables him to re-invent himself by appropriating not only Dickie's financial means and lifestyle, but his very identity. For Baldwin (2020: 144–145), this appropriation of identity enables Tom to lose his own identity, and the sense of 'grubbiness' he experiences when he is read as queer. Similarly, Haggerty (2006: 175) argues that by physically eliminating and impersonating Dickie, Tom does away both with his sense of shame (Dickie, in rejecting him, has caused him to fail), but also with himself, whom he hates for the impression of failure he has made on Dickie: 'hating Tom Ripley is after all the motivation behind the action in the novel' (176).

But I want to suggest that Tom's appropriation of Dickie's identity is less about shedding his own than a *merger* of identities. What Dickie's killing accomplishes, that is, is Tom's marriage to Dickie, in a kind of homo-marital union that turns the idea of 'till death do us part' right on its head. It takes a while for Tom to adjust (as it would for any newlywed) to this merging of identities, but then, in Paris, the magic happens: 'Now, from the moment when he got out of bed and went to brush his teeth, he was Dickie, brushing his teeth with his elbow jutted out' (Highsmith, 1985: 105). Do they not say, after all, that before long the partners in a couple start resembling each other? It is only appropriate that later, when Tom visits Venice, and stays at the Grand Hotel, and treats himself to a 'luscious and expensive' dinner, he experiences no longing to share the postcard romanticism with a loved one. For, having possessed Dickie so completely, they are already sharing it. No wonder then that Tom resolves to 'watch the gondolas drifting as lazily as they every drifted for any *honeymooner*, with the gondoliers and their oars silhouetted against the moonlit water' (Highsmith, 1985: 157, emphasis added).

It seems clear, too, that it is because Tom subconsciously can make-believe the reality of his union with the murdered Dickie that he can experience gratification at telling Marge that Dickie and he are probably going to live in Rome together 'for a while' (Highsmith, 1985: 90). Later, he reflects that perhaps Marge had 'caught on to the idea that Dickie was running away from her and that he wanted to be with Tom, alone. Maybe that had penetrated even *her* thick skull' (Highsmith, 1985: 135) The choice of verb – caught on to – is suggestive of Marge's realising less what Tom would like to mislead her into thinking is happening, than what actually *is*, in Tom's subconscious, happening. Just like Tom had to beat the reality of their mutual love into Dickie's head with the oar, now it is finally penetrating Marge's own skull. How satisfying, then, for Tom to read Marge's letter addressed to Dickie, whom she still believes to be alive, where she complains that he did not have the guts to tell her '*outright*' that he and his 'little chum' are cohabiting, inseparable (Highsmith, 1985: 136) – unwittingly validating Tom's own fantasy that they are. Marge's is the lament of a spurned lover, complete with the patronising arrogance of self-satisfied heterosexuality: 'I hope my telling you what you hadn't the courage to tell me relieves your conscience a little bit and lets you hold your head up' (Highsmith, 1985: 136).

Highsmith falls short of explicitly making Tom a victim of psychotic delusions, though Gordon (2000: 18) reads Tom as literally hallucinating. Be that as it may, it is clear that Tom's subconscious has a rather loose grip on reality. Is this merely a case of individual psychopathology? That might make TTMR a conservative work, one that would seem to reinforce the prevailing pathologisation of queerness in 1950s America (Gordon, 2000: 18; Trask, 2010: 585).[7] Peters (2016: 156) has noted that Highsmith, in an interview in which she may be referring to Ripley, stated that she tended to think that people who are capable of committing murder without remorse may be sexually maladapted (channelling into homicidal behaviour the violence that is inherent in sex), though Highsmith was careful to state that this was not something necessarily peculiar to queers. Peters (2016: 156), however, thinks that Highsmith trivialises and de-radicalises her own work by implying that it can be read in terms of individual psychopathology. I agree that reducing Ripley's story to a psychological 'case history' is reductive and even a misreading. Rather, TTMR can be read as an indictment of heteronormativity for the ways in which it may make an enduring same-sex relationship (of the kind that comes to fruition in TPOS) both an imaginative and practical near-impossibility.

The key to this reading can be found relatively early on in TTMR. On the same day when Dickie will, later, surprise Tom in Dickie's own clothes (shortly after Marge has suggested to Dickie that Tom is gay) an argument between Tom and Dickie causes Tom a sharp pang of pain, a feeling of loss, and betrayal. The scene is still in the village on the Amalfi Coast. After their argument, Tom starts behaving somewhat erratically as he and Dickie walk uphill in the direction of Dickie's house. Dickie looks puzzled, but Tom responds with a laugh. For that 'was reality, laughing it off, making it silly, something that was more important than anything that had happened to him in the five weeks since he had met Dickie, maybe that had ever happened to him' (Highsmith, 1985: 71). In light of the numerous clues about Tom's queerness, this passage can scarcely be read as anything other than social critique.[8] The message is clear: it is the forces homophobia and heteronormativity that foist unreality upon queerness under the pretence that same-sex desire is not real. Tom cannot admit to himself, let alone speak, of his homosexual attraction for Dickie; Dickie, on his part, can only speak of homosexuality with sneering distaste. Heteronormativity forces Tom to make 'silly' and unreal what is most 'important' and real to him – his pain at his and Dickie's drifting apart. This is what the 'reality' enforced by heteronormativity demands: that he should de-realise his same-sex desire, relegating it to the realm of subconscious fantasy.

---

7   But Thifault (2014: 316–317) has argued that any temptation on the reader's part to ascribe Tom's murders to 'a sensationalized view of homosexuality and the threat it might pose to the social order in postwar America' is 'purposely undercut by the readers' complicity in Ripley's crimes.

8   This, incidentally, undercuts Trask's (2010: 595–596, 608) elegantly made argument against reading Highsmith as motivated by a desire to denounce gay oppression, and his claim that the novel displays a politically incorrect 'determination to eroticise the closet as a locus of mystique'. Similarly it undercuts Hesford's (2018: 102) point about 'the impossibility of reading her novels as political ... [as] being interested in locating the distinction between what is and what could or should be'.

And that is just what Tom proceeds to do, starting with the de-realisation of Dickie himself, and going on to construct and live an elaborate subconscious or semi-conscious fantasy of their perfect union.

Neil Gordon argues that 'the psychotic split that allows Ripley to kill so easily is clearly articulated by Highsmith as the same necessary adaptation that allowed him to exist in the horrendous homophobia of '50s America. Just as Ripley denies … the unbearable reality of his homosexuality, he denies the fact of being guilty of murder' (Wilson, 2004: 453). I want to argue, however, that Tom's murder of Dickie *stands in* for their homosexual union, a union that heteronormativity makes impossible in the (fictional) real world of the 1950s painted in TTMR. That union can therefore only be realised through its absolute practical de-realisation (via Dickie's death) and, thereby, by being transposed to the level of Ripley's subconscious imaginings.

Highsmith's imaginative powers rivalled Ripley's vivid own. Jonathan Kent, who played Ripley in dramatised scenes from *Ripley Underground* (1970) produced for the *South Bank Show* in 1982 (Wilson, 2004: 390), happily found, upon meeting Highsmith, that she happened to fully approve of the casting. Kent reported that he got the impression that she liked him because she felt he '*was* Ripley': 'She was so curious about me, really liked me, in a way that had nothing to do with me: it had more to do with her vision of Ripley' (Wilson, 2004: 392).

For any readers who have come, despite themselves, to root for Ripley, TTMR ends on a happy note. Tom, arriving in Athens, receives a letter from Dickie's parents, who inform him they intend to carry out Dickie's last wishes (contained in a will forged by Tom himself) that Thomas Ripley should be the beneficiary of their son's estate. The policemen that Tom had sighted with apprehension at Piraeus turn out not to have been after him at all. Fantasising about the travels and experiences that now await him, he asks a taxi driver to take him to the best hotel in town (Highsmith, 2001: 211–215). Experiencing this ending as 'happy' is contingent on the reader's cathecting with Tom by mobilising an ethically inappropriate affective response, in accordance with the mechanisms that result in readers overcoming imaginative resistance to 'rough heroes' (Clavel-Vazquez, 2018). For queer readers, it is partly TTMR's implicit social critique – its indictment of homophobia and heteronormativity for how they force unreality upon same-sex desire – that enables such an affective response. In any case, the ending being affectively experienced by readers as happy does not cancel out the perversity of Tom escaping justice for his murders.

A genuine same-sex happy ending would have seen Dickie travelling together with Tom to Greece, as they had at one point planned to do. But by the end of the book Dickie is out of the picture. Tom's own same-sex happy ending – the kind that Highsmith idealised, where the partners bring off the kind of enduring romance promised at the end of TPOS – takes place about one third into TTMR, when, by killing Dickie, Tom merges their two identities in an ever-after, homo-marital union. But the idea of happiness, here, is turned on its head.

Its pre-condition is – so heteronormative imperatives demand – the tragedy of the physical elimination of Dickie, through Tom's insane conflation of erotic and murderous passion. Gordon (2000: 19) argues that Tom shows a 'psychotic relativism toward the truth' in being able to deny both his sexuality and relieve himself from guilt for the murders he accomplished. On my reading, that relativism towards the truth manifests itself in Tom's sub-conscious experience of homo-marital oneness with Dickie, whose inanimate body he has in fact consigned to the waters of the Mediterranean.

Conclusions

Highsmith's lesser susceptibility – relative to other authors of mid-century queer fiction – to heteronormative constraints meant not only that she was able to make-believe same-sex happy endings, but also that she successfully resisted adopting heterosexual marriage as one of her life's comprehensive goals (as demonstrated in her calling off her plan to marry Marc Brandel). Throughout the 1950s, several prominent discourses (advertising, popular magazines, schooling, social sciences) conspired to shepherd women into finding fulfilment in marriage and housewifery, only for many of these women to find themselves profoundly dissatisfied (Friedan, 1963). Given this gap between the imaginative activity prescribed by these discourses (heteronormative domesticity as an unqualified good for all women) and the negative experiences reported by many married women at the time, Highsmith's life choices, in rejecting marital domesticity, can be seen as paralleling, in the context of her own life, the paradigmatic case of readers' imaginative resistance in the fictional context. This, it will be remembered, is the case to which Gendler (2000: 56) first drew attention in her discussion of the puzzle of imaginative resistance, where imaginative resistance figures as our unwillingness to engage with a story containing what we take to be moral non-truths, due to a desire not to be manipulated into changing our appreciation of moral truth.[9] Readers who are competent knowers of moral truths will tend to reject a prescription to imaginatively engage with a morally deviant fictional world. Similarly, Highsmith was not prepared to go along with social discourses prescribing her to make-believe an idea – that heterosexual marriage would be good for her – which ran counter to her own appreciation of the good life.

---

9   Gendler (2000: 64–74) argues that resistance is not a matter of our finding it *impossible* to assent to moral non-truths on the ground of their conceptual impossibility: for we can both be made to make-believe impossible things (as their impossibility can be disguised in a story), and we can will ourselves to make-believe them even if we know them to be impossible. In any case, resistance can be experienced even in the absence of conceptual impossibilities. So, she argues, it is *unwillingness* that must be at the heart of imaginative resistance; and such unwillingness is motivated by a desire to avoid manipulation into exporting those beliefs to the real world.

Highsmith's resistance to making heterosexual marriage and housewifery her comprehensive goal enabled her to have a good life on her own terms. Had she not rejected these heteronormative prescriptions, she would have compromised her well-being by finding herself – like many other women at the time (Friedan, 1963) – alienated from her own goals. It might be tempting to radicalise this argument and claim that Highsmith had a good life not only in being true to her desire not to participate in heteronormative domesticity, but also to the extent that circumstances frustrated her desire for an enduring, dyadic same-sex affair. One might argue here that her creativity might have been dampened by a more settled romantic life; or that her desire for an enduring, dyadic same-sex relationship was itself – as a hankering towards homonormativity – a kind of heteronormative hangover that she was better off not being able to satisfy.

But the conception of well-being adopted in this book does not authorise us to make such a move. The philosophical concept of well-being captures the idea of how one's life goes overall *from the perspective of the person who leads it.* To be sure, I have rejected a desire-based conception of well-being that would take at face value all of a person's goals/desires, regardless of how worthy they may be. I have, instead, defended an autonomy-based conception that enables us to discriminate between morally unacceptable goals/desires (which do not contribute to well-being) and morally acceptable ones (which do). But, beyond that basic discrimination, an autonomy-based conception of well-being requires us to judge the quality of a person's life on the basis of her success in pursuing the (morally acceptable) comprehensive goals she happens to be genuinely committed to. It is irrelevant that we may believe that that person should have preferred other, more radical, goals; or that we (or others) might have committed to different goals if we had been in her shoes.

The implication of this, in respect of the argument that a less volatile romantic life might have adversely affected Highsmith's creativity, is clear. Quite apart from the fact that widespread value incommensurabilities suggest that it makes little sense to speculate on the worth of a creative life relative to that of an emotionally settled one, it is not for us to say that Highsmith should have been content with her success as a writer, when her comprehensive goals appear to have included succeeding not just as a writer, but also at an enduring same-sex relationship. Similarly, it is not up to us to say that Highsmith fared well in her love life because she managed to eschew homonormativity, if one of her comprehensive goals was – as it genuinely seemed to be – her (morally acceptable) commitment to an enduring, dyadic same-sex romance. In short, just because we can say that Highsmith's resistance to making heteronormative domesticity one of her comprehensive goals enabled her to have a good life, we are not thereby authorised to say that she would not have enjoyed a greater quality of life if she had managed to bring off the kind of enduring same-sex affair she yearned for.

Highsmith's psychic alignment with the marginal and queer created the enabling conditions not only for resisting, in her own life, the social prescription that biology is (heteronormative) destiny, but also for curious denouements in her same-sex themed fiction. Well before conceiving TPOS or TTMR, Highsmith planned a story with a homosexual theme, involving a gay man whose diary goes missing. Believing his mother has read it and is now aware of his sexuality, he commits suicide, only for the reader to discover that the mother, finding the diary after her son's death, decides against reading it, out of respect for her son's privacy (Wilson, 2004: 96). Gay suicide is the mid-century queer tragic ending par-excellence, yet the ironic twist in Highsmith's sketched story subverts the tragedy by making the suicide come across as pathetically self-defeating.

If this is an example of an ironic tragic ending, in TTMR Highsmith offers a perverse happy ending. But it is in TPOS's more straightforward, unreconstructed happy ending that Highsmith's imaginative powers show a reach that other authors of mid-century queer fiction could not manage. Indeed, some argue that TPOS's ending is *too* happy. Peters (2016: 128–129, 134) maintains that the promise of a fulfilling union between Carol and Therese, of their mutual completion, in particular, detracts from Highsmith's powerful analysis of the ultimate impossibility of fulfilling relationality and intimacy, an analysis which underwrites the writer's portrayal of heterosexual relationships. Peters (2016: 155) concludes that Highsmith 'cannot write love', that 'when she focuses on love … her work becomes profoundly and deeply unconvincing'. But, as I have already argued, Therese's and Carol's happy ending is the suggestion of their relationship's power to endure, rather than a promise of pure bliss. Peters invokes Lacan's insistence on the '*impossibility* of the sexual *relation*ship as such' (Peters, 2016: 135), an impossibility that she thinks TPOS's happy ending violates. I would argue, however, that that 'impossibility' should be understood as metaphorically as one should take the ideas of mutual completion associated with the ideal of romantic love itself.

Admittedly, Therese's attraction to Carol in the first part of the novel belongs to what Fink's (2015: 83) gloss on Lacan on love characterises as 'the register of passion, often uncontrolled and uncontrollable passion', namely, the register of the imaginary, when 'we fall in love with people … who resemble an ideal we have for ourselves, who seem to be what we ourselves want to be'. Since this ideal, in Lacanian terms, is an imaginary projection, there is a delusional structure to the experience of falling in love (Fink, 2015: 84). Carol is aware that something like this inauspicious logic governs Therese's attraction to her when they first meet – hence her rebuke, which we have already seen, that Therese has 'a private conception' of Carol herself (Highsmith, 2010a: 186). But Therese's attraction to Carol at the end of the novel is of a different order. As Fink (2015: 65) puts it, on the register of the symbolic rather than the register of the imaginary, '[t]o love someone is to convey in words to that person that we lack – preferably big time – and that he or she is intimately related to that lack. We need not suggest that he or she fills in absolutely every respect, that he or she can *saturate* our lack one hundred percent'. Or, 'to say "I *love* you" is to say, "I lack and you speak to my lack." (It is not to say, "'I lack and you complete me")' (Fink, 2015: 69). This is just the kind of desire-based, rather than passion-based, relationship that Therese and Carol share at the end of the novel, when Therese makes a deliberate choice to go back to Carol, despite having deeply felt Carol's betrayal and mused over it (and hence despite being no longer able to make her into an image of her ego-ideal). As Esteve (2012) notes, Therese's agency moves through 'perplexity and subsequent assessment and claiming of her desire'; this movement 'marks intersubjective happiness as something humanly willed rather than miraculously caused'.

Thus, the psychic journey that precedes Therese's return to Carol does not portend the promise of an impossible relational totality. Highsmith's (2010: 311) own intentions, as they transpire from her afterword to the Bloomsbury edition of the novel, make this clear, clarifying that TPOS's happy ending is less a promise of Therese and Carol's living happily ever after than their 'try[ing] to have a future together'. It follows that TPOS is not vulnerable to Peters' (2016: 134) charge that it places lesbianism 'within a particularly heterosexual fantasy of romantic love, exclusivity and completion', writing completion 'as possibility rather than *impos*-sibility, thus replacing the fantasy of completion with completion itself'.

Tom Ripley's erotic attraction to Dickie, on the other hand, plays out wholly on the register of the imaginary. Indeed, Tom's denial makes it impossible for him to articulate his attraction in the terms of the symbolic – of words – as 'love'. Again, Fink's (2015: 83) gloss on Lacan explains that 'insofar as love is the narcis-sistic aim to make one of two, to fuse into one, it aims at the annihilation of dif-ference'; this 'is a chimerical project at best, but one that unleashes more passion in most of us than we experience at any other moment (except perhaps that of murderous rage)'. Tom accomplishes his longed-for merging with Dickie by eliminating and disposing of what remains recalcitrant to the fusion (Dickie's body, but also his rejection of Tom), while claiming whatever of Dickie's is susceptible to appropriation: clothes, identity documents, income, voice, mannerisms, charm, éclat. By collapsing the space between erotic passion and murderous rage, Tom's subconscious engineers his own, chimerical, happy ending.

References

Abel, M (2007) *Violent Affect: Literature, Cinema, and Critique after Representation* (Lincoln, NE: University of Nebraska Press).

Baldwin, C (2020) *Anxious Men: Masculinity in American Fiction of the Mid-Twentieth Century* (Edinburgh: Edinburgh University Press).

Cheng, CC (2019) 'Ripley's Transgression, Highsmith's Art', *Critique: Studies in Contemporary Art*, vol 60(4), 409–418.

Clavel-Vazquez (2018) 'Sugar and Spice, and Everything Nice: What Rough Heroines Tell Us about Imaginative Resistance', *The Journal of Aesthetics and Art Criticism*, vol 76(2), 201–212.

Dill, S (2014) 'Visions of Violence: Christianity and Anti-Humanism in Patricia Highsmith's Ripliad', *Christianity and Literature*, vol 63(3), 373–390.

Eco, U (1990) *I Limiti dell'Interpretazione* (Milano: Bompiani).

Esteve, M (2012) 'Queer Consumerism, Straight Happiness: Highsmith's "Right Economy"', *Post45* https://post45.org/2012/12/queer-consumerism-straight-happiness-highsmiths-right-economy/.

Fink, B (2015) 'Love and Psychoanalysis: A Commentary on Lacan's Reading of Plato's Symposium in Seminar VIII: Transference', *Psychoanalytic Review*, vol 102(1), 59–91.

Friedan, B (1963) *The Feminine Mystique* (New York: WW Norton).

Gendler, TS (2000) 'The Puzzle of Imaginative Resistance', *Journal of Philosophy*, vol 97(2), 55–81.

Gordon, N (2000) 'The Talented Miss Highsmith', *The Threepenny Review*, vol 81, 16–19.

Haggerty, G (2006) *Queer Gothic* (Urbana, IL and Chicago: University of Illinois Press).

Halley, J (2006) *Split Decisions: How and Why to Take a Break from Feminism* (Princeton and Oxford: Princeton University Press)

Harrison, P (1997) *Patricia Highsmith* (New York: Twayne).

Hesford, V (2005) 'Patriotic Perversions: Patricia Highsmith's Queer Vision of Cold War America in "The Price of Salt", "The Blunderer", and "Deep Water"', *Women's Studies Quarterly*, vol 33(3/4), 215–233.

Hesford, V (2018) 'Tom Ripley, Queer Exceptionalism, and the Anxiety of Being Close to Normal', *Angelaki: Journal of the Theoretical Humanities*, vol 23(1), 102–115.

Highsmith, P (2010) 'Afterword' in Highsmith, P, *Carol* (London: Bloomsbury) 308–311.

Highsmith, P (2010a) *Carol* (London: Bloomsbury).

Highsmith, P (1966) *Plotting and Writing Suspense Fiction* (Waukesha, WI: Kalmbach).

Highsmith, P (1970) *Ripley Underground* (New York: Doubleday).

Highsmith, P (2001), *The Boy Who Followed Ripley* (London: Vintage).

Highsmith, P (1985) *The Mysterious Mr Ripley* (London: Penguin).

McDermid, V (2010) 'Foreword' in Highsmith, P, *Carol* (London: Bloomsbury).

Messent, P (2013) 'Liminality and Patricia Highsmith's The Talented Mr Ripley', *Clues: A Journal of Detection*, vol 31(2), 67–77.

Peters, F (2016) *Anxiety and Evil in the Writings of Patricia Highsmith* (Abingdon, UK: Routledge).

[Prime-Stevenson, E] Mayne, X (1906) *Imre: A Memorandum* (Naples: The English Book Press).

Radicalesbians (1970) *The Woman-Identified Woman* (Pittsburgh: Know).

Rubin, EL (1988) 'Putting Rational Actors in their Place: Economics and Phenomenology', *Vanderbilt Law Review*, vol 51, 1705–1727.

Shannon, EA (2004) '"Where Was the Sex?" Fetishism and Dirty Minds in Patricia Highsmith's "The Talented Mr. Ripley"', *Modern Language Studies*, vol 34(1/2), 16–27.

Thifault, P (2014) 'The Boy Ripley Followed: "Pym" as a source for Highsmith's Killer', *November*, vol 76(3), 312–319.

Trask, M (2010) 'Patricia Highsmith's Method', *American Literary History*, vol 22(3), 584–614.

Tuss, A (2004) 'Masculine Identity and Success A Critical Analysis of Patricia Highsmith's The Talented Mr. Ripley and Chuck Palahniuk's Fight Club', *The Journal of Men's Studies*, vol 22(3), 93–102.

Wagers, K (2013) 'Tom Ripley, Inc.: Patricia Highsmith's Corporate Fiction', *Contemporary Literature*, vol 54(2), 239–270.

Wilson, A (2004) *Beautiful Shadow: A Life of Patricia Highsmith* (London: Bloomsbury).

Conclusions

In both Britain and the United States, the social salience of same-sex desire appears to have increased in the postwar years. This was largely a result of the war itself, combined with the growing prestige of psychiatry. The homosociality of the armed forces, the 'suspension' of peacetime morality, the relaxation – in some instances – of coercive social control over sexual morality, the continuous injection into certain port cities of young bodies seeking temporary relief and distraction from the rigours of the army and the horrors of war, and the way commercial establishments responded to this quest created the conditions for an unprecedented flourishing of same-sex intimacy during WWII.

Meanwhile, the discourse of psychiatry became increasingly influential. Psychiatry's services were enlisted in the war effort to assist in managing same-sex desire in the armed forces, particularly in the US. During the postwar years, psychiatry was also used to manage same-sex desire in society at large on both sides of the Atlantic, in the context of new anxieties about rapid social change and the threat of the cold war. This turn to medical discourses affected same-sex attracted people's self-conception, consolidating identity-based understandings of same-sex desire, which in the event proved useful in giving impetus to gay political organisation and mobilisation. In the US, this mobilisation was, in part, a response to new punitive laws. On both sides of the Atlantic, but more markedly so in America, gay mobilisation was also a reaction to ideological scapegoating. Finally, it was also a response to authorities' renewed energy in the legal enforcement of laws against same-sex intimacy. This punitive zeal was itself, partly, triggered by the proliferation of gay bars and the greater visibility of gay life in the wake of the war, as well as, in the UK, by the perceived greater incidence of same-sex intimacy, especially male same-sex intimacy, in public spaces.

This complex picture made same-sex desire socially and politically salient to postwar America and Britain, generating the conditions for its express thematisation, among others, in numerous works of fiction, though queer fictional output petered out in the US after the early fifties, in response to both official and activist forms of censorship. The postwar years, therefore, with their flourishing of gay and lesbian-themed expression under conditions of considerable (hetero)normative constraints, offer a fruitful context in which

DOI: 10.4324/9781003188797-7

to investigate the expanded concept of imaginative resistance pursued in this book. Rather than focusing on readers' experience of reading fiction, this expanded understanding of imaginative resistance foregrounds authors' experience of writing it, and, by extension, practical agents' experience of scripting the story of their own lives.

As expanded and used in this book, the concept of imaginative resistance helps us focus our thought on the ways in which normative constraints make it hard (not, of course, impossible) for authors to make-believe, and therefore commit to, certain fictional outcomes in their books. Authorial imaginative resistance then provides the model for an appreciation of how normative constraints may also make it hard for practical agents to make-believe, and hence commit to, certain practical outcomes in the real word. In respect of postwar Anglo-American queer novels, imaginative resistance, thus understood, offers a more convincing explanation for their quasi-obligatory tragic or miserable endings than commonly proposed alternative explanations – such as a putative requirement, imposed by publishers, that queer stories should end tragically, or authors' internalised homophobia, or authors' desire to elicit in their readership the kind of emotional response serviceable to social and legal change (though the last of these factor may well have played a role on some occasions). In illustrating, in relatively stark form, the effect of (hetero)normative constraints on queer imagination, the example of mid-century queer fiction makes it plausible to hypothesise that heteronormativity may also stunt our ability to make-believe same-sex happy endings in the real world, and hence to make them happen in our own lives.

This is a hypothesis that – to borrow from Sedgwick (1990: 12) – is more liable to being 'deepened and broadened' rather than proved or disproved, though it is not inconceivable that qualitative, and even quantitative, empirical work could be designed having it in mind. Indeed, this book itself made the findings of two qualitative interviews bring to bear on the case studies used in an attempt to thicken the hypothesis. Those case studies revolve around four texts of mid-century Anglo-American queer fiction. An analysis of the ways in which fictional outcomes in these novels were constrained by the heteronormativity of the times gives texture, albeit indirectly, to the hypothesis that heteronormativity may similarly shackle the imagination when it comes to using our practical reason in order to select and pursue our comprehensive goals.

The choices (or compulsions) that steered both Charles Jackson's and Patricia Highsmith's personal lives similarly illustrate my claim that under conditions of homophobia and heterosexism, or marked heteronormativity, same-sex attracted practical agents may experience imaginative resistance of a kind that interferes with their success in having a good life. Jackson's marriage did not prevent him from enjoying same-sex intimacy, at least now and again. But the marriage was evidently very trying to his wife, was marred by his addictions, and even he came to the belated conclusion that a separation was in order, after which he proceeded to live it up briefly as a queer man and settle, apparently happily, with a same-sex lover. This indeed made, *in extremis,* for a happy ending – one that gave Rhoda Jackson the breathing space and serenity she needed to be able, eventually, to look back on her life with her husband Charles without regret, and even fondness; and one that gave Jackson himself a last-ditch chance, however short-lived, to experience the sort of life he could not make-believe and commit to until it was almost too late.

It seems clear, however, that both Charles and Rhoda Jackson's lives were not as successful as they might have been: not because their comprehensive goals – heterosexual marriage, a life with children, Jackson's writing career – were bad ones in themselves, but because the first (heterosexual marriage) was not good for Jackson. It seems clear that Jackson was pushed into marrying by societal homophobia and heteronormativity. These robbed him of the willingness to imagine for himself, as a realistic possibility, the kind of life that he managed to live only decades later, during the last few months of his life – a life shared with a same-sex, rather than a different-sex, lover. Jackson's feeling – conveyed in his letters to his daughters – that his writing career was not what it might have been because of his addictions, on which his creativity became dependent, also suggests a relative failure to bring off his professional aspirations. And if his addictions had anything to do with his repressed sexuality, then the constraints of heteronormativity were also, indirectly, implicated in his limited professional success, not just the problems in his relational life. Heteronormativity affected, that is, more than one of his comprehensive goals.

As to Highsmith, it is true that there may have been a biological basis to her failure to realise the kind of enduring love affair she aspired to. Her friend Vivienne de Bernardi, an educational therapist, expressed a belief that Highsmith had 'a form of high-functioning Asperger's syndrome', and imputed the writer's short-lived love affairs to the communication difficulties associated with it (Wilson, 2004: 394). But it would be implausible to exonerate heteronormativity from also having had a hand in making Highsmith's romantic life quite as tormented as it turned out to be. Highsmith's choosing, at one point, to undergo therapy in the belief that it might fit her for heterosexual marriage suggests her difficulties in imagining herself as the protagonist of an enduring same-sex love affair in the real world – for all that, as I have noted, her marginality, eccentricity or genius enabled her to make-believe such affairs in the world of fiction. Indeed, it seems significant that, as originally envisaged, even *The Price of Salt* was due for a tragic ending. Additionally, when writing a commissioned piece entitled 'First Love' for the *Sunday Times* in 1974, Highsmith declared: 'If I don't speak of happy or successful first love, it is because I can't imagine it easily' (Wilson, 2004: 339).

Highsmith expressly connected homosexuality with transitory love affairs already several decades before, when she first became sexually active (Wilson, 2004: 9999). Then, in 1962 she observed that 'the conscience-stricken young homosexual' is forced to conceal 'not only ... his sex objectives, but .. his humanity and natural warmth of heart as well' (Wilson, 2004: 53). This suggests that she intuited the role that homophobia and heteronormativity had played in frustrating her successful pursuit of an enduring same-sex romance, much as she rightly insisted that 'we all become reconciled to being queer and prefer life that way' (Wilson, 2004: 307).

I think Jackson's and Highsmith's cases give credibility to the expanded understanding of imaginative resistance I proposed in this book – one, that is, whereby normative constraints may interfere with the authorship of one's life not, or not only, through coercion (whether legal or social), but by failing to sustain the imaginative capacities that are a pre-condition to leading an autonomous life. Naturally, the scope of application of this understanding of imaginative resistance exceeds the case of queer people living under conditions of heteronormativity. For instance, with the aetiology of social inequalities likely to be co- or over-determined, imaginative resistance engendered by race- and class-based regulatory regimes may be a plausible part of the explanation for why laws guaranteeing formally equal opportunities, and in some cases even affirmative action programmes, are not necessarily accompanied by the high levels of social mobility they are supposed to foster.

This analysis of imaginative resistance assumes that one's failure to bring off certain outcomes is in part a function of the failure to make-believe them as possibilities in one's own life. Of course, the concept of imaginative resistance should not distract us from the fact that in many cases it is the coercive nature of relevant normative constraints that is primarily to blame, so that even if I could fully make-believe a certain outcome in my life, I simply could not bring it off, either because my efforts would be thwarted, or because the price of bringing it off would be intolerable legal or social penalties. An example of the former – the practical impossibility, due to coercive constraints, to bring off a certain outcome – is the way in which heteronormative immigration laws may prevent same-sex partners of different nationalities from sharing a life together. An example of the latter – the imposition of intolerable sanctions – is the ways in which, in certain cultural contexts, social homophobia may prevent same-sex partners from living openly together as such. In these two examples, it is less a case of regulatory regimes making certain options unavailable to the imagination, than their making those options practically unavailable, by imposing legal or social disabilities through force or the threat thereof.[1]

In both the US and Britain, taken as national contexts, the heteronormative legal regime that coercively imposed legal and social disabilities on lesbians and gay men in the postwar years has now been largely dismantled, although social (no longer legally sanctioned) constraints remain very much alive in some American or British local or subcultural contexts. As legal pluralists propose, just because such forms of regulation are not (or no longer) grounded in State law does not necessarily mean they are any less central to people's lives (Kleinhans and Macdonald, 1997; Davies, 2005), nor indeed any less coercive, for they may be backed up by social and community violence. In any case, in both Britain and the US heteronormativity also survives as a more diffused

---

1   Other kinds of constraints (not normative, or not primarily normative, in nature) may also affect our well-being following a similar logic of imposing absolute or near-absolute social disabilities – as in the case of certain health conditions, or material deprivation.

phenomenon, the kind that, without *practically* robbing one of options, may engender imaginative resistance to them. Plenty of indicators that this remains the case could be given: one that caught my eye today – as I type the first draft of these Conclusions – is viewers' complaints received by the BBC after broadcasting a same-sex kiss in the Canadian teenage show *The Next Step* (Parsons, 2020).

Heteronormativity, and indeed heterosexism and homophobia, are socially prevalent in many national contexts beyond the US and Britain too, and they continue overtly to structure the laws of many countries world-wide. The analytical model proposed in this book, whereby heteronormativity, even when it falls short of making certain options practically and coercively unavailable, may act as a constraint on the imagination and hence affect queer quality of life, is fully applicable in these contexts. However, the ways in which heteronormative dynamics operate to generate queer imaginative resistance will, necessarily, be mediated by local conditions and histories, and the ways in which they interact with globalised discourses.

Contemporary Japan, for example, remains a highly heteronormative society (Sunagawa, 2006). To be sure, in Japan same-sex sexual activity is perfectly legal (Amnesty International, 2017: 5). McLelland, Suganuma and Welker (2007: 24) also note that 'there was never any organized police persecution' of queers. Some local authorities have also started to introduce policies that are protective of lesbians and gay men (Sunagawa, 2006; Amnesty International, 2017: 5). Yet State law fails to formally provide for any form of legal recognition of same-sex relationships, even for limited *ad hoc* purposes, nor does it afford comprehensive protection against discrimination on the ground of sexual orientation (Amnesty International, 2017: 9, 16–17).[2] Where specific anti-discrimination provisions exist, they may be ignored with relative impunity (McCurry, 2020). Discrimination in employment also remains common (Amnesty International, 2017: 11) and coming out challenging (Anonymous, 2020). Homophobic hate crime is rare (Amnesty International, 2017: 5), but not unheard of (Sunagawa, 2006). Media stereotyping is rife (McLelland, 2000; Soushi, 2008). Notoriously, finding rental accommodation for same-sex couples, or lenders prepared to provide their services to them, can be a challenge (Anonymous, 2017).

Nonetheless, a number of factors arguably counteract the effect of heteronormative constraints on make-believing same-sex happy outcomes in the domain of fiction in Japan. These include the historical institutionalisation of age and class-differentiated male same-sex relationships (McLelland, Suganuma and Welker, 2007: 17; McLelland, 2000: [10]); the fact that Japan's brand of heteronormativity lacks the virulently homophobic and sex-phobic connotations that have accompanied it in Judaeo-Christian cultures (Soushi, 2008; McLelland, 2000: [30], [36]); and the development of a manga and popular culture industry producing a variety of genres centring gender and sexual nonconformity, catering to niche interests, and pushing the boundaries of the fictionally imaginable (McLelland, 2000; Zanghellini, 2009a).

---

2   A draft LGBT Equality Act is, at the time of writing, under consideration by the Diet, but it only seeks to promote understanding, failing to outlaw discrimination (Worden and Doi, 2021).

In such a context, despite widespread societal and legal heteronormativity, one would not necessarily expect tragic endings to be characteristic of contemporary Japanese same-sex themed fictional production in the same way in which they were in post-war Britain and America. One may expect, however, genre to make a difference. Same-sex story lines with unambiguously happy endings may well be more imaginable in so-called 'boys' love' stories – gay-themed manga and anime produced (mainly) by heterosexual women for heterosexual girls and women, which reflect their audience's romantic expectations – than in anime and manga produced by queers for queers, many of whom are used to negotiating the daily compromises and indignities of discrimination and the closet. Same-sex happy endings may also be more imaginable in manga/anime than in literary fiction (see, for example, Kastel, 2017), where make-believing will often tend to track what is, so to speak, realistically imaginable, rather than what can be merely fantasised about from a more detached vantage point.[3]

If same-sex happy endings may not trigger imaginative resistance in many (if not all) fictional domains in Japan, it is quite a different matter, however, when it comes to many Japanese queers' lives. Many lesbians and gay men in Japan continue to live in the closet (McLelland, 2000: [8]; Amnesty International, 2017: 6, 11) and lgbt Japanese people are at high risk of committing suicide (Amnesty International, 2017: 6). Anecdotal evidence suggests that it is not necessarily infrequent for Japanese same-sex attracted people to marry hetero-sexually and pursue same-sex intimacy in secret (Abe, 2011: 199, 202; McLelland, 2000: [24], [29]; 46; Soushi, 2008). For some Japanese queers who marry heterosexually, doing so may be part of an elaborate attempt to pass. For others it may simply be a matter of satisfying a desire for social conformity (McLelland, 2000: [29]) – like Carol in Highsmith's (2010: 82) novel, who declares that she married 'because it was the thing to do, when you were about twenty, among the people [she] knew'. Of course, these sorts of arrangements – a straight, married public persona and a same-sex desiring private one – may be experienced as a satisfactory or even a reasonably fulfilling pragmatic compromise by those who choose them. But the analytical lens of imaginative resistance suggests that such an assessment ('satisfactory', 'fulfilling') for many may be largely contingent, under conditions of profound heteronormativity, on a resistance to make-believing, as one's comprehensive goal, a life shared with a same-sex partner.[4]

---

3   This distinction between what is realistically imaginable and what can be made an object of pure fantasy is relevant to the fact, noted by Bergman (2004: 52), that in US same-sex themed porn from the 1950s one finds the happy endings missing from 'proper' novels. The constraints of what is realistically imaginable better explain, I think, queer novels' tragic endings than Bergman's (2004: 52) own suggestion that such endings were chosen as a matter of professional expediency by queer novelists aspiring to 'literary respectability'.

4   This is to say nothing of the fact that, unless one's heterosexual spouse-of-convenience is agreeable to the arrangement, one's marriage of (unilateral) convenience would be marred by deceit and subterfuge, detracting from the well-being of the two participants to that relationship.

Clearly, not all gay people – whether in Japan or elsewhere – care to make the pursuit of a committed same-sex relationship one of their comprehensive goals. Yet some do, and presumably many more would if such relationships were both a practical possibility and within the bounds of what can realistically be imagined for one's own life plan. Importantly, as we have seen in the introduction, it is precisely when integrated with one's comprehensive goals that hedonic pleasure, including gay sex, comes to matter to one's well-being. While experiencing hedonic pleasure is consistent with one's well-being even when not integrated with comprehensive goals, it does not contribute to how well one's life goes overall unless it is so integrated (Raz, 1999: 325). Committed intimate relationships are one of the typical ways in which many of us around the world integrate hedonic pleasure with one of our comprehensive goals – this goal being the committed relationship itself. In other words, in committed sexually intimate relationships, sex can be brought to bear on well-being, becoming a constitutive component of a valuable form of life.

If same-sex marriage resonates as a political goal for lesbians and gay men worldwide, it is precisely because committed relationships[5] offer one obvious way (not necessarily the only way) in which sexual activity may come to matter to people's well-being. On this view, societies where committed intimate relationships feature among their (often central) social forms, but which fail adequately to sustain same-sex attracted people's imagination in make-believing (and hence bringing off) committed same-sex relationships, reduce the range of the comprehensive goals available to same-sex attracted people's intimate life below an acceptable minimum.

Raz (1986: 206) argues that to the extent that societies that recognise same-sex marriage offer same-sex attracted individuals 'the option of benefitting from an existing social framework', they 'make it possible for individuals to have an autonomous life'; as such, the existence of an option such as same-sex marriage is 'intrinsically valuable'. The point is an important one, but in light of queer and feminist critiques of marriage (Barker, 2012), Raz's (1986: 206) statement should be unpacked. First, we should move away from the politically fraught terminology of same-sex marriage, and concentrate on the substantive form of relationship that, I have argued, accounts for why same-sex marriage rhetoric is so powerful in the first place: a sexually-intimate, adult, committed relationship. Secondly, the claim that societies that recognise committed same-sex relationships 'make it possible for individuals to have an autonomous life' (Raz, 1986: 206) is not necessarily the same as advocating for comprehensive legal recognition of same-sex (and different sex) sexually-intimate, adult, committed relationship through full-blown institutions such as marriage or civil unions.

The point is, rather, that the existence of conjugal relationships provides a distinctly valuable form of life (among others) by attaching a set of expectations (say: a shared life, mutual material and emotional support, loyalty, cooperation,

---

5   Committed relationships need not take the form of marriage, of course, but marriage is a widespread mode of organising and announcing relational commitment.

etc) to a sexually-intimate adult relationship. Given this, a society that does not treat those relationships as the preserve of heterosexuals enables same-sex attracted people to choose a valuable form of life that is precluded to them in other, more homophobic, heterosexist, or heteronormative societies. True, some people in sexually-intimate same-sex relationships may still be able to create a shared life involving mutual support, loyalty, cooperation, etc, even in a homophobic society that actively interferes with their efforts to do so, or in a heteronormative one that tolerates such efforts as quaint. But for many – less privileged and/or less imaginative – others, such societies hinder their pursuit of that comprehensive goal not only in practical ways, but also by engendering resistance to make-believing a committed same-sex relationship as one's comprehensive goal in the first place.

No part of this argument rests on the idea that sexually-intimate committed relationships (gay or straight) should necessarily be legally recognised for *all* the purposes that present-day societies commonly treat conjugal relationships relevant to. Nor does it rest on the idea that conjugal relationships should be legally privileged vis-à-vis other relationships involving interdependency and care. Neither of these ideas could be defended from a perspective of progressive feminist or queer politics (Stychin, 2006; Barker, 2012); nor would it be consistent with the variety of ways (in some cases pioneered by lesbians and gay men) in which interdependency and care is managed in the 21st century (Barker, 2015). For some, these may involve a de-centring of sexually intimate bonds and/or an emphasis on friendship (Roseneil and Budgeon, 2004; Monk, 2016).

But societies may sustain the imaginative and practical pursuit of same-sex committed relationships in ways that fall short of legally recognising conjugal same-sex relationships in the privileged form of full-blown legal institutions such as marriage or civil unions. Consider, for example, a State that does not criminalise gay sex; guarantees, both on paper and in practice, access to jobs, accommodation and services without discrimination on the ground of sexual orientation and relationship status; recognises committed same-sex relationships for the purposes of immigration/family reunification; robustly pursues homophobic crime; and does not censor the representation of same-sex intimacy and same-sex relationships as a valuable form of life. Such a state may be doing enough, on the legal plane at least, to create the conditions under which the option to pursue committed same-sex relationships is both realistically imaginable and practically achievable, even if it fails to introduce the legal institution of same-sex marriage or civil partnerships.

Neither Britain nor the US measured up to this standard in the postwar years, and to that extent they unjustly deprived many (not all) lesbians and gay men of the option to form committed same-sex relationships – an option that should have been available to them on the ground of the value of their having an autonomous life. Britain and the US made it, that is, practically too difficult for many lesbians and gay men to have such relationships, or even to be able to imagine themselves in such relationships. Many countries around the world today are guilty of the same offence. Legal and/or social heteronormativity either coercively robs many of their same-sex attracted citizens of the option to safely create and sustain committed same-sex relationships, or it makes their imagination resistant to entertaining their participation in such relationships.

Thus, one of the normative implications of this book's analysis of imaginative resistance is that it bolsters the case for global gay rights. In a critical scholarly context, however, advocating legal protections for same-sex attracted people in a global context immediately raises the question of the purity of one's political investments and motivations. Building on the work of Massad (2002), Puar (2007), and others, such as Haritaworn, Kuntsman, and Posocco (2015), there is now a growing body of literature concerned with the missionary zeal of projects directed at exporting western models of gay identity on non-western others (see e.g. Wahab 2016; Wahab 2016a). Broadly, scholarship in this vein argues that the global 'exportation' of gay rights is contingent on an assertion of Western exceptionalism that is serviceable to Western nation-building/consolidation, and predicated on the devaluation of non-Western others as irreducibly primitive, homophobic and in need of control. At worst, this literature argues, homonationalist dynamics entail the disposability of the lives of non-Western others.

As I have explained elsewhere (Zanghellini, 2012) this literature is sometimes valuable in identifying certain tendencies in the context of complex deployments of rights discourse, and in prompting self-reflection and soul-searching on the part of those involved in those deployments. Yet, it tends to rely on problematic dichotomies that too often yield reductive readings of LGBT politics and social dynamics, and its evidential basis is sometimes in inverse relation to its rhetorical power. More significant than any analytical pitfalls, however, are the performative effects of this body of scholarship: notably, the ways in which it may either put local arrangements surrounding the treatment of same-sex desire beyond critique by presuming their benign quality, or deflect attention away from these arrangements, or cast non-western queer folks critical of these arrangements as self-interested collaborators, or passive victims of Western queers' manipulation (Habib, 2010: xviii–xix; Zanghellini, 2012).

It is by jettisoning the question of what States and societies owe to the well-being of their same-sex attracted body politic that these analytical moves, their rhetorical investments, and their performative effects become possible. Massad's (2002) argument that the so-called 'Gay International' harms same-sex attracted Arabs, for example, combines a defensible, if sketchy, argument about how not to go about promoting gay rights in the Middle East,[6] with a much more controversial contention about the illegitimacy of promoting them at all. This contention, however, discounts the possibility of a practice of queer international solidarity 'as a joyful affirmation of our desire to live well' (Trott, 2014: 228). It is also contingent on obfuscating the value, for same-sex attracted people, of the option to integrate same-sex desire within committed same-sex

6   This argument was later developed with greater clarity and nuance by Awwad (2010).

relationships: just because current social arrangements might trigger my imaginative resistance to such an option does not mean my well-being does not entitle me to its availability.

Both the positive analysis and normative implications of this book's argument about imaginative resistance in queer lives, therefore, reject as mistaken many of the assumptions of the queer postcolonial literature just discussed, as well as the claims that flow from these premises. My analysis, on the other hand, is consistent with recent postcolonial scholarship – such as Wan, 2020; Karimi, 2018; Lee, 2016; Obadare, 2015 – that treats global gay rights as a discursive resource that same-sex attracted people creatively engage with in a variety of national contexts in order to sustain their aspirations to a good life.

Karimi (2018), for example, starts by noting the 'disparate discourses' that same-sex attracted Iranians can access: 'current homophobic Iranian culture, emerging youth culture, Iranian diaspora's viewpoints, and Western emancipatory discourses that carry racist-orientalist components'. He goes on to detail how Iranians gay men seek to improve their quality of life (as same-sex desiring people) by engaging the family – which is the primary site of ideological regulation by the State – rather than through public political activism. This means, primarily, investing in the idea of committed same-sex relationships, ones where desire escalates to the level of love and emotional bonds, which anchor gay identities to family values and make gay men acceptable to their family members. Some of Karimi's (2018) research participants (all of whom carefully negotiated their coming out to safeguard their psychological and physical safety) were able to live with their lovers because the presumption of heterosexuality in Iran makes male cohabitation fairly unremarkable. Karimi (2018) also notes that many Facebook profiles of Iranian gay men indicate their committed relationship status, though generally without displaying pictures.

Karimi's (2018) fascinating study is illuminating in many ways. First, it illustrates the fact that imaginative resistance to same-sex happy endings is not automatic, even in contexts which are institutionally inimical to same-sex desire, failing as they do to meet many of the conditions I enumerated above (no sodomy laws; anti-discrimination legislation on the grounds of sexual orientation/relationship status; no censorship of representations of same-sex intimacy as a valuable form of life, etc.). In Iran, the way in which institutional homophobia clashes with, or is modulated by, the other discourses Karimi (2018) identifies, and the way in which heteronormativity disciplines same-sex attracted folks through family ideology create an imaginative space for make-believing committed same-sex relationships. Secondly, the society's very heteronormativity, to the extent that it generates a presumption of heterosexuality, provides same-sex attracted men with the opportunity to practically sustain, and not simply make-believe, committed relationships with other men, as male cohabitation easily passes under the radar.[7] Iran's case,

7   This situation, where the presumption of heterosexuality has a protective effect on committed same-sex relationships, appears to contrast with the postwar years in the US. There, as we saw, the way in which war brought same-sex desire out into the

then, suggests that under certain conditions heteronormativity may have the effect of generating a kind of imaginative resistance, concerning same-sex relationships, which affects the general population but not same-sex attracted folks themselves – a state of affairs that ironically turns out to have protective value for the latter.

Iran's case, however, also shows that just because committed same-sex relationships may both be imaginable and practically achievable in some form under conditions of intense heteronormativity does not mean that society is thereby doing enough by way of supporting the well-being of its same-sex attracted members. First, any society that forces same-sex attracted people and their committed relationships into the closet strikes at the core of their well-being: for being the authors of our lives requires that we should not be consumed by concerns about our own safety and survival (see Raz 1986: 374). Secondly, the Facebook profiles discussed by Karimi (2018), where same-sex attracted Iranians proudly announce their relationship status, illustrate how same-sex love clamours for publicity. This is consistent with the idea that our experience of value is mediated through social forms, and that these are inter-subjectively validated. Since this process of inter-subjective validation requires communicability, a heteronormative society is unjust to the extent that it forces anonymity on same-sex attracted people seeking publicity for their relationships.

The way in which this book has centred committed same-sex relationships may not resonate with queer critiques of the ways in which heteronormativity ratifies queer relationships that look sufficiently like idealised heterosexual marriages – dyadic, stable, monogamous, etc – while de-authorising alternative forms of intimacy, or even making them unintelligible. But note that the kind of committed relationships that make for a same-sex happy ending as conceived in this book need not be sexually monogamous[8] (despite the fact that as already noted, sexual monogamy can be, for some of us, a powerful way of

---

open, followed by both cold war paranoia about the (gay) 'enemy within' and by the findings of the Kinsey report about the pervasiveness of same-sex desire, was rather more apt to disrupt the presumption of heterosexuality. This does not mean, of course, that even in McCarthyite America it was *impossible* for queers to both make-believe and bring off committed same-sex relationships. Imaginative resistance, after all, is not about impossibility; and Highsmith (2010: 311), following publication of her lesbian romance, received letters of appreciation from readers who were relieved to read about hopeful representations of same-sex relationships, and who found them to resonate with their own experience.

8 Indeed, polyamorous participants to a recent study reported experiencing greater nurturance with their primary partners than their monogamous counterparts – but the researchers go on to add that 'various negative cross-partner effects … provide little evidence for the claim that diversifying needs across partners may benefit relationships' (Balzarini et al., 2019: 197). These cross-partner effects include the fact that 'greater eroticism with a primary partner was associated with less closeness and sexual satisfaction for a secondary, while greater eroticism with a secondary partner was associated with less sexual satisfaction with a primary partner' (ibid). Previous 'research [similarly] suggests that diversifying needs across partners can have both detrimental and beneficial effects' (188).

expressing commitment). Committed relationships of the kind envisaged in this book also need not be dyadic (though, in practice, because value is mediated by social forms, in cultures that value couple-based intimate relationships, one would expect same-sex attracted people seeking commitment to gravitate towards exclusively or primarily dyadic relationships).[9] In any case, if we have little reason to ideologically privilege dyadic and sexually monogamous relationships, it is no less problematic, as Ruddick (2015) notes, for critical theory to indulge the urge to discount 'the idea of valuing a lover for the one being he or she is, with the inner richness and consistency that could make for an "integral" relationship'. More broadly, the ways in which I have insisted, in this book, on the potential that same-sex committed relationships have for contributing to personal well-being is continuous with a theoretical project aimed at problematising the link between queer theory and counternormativity (Zanghellini, 2009b) – a move that has gained more and more currency in recent years (Wiegman and Wilson, 2015; Ruti, 2016; Zanghellini, 2020).

Yet, I also agree that we should be mindful of how certain discursive engagements surrounding not only monogamy, but also polyamory may de-authorise 'more sex- or pleasure-centred forms of non-monogamy' (Klesse, 2006: 565). Consistent with this, at no point did my argument in this book rely on the idea that gay sex needs to be redeemed by, or elevated through, committed relationships (whether monogamous or polyamorous), or that sex that is not embedded in such relationships is bad, or detracts from our well-being, or is not fun, or not worth having. Instead, my argument turned on the ideas that sexual pleasure (like other episodical experiences of pleasure and pain) tends to matter to how our life goes overall only to the extent that it is integrated with comprehensive goals; and that sexually intimate, committed same-sex relationships offer an obvious – not the only – way to so integrate it.

As I argued in the introduction, as an empirical matter, many same-sex attracted people care about embedding sex within committed relationships. It would be reductive to write this off as same-sex attracted folks buying into dominant ideology. Rather, queer attachment to the ideal of sexually intimate committed relationships is consistent with the fact that human well-being is a function of the success in pursuing autonomously chosen comprehensive goals, coupled with the fact that to count as one's *comprehensive* goal, a sexually intimate relationship (like any other kind of interpersonal relationship) needs to be sufficiently close and durable.

It might be objected, once again, that the idea of durability imports a heteronormative logic of – to borrow from Halberstam – 'narrative coherence' (Dinshaw et al., 2007: 182) into same-sex affairs. Isn't such chronological linearity at odds with queer temporality conceived as, say, the circular recurrence of cruising routines, or – to draw on Edelman's (2004: 27) account of queer anti-futurity – the senseless (because non-procreative, and hence non-teleological) repetition of thrusts

9 Consistent with this, even the majority of polyamorists – in America at least – tend to pursue primary-secondary relationship arrangements (Balzarini et al., 2019: 187).

and retreats during gay sex? But such queer theoretical invocations of counternormativity (manifesting, here, in the language of countertemporality) are too vague to take us far. Just like 'asynchrony, multitemporality and non-linearity', as Jagose notes, 'might as easily be lived in the register of brutalizing normativity as queer radicality' (Dinshaw et al., 2007: 191), so there is nothing essentially heteronormative about the chronological linearity implied by a committed relation's durability.

To the extent that they may occlude an appreciation of how committed sexual relationships may contribute to personal well-being, queer-theoretical critiques of the homonormativity of committed same-sex relationships should be treated with caution. Among other things, such critical moves may preclude an appreciation of how the logic of both formal legal prohibition against same-sex sexual activity and social disfavour for queer sex have a disparate impact on sexually intimate, committed same-sex relationships, as distinct from queer sex per se. After all, same-sex attracted people have always found ways of seizing sexual pleasure despite such prohibitions and disfavour. Indeed, prohibition, in de-authorising queer sex, may paradoxically enhance the good-making property of gay sex as a pleasure-giving activity (a circumstance that probably partly explains queer attachments to counternormativity). Conversely, legal prohibition of, or social disfavour towards, gay sex, in de-authorising committed, sexually intimate, same-sex relationships by forcing invisibility upon them and denying them publicity, prevents them from being intersubjectively validated, and hence from officially (and, to a certain extent, practically) working as a valuable social form. From this perspective it makes little sense to treat sex unmoored from commitment as a more authentically queer option (in the sense of its potential for subverting the mainstream heteronormative order) than sexually intimate, committed same-sex relationships. Or at least this must be so in societies where legal prohibition of and/or pervasive disfavour towards gay sex persist, or where their legacy lingers.

Ultimately, any queer critique that objects to the normativity of certain same-sex relationships simply on the ground that they are committed, and/or dyadic, and/or durable seems a case of critical theory's mistaking 'good matters of fact' for 'bad ideological biases' (Latour, 2004: 227). Murdoch's (1992: 216) exhortation not to cut theory off from the everyday perspectives functional to our day-to-day existence is apt here. Like Therese and Carol in *The Price of Salt*, and Reggie and Dick in *The Leather Boys*, many same-sex attracted people today equate same-sex happy endings with success in bringing off a sexually intimate, committed relationship. This, if I am right, has less to do with their longing for the social rewards of embracing normativity, than with an intuitive appreciation of some of the conditions under which same-sex desire can be brought to bear on our well-being.

References

Abe, H (2011) 'A Community of Manners: Advice Columns in Lesbian and Gay Magazines in Japan' in Bardsley, J and Miller, L (eds) *Manners and Mischief: Gender, Power, and Etiquette in Japan* (Berkeley: University of California Press) 192–212.

Amnesty International (2017) *Human Rights Law and Discrimination Against LGBT People in Japan* (Amnesty International).

Anonymous (2017) 'Housing Website to Offer LGBT Support in Finding Tolerant Landlords', *Japan Today*https://japantoday.com/category/features/lifestyle/hou sing-website-to-offer-lgbt-support-in-finding-tolerant-landlords.

Anonymous (2020) 'Survey Reveals Few LGBT Employees Coming out in Japan', *Nippon.com*www.nippon.com/en/japan-data/h00851/.

Awwad, J (2010) 'The Postcolonial Predicament of Gay Rights Discourse in the Queen Boat Affair', *Communication and Critical/ Cultural Studies*, vol 7(3), 318–336.

Balzarini, RN, et al. (2019) 'Eroticims versus Nurturance: How Eroticism and Nurturance Differs in Polyamorous and Monogamous Reationships', *Social Psychology*, vol 50 (3), 185–200.

Barker, N (2012) *Not the Marrying Kind: A Feminist Critique of Same-Sex Marriage* (Basingstoke, UK: Palgrave MacMillan).

Barker, N (2015) 'After the Wedding, What Next? Conservatism and Conjugality' in Barker, N and Monk, D (eds) *From Civil Partnership to Same-Sex Marriage: Interdisciplinary Reflections* (Abingdon, UK: Routledge).

Bergman, D (2004) *The Violet Quill and the Making of Gay Culture* (New York: Columbia University Press).

Davies, M (2005) 'The Ethos of Pluralism', *Sydney Law Review*, vol 27(1), 87–112.

Dinshaw, C et al. (2007) 'Theorizing Queer Temporalities: A Roundtable Discussion', *GLQ*, vol 13(2-3), 177–195.

Edelman, L (2004) *No Future: Queer Theory and the Death Drive* (Durham, NC: Duke University Press).

Habib, S (2010) 'Introduction' in Habib, S (ed.) *Islam and Homosexuality* (Santa Barbara, CA: Praeger) xvii–lxii.

Haritaworn, J, Kuntsman, A and Posocco, S (eds) (2015) *Queer Necropolitics* (Abingdon, UK: Routledge).

Highsmith, P (2010) *Carol* (London: Bloomsbury).

Karimi, A (2018) 'Hamjernsgara belongs to family; exclusion and inclusion of male homosexuality in relation to family structure in Iran', *Global Studies in Culture and Power*, vol 25(4), 456–474.

Kastel (2017) 'The Quiet Revolution of Contemporary Japanese Queer Novels', *Anime Feminist*https://animefeminist.com/perspectives-quietrevolutions-contemporary-japa nese-quer-novels/#disqus_thread.

Kleinhans, MM and Macdonald, RA (1997) 'What is Critical Legal Pluralism?', *Canadian Journal of Law & Society*, vol 12(2), 25–46.

Klesse, C (2006) 'Polyamory and its "Others" Contesting the Terms of Non-Monogamy', *Sexualities*, vol 9(5), 565–583.

Latour, B (2004) 'Why Has Critique Run Out of Steam? From Matters of Fact to Matters of Concern', *Critical Inquiry*, vol 30, 225–248.

Lee, PH (2016) 'LGBT Rights versus Asian Values: De/Re-Constructing the Universality of Human Rights', *The International Journal of Human Rights*, vol 20(7), 978–992.

Massad, J (2002) 'Re-Orienting Desire: The Gay International and the Arab World', *Public Culture*, vol 14(2), 361–385.

McCurry, J (2020) 'Japan's Love Hotels Accused of Anti-Gay Discrimination', *The Guardian* (30 October).

McLelland, M (2000) 'Male Homosexuality and Popular Culture in Modern Japan', *Intersections*, vol 3.

McLelland, M, Suganuma, K and Welker, J (2007) 'Introduction' in McLelland, M, Suganuma, K and Welker, J (eds) *Queer Voices from Japan First Person Narratives from Japan's Sexual Minorities* (Lanham, MD: Lexington Books) 1–29.

Monk, D (2016) '"Inheritance Families of Choice"? Lawyers' Reflections on Gay and Lesbian Wills', *Journal of Law and Society*, vol 43(2), 167–194.

Murdoch, I (1992) *Metaphysics as a Guide to Morals* (London: Chatto & Windus).

Obadare, E (2015) 'Sex, Citizenship and the State in Nigeria: Islam, Christianity and Emergent Struggles over Intimacy', *Review of African Political Economy*, vol 42, 62–76.

Parsons, V (2020) 'BBC Swamped with Complaints for Showing Two Girls Kissing on Teen Drama The Next Step', *PinkNews* www.pinknews.co.uk/2020/08/02/the-next-step-bbc-complaints-two-girls-kissin-teen-drama/.

Puar, J (2007) *Terrorist Assemblages* (Durham, NC: Duke University Press).

Raz, J (1999) *Engaging Reason: On the Theory of Value and Action* (Oxford: Oxford University Press).

Raz, J (1986) *The Morality of Freedom* (Oxford: Oxford University Press).

Roseneil, S and Budgeon, S (2004) 'Cultures of Intimacy and Bare Beyond 'the Family': Personal Life and Social Change in the Early 21st Century', *Current Sociology*, vol 52(2), 135–159.

Ruddick, L (2015) 'When Nothing is Cool', *The Point* https://thepointmag.com/criticism/when-nothing-is-cool/.

Ruti, M (2016) 'The Bad Habits of Critical Theory', *The Comparatist*, vol 40(1), 5–27.

Sedgwick, EK (1990) *Epistemology of the Closet* (Berkeley: University of California Press).

Soushi, S (2008), 'Japan and Sexual Minorities', *FOCUS*, vol 52, http://hurights.or.jp/archives/section2/2008/06/japan-and-sexual-minorities.html.

Sunagawa, H (2006) 'The Social Situation Facing Gays in Japan' (Mark McLelland trans) *Intersections*, vol 12, 30–33.

Stychin, C (2006) '"Law Vegas Is not where We Are": Queer Readings of the Civil Partnership Act', *Political Geography*, vol 25(8), 899–920.

Trott, B (2014) 'A Spinozist Sort of Solidarity: From Homo-Nationalism to Queer Internationalism', *Interface: A Journal for and about Social Movements*, vol 6(2), 224–229.

Wahab, A (2016) 'Calling 'Homophobia" into Place (Jamaica): Homo/Trans/Nationalism in the Stop Murder Music (Canada) Campaign', *International Journal of Postcolonial Studies*, vol 18(6), 908–928.

Wahab, A (2016a) '"Homosexuality /Homophobia Is Un-African?": Un-Mapping Transnational Discourse in the Context of Uganda's Anti-Homosexuality Bill/Act', *Journal of Homosexuality* vol 63(5), 685–718.

Wan, M (2020) 'The Invention of Tradition: Same-Sex Marriage and its Discontents in Hong Kong', *International Journal of Constitutional Law*, vol 18(2), 539–562.

Wiegman, R and Wilson, EA (2015) 'Introduction: Antinormativity's Queer Conventions', *differences*, vol 26(1), 1–25.

Wilson, A (2004) *Beautiful Shadow: A Life of Patricia Highsmith* (London: Bloomsbury).

Worden, M and Doi, K (2021), 'Japan's Ruling Party LGBT Bill Falls Short', *Human Rights Watch* (7 May), https://www.hrw.org/news/2021/05/07/japans-ruling-party-lgbt-bill-falls-short.

Zanghellini, A (2009a) 'Underage Sex and Romance in Japanese Homoerotic Manga and Anime', *Social & Legal Studies*, vol 18(2), 159–177.

Zanghellini, A (2009b) 'Queer, Anti-Normativity, Counter-Normativity and Abjection', *Griffith Law Review*, vol 18(1), 1–16.

Zanghellini, A (2012) 'Are Gay Rights Islamophobic? A Critique of Some Uses of the Concept of Homonationalism in Activism and Academia', *Social and Legal Studies*, vol 21(3), 357–374.

Zanghellini, A (2020) 'Antihumanism in Queer Theory', *Sexualities*, vol 23(4), 530–548.

Index

For Product Safety Concerns and Information please contact our EU
representative GPSR@taylorandfrancis.com
Taylor & Francis Verlag GmbH, Kaufingerstraße 24, 80331 München, Germany

www.ingramcontent.com/pod-product-compliance
Lightning Source LLC
Chambersburg PA
CBHW071517100726
47908CB00004B/1197

* 9 7 8 1 0 3 2 0 3 7 5 0 9 *